Cassell's Sports Quotations

Cassell's Sports Quotations

DAVID PICKERING

CASSELL&CO

For Dad – Donald Pickering and his team,
Worcestershire County Cricket Club

Cassell & Co
Wellington House, 125 Strand, London WC2R OBB

first published 2000

British Library Cataloguing-in-Publication Data
A catalogue entry for this book is available from the British Library.

ISBN 0-304-35384-1

Designed by Gwyn Lewis

Printed and bound in Great Britain by MPG Books Ltd, Bodmin, Cornwall

Contents

Introduction

There has been an explosion in sports publishing in recent years but relatively few attempts have been made to compile comprehensive, properly sourced collections of quotations relating to the whole sporting arena. This book aims to fill the gap, representing a selection of the funniest and most memorable quips and reflections on sport, drawn primarily from dozens of existing publications, newspapers, radio, television and the internet. To the familiar classics inherited from a wide variety of older publications have been added many newly minted nuggets deemed worthy of inclusion among the all-time greats. The author is happy to acknowledge his debt to those few hardy souls who have tilled the same soil over the years, notable amongst them such contemporary luminaries as Barry Liddle, Colin Jarman, Phil Shaw and the late Peter Ball.

The author would like to thank everyone at Cassell for their assistance and, as ever, Jan, Edward and Charles for their support from the terraces.

David Pickering
BUCKINGHAM, July 2000

Note In the source notes, 'American football player' or 'American football coach' indicates someone who plays or coaches American, rather than Association, football. All other allusions to 'footballers' of other nationalities refer to Association football.

Henry ('Hank') AARON

US baseball player (1934–) remembered for hitting a
record 755 home runs.

Quotes about Hank Aaron

Throwing a fastball by Hank Aaron is like trying to sneak the sunrise past
a rooster.

Curt Simmons (1929–), US baseball player.

Quotes by Hank Aaron

My motto was always to keep swinging. Whether I was in a slump or feeling
badly or having trouble off the field, the only thing to do was keep swinging.

Attributed.

I don't want people to forget Babe Ruth. I just want them to remember
Henry Aaron.

Referring to his achievement in breaking Babe Ruth's record of 714
home runs.

See also INCOMPETENCE; RETIREMENT.

Action replays

The action replay showed it to be worse than it actually was.

Ron Atkinson (1939–), English football manager. ITV television
football commentary.

Strangely, in slow-motion replay, the cricket ball seemed to hang in the air for even longer.

David Acfield (1947–), English cricketer and television sports
commentator. BBC television cricket commentary.

We don't always get from slow-motion the pace at which they play.

John Barrett (1931–), British television sports commentator. BBC
television tennis commentary.

The slow-motion replay doesn't show how fast the ball was really travelling.

Richie Benaud (1930–), Australian cricketer and television sports
commentator. BBC television cricket commentary.

See also TELEVISION.

Advice

If you wish to be a good sport, you must let people teach you a lot of things that you already know.

Anonymous.

Six Rules for a Happy Life –

1. Avoid fried meats which angry up the blood.
2. If your stomach disputes you, lie down and pacify it with cool thoughts.
3. Keep the juices flowing by jangling around gently as you move.
4. Go very lightly on vices such as carrying on in society. The social ramble ain't restful.
5. Avoid running at all times.
6. Don't look back. Something may be gaining on you.

Leroy 'Satchel' Paige (1906–82), US baseball player. Advice printed
on the back of his autograph card, quoted in *Collier's Magazine*,
13 June 1953.

You're only here for a short visit, so don't hurry, don't worry, and be sure to stop and smell the flowers along the way.

Walter Hagen (1892–1969), US golfer.

You can't climb up to the second floor without a ladder. When you set your aim too high and don't fulfil it, then your enthusiasm turns to bitterness.

Try for a goal that's reasonable, and then gradually raise it. That's the only way to get to the top.

Emil Zatopek (1922–), Czech middle-distance runner.

I would advise anyone coming to the match to come early and not leave until the end, otherwise they might miss something.

John Toshack (1950–), Welsh footballer and football
club manager.

If there is any game in the world that attracts the half-baked theorist more than cricket I have yet to hear of it.

Fred Trueman (1931–), English cricketer and cricket commentator.
Freddie Trueman's Book of Cricket (1964).

Cricket is full of theorists who can ruin your game in no time.

Ian Botham (1955–), English cricketer. *Ian Botham on
Cricket* (1980).

Don't take advice from people with missing fingers.

Henry Beard, US humorist. Advice to anglers in *An Angler's
Dictionary* (1983).

See also TECHNICAL TIPS.

Aerobics *See* EXERCISE.

Age

Running races should be absolutely forbidden to men over 27 years of age. Between 30 and 40, a man may indulge in running at a moderate pace for exercise, but not in races. Men over 60 years of age should never run at all for anything, not even to catch a train.

James Cantlie (1851–1926), Scottish physician and writer.
Physical Efficiency (1906).

I am getting to an age when I can only enjoy the last sport left. It is called hunting for your spectacles.

Edward Grey (1st Viscount Grey of Fallodon; 1862–1933), British
Liberal politician.

Age is a mighty important subject for a champion, because it is the one opponent he can't lick.

Wilfrid Diamond (1931–), US sportswriter. *This Guy Marciano* (1955).

There are compensations for growing older. One is the realisation that to be sporting isn't at all necessary. It is a great relief to reach this stage of wisdom.

Cornelia Otis Skinner (1901–79), US actress and humorist.

At another year, I would not boggle,
Except that when I jog, I joggle.

Ogden Nash (1902–71), US poet.

I'm throwing just as hard as I ever did. The ball's just not getting there as fast.

Vernon 'Lefty' Gomez (1908–89), US baseball player, lamenting his decreasing power as a pitcher.

You're not old until it takes you longer to rest up than it does to get tired.

Dr Phog Allen (1885–1974), US basketball coach. A comment made by him at the age of 79, and quoted in 'Scorecard', *Sports Illustrated*, 6 September 1965.

When I was 40 my doctor advised me that a man in his forties shouldn't play tennis. I heeded his advice carefully and could hardly wait until I reached 50 to start again.

Hugo L. Black (1886–1971), US judge.

Not bad. Most people my age are dead. You could look it up.

Charles 'Casey' Stengel (1890–1975), US baseball player and manager. He was speaking in response, as an old man, to an inquiry after his health.

Age is a question of mind over matter. If you don't mind, age don't matter.

Leroy 'Satchel' Paige (1906–82), US baseball player.

Some of these legends have been around golf a long time. When they mention a good grip, they're talking about their dentures.

Bob Hope (1903–), US comedian.

I've always been quite an athlete myself – big chest, hard stomach. But that's all behind me now.

Bob Hope (1903–), US comedian.

Everyone keeps telling me I'm 31, and now I start to worry about my strokes. Now I'm thinking, two or three times, before I hit each shot. Before I just used to play and everything came naturally.

Ilie Nastase (1946–), Romanian tennis player.

He now floats like an anchor, stings like a moth.

Ray Gandolfo, referring in 1982 to US boxer Muhammad Ali's continued appearances in the ring at the advanced age of 39. The comment parodies Ali's own 'Float like a butterfly, sting like a bee.'

His nerves. His memory. And I can't remember the third thing.

Lee Trevino (1939–), US golfer. Listing the three things a golfer loses as he grows older. Quoted in Jeff Parietti, *The Book of Truly Stupid Sports Quotes* (1996).

When you get old, everything is hurting. When I get up in the morning, it sounds like I'm making popcorn.

Lawrence Taylor (1959–), American football player.

I no count the years. Men may steal my chickens, men may steal my sheep. But no man can steal my age.

Miruts Yifter (1938–), Ethiopian athlete, nicknamed 'Yifter the Shifter'.

I'm between the twilight and the no-light of my career.

Billy Olson, US pole vaulter.

By the time I was sixteen I was a has-been.

Mary Decker (1958–), US middle-distance runner.

I was 18 about six years ago – I'm 28 now.

Frank Bruno (1961–), British heavyweight boxer, *c.*1989.

The older you get the stronger the wind gets – and it's always in your face.

Jack Nicklaus (1940–), US golfer. Quoted, on the occasion of his 50th birthday, in the *International Herald Tribune* (Paris), 28 February 1990.

He must have discovered euthanasia. He never seems to get any older.

John Francome (1952–), British jockey and trainer, referring
to a youthful-looking jockey during a Channel 4 Racing
television broadcast.

You're never too old to stop learning.

Ian Botham (1955–), English cricketer.

You are not too old to play cricket at 35-plus. But you've got to be about
60-plus if you want to administer the game or administer the team at
international level. So you walk around a field for about 20 years and
forget everything you've learned. It doesn't make any sense.

Ian Botham (1955–), English cricketer.

For a while you're a veteran, and then you're just old.

Lance Alworth (1940–), American football player.

Your body is like a bar of soap. The more you use it, the more it wears
down.

Dick Allen (1942–), US baseball player.

When a player gets to 30, so does his body.

Glenn Hoddle (1957–), English football manager.

See also YOUTH.

Agents

What do you have when you've got an agent buried up to his neck in the
sand? Not enough sand.

Pat Williams (1972–), US basketball player.

Agents do nothing for the good of football. I'd like to see them lined up
against a wall and machine-gunned ... some accountants and solicitors
with them.

Graham Taylor (1944–), English football manager.

Dogs, worms, vermin.

Joe Kinnear (1947–), Irish football manager, 1995.

If God had an agent, the world wouldn't be built yet. It'd only be Thursday.

Jerry Reynolds (1970–), American football player.

The terrible thing about my job is that players get 80% of my earnings.

Eric Hall (1937–), English football agent. Quoted in Mark
Reynolds, *The Wrong Kind of Shirts* (1998).

Alcohol

Large wine glasses and such things will lose you a race sooner than anything else.

G. Morrison, British rower, speaking as President of the Oxford
University boat crew in 1865.

If you foozle with your cleek,
And your putts are let's say – weak.
If your drives, for all to see,
Do not always leave the tee.
And to slice them is a habit,
If, in short, you're a rabbit,
Do not put your clubs away
Drink a Guinness every day.

Advertisement for Guinness, aimed at golfers, early 20th century.

Moderation is essential in all things, madam, but never in my life have I failed to beat a teetotaller.

Harry Vardon (1870–1937), British golfer.

Golfing excellence goes hand in hand with alcohol, as many an open and amateur champion has shown.

Henry Longhurst (1909–79), British golf writer and broadcaster.

The modern professional cricketer does not get drunk at Lord's or often get a century there, or anywhere else, before lunch.

Sir Neville Cardus (1889–1975), British journalist and writer. He was
referring to the batsman Billy Barnes, who once scored a century at
Lord's despite being somewhat the worse for drink. Sir Neville
Cardus, *Autobiography* (1947).

Sure I eat what I advertise. Sure I eat Wheaties for breakfast. A good bowl of Wheaties with Bourbon can't be beat.

Jay 'Dizzy' Dean (1911–74), US baseball player. Quoted in the *Guardian*, 'Sports Quotes of the Year', 1978.

If you drink, don't drive. Don't even putt.

Dean Martin (1917–95), US film actor and singer.

If the crowd throw bottles at us, we'll hurl 'em straight back – unless they are full of course.

Rachael Heyhoe-Flint (1939–), English cricketer, commenting upon anticipated crowd trouble during a tour of the West Indies in 1970.

Beer and Rugby are more or less synonymous.

Chris Laidlaw (1943–), New Zealand rugby player and sportswriter. *Mud in Your Eye: A Worm's Eye View of the Changing World of Rugby* (1973).

The pub is as much a part of rugby as the playing field.

John Dickinson (1943–), *A Behavioural Analysis of Sport* (1976).

Drink is a serious problem, particularly on cricket tours, for it can be said, without fear of contradiction, that nothing yet devised by man is worse for a sick hangover than a day's cricket in the summer sun.

Michael Parkinson (1935–), British television chat show host. *Bats in the Pavilion* (1977).

Alcoholism v Communism.

Banner waved by Scottish fans when the Scotland football team met the USSR in the 1982 World Cup.

I had a bash at positive thinking, yoga, transcendental meditation, even hypnotism. They only screwed me up, so now I'm back to my normal routine – a couple of lagers.

Leighton Rees (1940–), Welsh darts player.

I have been to many great functions where some of the great cricketers of the past have been present ... to see them sink their drink is to witness performances as awe-inspiring as ever any of them displayed on the cricket field.

Ian Botham (1955–), English cricketer, in response to media criticism of his use of marijuana in 1986.

It took a lot of bottle for Tony to own up.

Ian Wright (1963–), English footballer. He was referring in 1996 to news that his team-mate Tony Adams had admitted publicly to having an alcohol problem.

In America once you're famous, you're famous for the rest of your life. And they make great pina coladas.

Paul Gascoigne (1967–), English footballer, detailing his reasons for considering a move to the USA in the late 1990s. Quoted in Mark Reynolds, *The Wrong Kind of Shirts* (1998).

I only drink when we win a trophy. Maybe people think I'm an alcoholic.

Ian Ferguson (1967–), Scottish footballer. Quoted on receiving his 23rd cup- and league-winner's medal with Glasgow Rangers.

Some of the younger players think that lager makes you invisible.

Craig Brown (1940–), Scottish football manager, speaking as manager of Scotland in 1999.

Muhammad ALI

US heavyweight boxer (Cassius Marcellus Clay; 1942–) who amply justified his reputation as 'the greatest' by winning a record three world heavyweight titles.

Quotes about Muhammad Ali

Richard Dunn's not overawed by this Muhammad Ali. Why, we've got far too many of those black chat merchants back home in Bradford. He's right used to seeing them dance up and down Westgate with their tambourines every Saturday.

Jimmy Devanney, British boxing trainer, assessing his protégé Richard Dunn's chances against Ali in 1976.

Muhammad Ali isn't a puncher. He just hit me so many times I didn't know where I was.

Brian London (1934–), British heavyweight boxer.

That was always the difference between Muhammad Ali and the rest of us. He came, he saw, and if he didn't entirely conquer – he came as close as anybody we are likely to see in the lifetime of this doomed generation.

Hunter S. Thompson (1939–), US journalist. 'Last Tango in Vegas: Fear and Loathing in the Far Room', in *Rolling Stone* (New York), 18 May 1978.

I got into the ring with Muhammad Ali once and I had him worried for a while. He thought he'd killed me!

Tommy Cooper (1922–84), British comedian.

He was like God with a custard pie up his sleeve.

Joseph O'Brian.

When it comes to ballyhoo, Muhammad Ali made Barnum and Bailey look like non-starters, and he had the incandescent quality of the real star which would have made him famous, even if his gift was knitting not fighting.

Michael Parkinson (1935–), British television chat show host.

Quotes by Muhammad Ali

I am the greatest!

A phrase frequently repeated by Ali in media appearances. He admitted borrowing it originally from the Las Vegas wrestler 'Gorgeous' George Wagner (1915–63). Ali once confessed, however, 'I'm not really the greatest. I only say I'm the greatest because it sells tickets.' Quoted in the *Louisville Times*, 16 November 1962.

Float like a butterfly, sting like a bee.

Repeated by Ali on a number of occasions when discussing his boxing style and indelibly associated with his name, this most famous slogan should perhaps be more correctly attributed to Ali's trainer Drew 'Bundini' Brown, who said it at the weigh-in before a title bout against Sonny Liston in Miami, Florida, on 25 February 1964. Brown's fuller version ran 'Float like a butterfly, sting like a bee; his hands can't hit what his eyes can't see.' Quoted in George Sullivan, *The Story of Cassius Clay* (1964).

The man who will whip me will be fast, strong and hasn't been born yet.

Quoted at the height of his career.

When you're as great as I am, it's hard to be humble.

Acknowledging his own lack of humility.

At home I am a nice guy: but I don't want the world to know. Humble people, I've found, don't get very far.

Sunday Express, 13 January 1963.

I'm so fast I could hit you before God gets the news.

Attributed.

I'm not only a great boxer, I'm a genius. I ain't just a dumb negro boxer. I'm a great writer, too.

Attributed.

It's gonna be a thrilla, a chilla, and a killa,
When I get the gorilla in Manila.

Looking forward in 1975 to what became known as 'the Thrilla in Manila', the celebrated bout in which Ali narrowly beat Joe Frazier.

See also AGE; BOXING; CONFIDENCE; EDUCATION; Joe FRAZIER; INJURIES; Joe LOUIS; MARRIAGE; PHYSIQUE; PREDICTIONS; SEX.

All Blacks

The invariably formidable New Zealand national rugby union team, named after their all-black playing strip.

Subdue and penetrate.

The motto of the All Blacks.

New Zealand rugby is a colourful game since you get all black ... and blue.

Anonymous.

You can go to the end of time, the last World Cup in the history of mankind, and the All Blacks will be favourites for it.

Phil Kearns (1967–), Australian rugby union player. *The Sunday Times*, 19 October 1999.

Amateurs

We swing with girded hips,
And lightened are our eyes,
The rain is on our lips,
We do not run for prize.

Charles H. Sorley (1895–1915), Scottish poet.

Amateur: one who plays games for the love of the thing. Unlike the professional, he receives no salary, and is contented with presents of clothes, clubs, rackets, cigarettes, cups, cheques, hotel expenses, fares, and so on.

Beachcomber (J.B. Morton; 1893–1979), British humorist. Quoted in
the *Daily Express*.

No one is more sensitive about his game than a weekend tennis player.

Jimmy Cannon (1910–73), US sportswriter. 'Nobody Asked Me,
But...', *New York Post*, c.1955.

The only true sport is amateur.

René Maheu, Director-General of the United Nations. 'Cultural
Anthropology' in E. Jokl and E. Simon, *International Research in
Sport and Physical Education* (1964).

The only true amateurs in sport these days are those who are no good at it.

Chris Brasher (1928–), British middle-distance runner. *Mexico
1968: A Diary of the XIXth Olympiad* (1968).

The only real amateur, in my book, is the one who pays his own expenses.

Vivian Jenkins (1918–), Welsh rugby player. Quoted in *Rugby
World*, March 1972.

One of the last of his kind – and certainly the finest specimen of it – the
amateurs, the smiling gentlemen of games, intensely devoted to the skill
and the struggle, but always with a certain gaiety, romantic at heart, but
classical in style.

J.B. Priestley (1894–1984), British playwright, referring to the
English cricketer, footballer and athlete C.B. Fry (1872–1956) in
The English (1973).

See also PROFESSIONALISM; VILLAGE SPORTS.

American football

Outlined against a blue-grey October sky, the four horsemen rode again.
In dramatic lore they were known as Famine, Pestilence, Destruction and
Death. These are only aliases. Their real names are Stuhldreher, Miller,
Crowley and Layden.

Grantland Rice (1880–1954), US sportswriter, describing the
legendary line-up of Notre Dame in a match against Army in 1924;
his most celebrated report.

To watch a football game is to be in prolonged neurotic doubt as to what you're seeing. It's more like an emergency happening at a distance than a game.

Jacques Barzun (1907–), US educationalist.

There are several differences between a football game and a revolution. For one thing, a football game usually lasts longer and the participants wear uniforms. Also, there are usually more casualties in a football game. The object of the game is to move a ball past the other team's goal line. This counts as six points. No points are given for lacerations, contusions, or abrasions, but then no points are deducted, either. Kicking is very important in football. In fact, some of the more enthusiastic players even kick the ball, occasionally.

Alfred Hitchcock (1899–1980), British film director.

College football today is one of the last great strongholds of genuine old-fashioned American hypocrisy.

Paul Gallico (1897–1976), US journalist, novelist and short-story writer. *Farewell to Sport* (1938).

Football is not a contact sport. It's a collision sport. Dancing is a good example of a contact sport.

Duffy Daugherty (1915–87), American football coach.
'Scorecard', *Sports Illustrated*, 14 October 1963.

Football is an incredible game. Sometimes it's so incredible, it's unbelievable.

Tom Landry (1924–), American football player.

You have to be somewhat crazy to play the game; crazy about the game.

Joe Montana (1956–), American football player.

Football is the only game you come into with a semblance of intelligence and end up a babbling moron.

Mike Adamle (1950–), American football player and sports commentator.

Rugby is a beastly game played by gentlemen. Soccer is a gentleman's game played by beasts. Football is a beastly game played by beasts.

Henry Blaha, 1972.

People stress the violence. That's the smallest part of it. Football is brutal only from a distance. In the middle of it there's a calm, a tranquillity. The players accept pain. There's a sense of order even at the end of a running play with bodies strewn everywhere. When the systems interlock, there's a satisfaction to the game that can't be duplicated. There's a harmony.

Don DeLillo (1926–), US writer and novelist. *End Zone* (1972).

They say football is America's greatest game, but it's not. The greatest game in America is called opportunity. Football is merely a great expression of it.

Joe Kapp (1938–), American football player and coach. Quoted in
James Lawton, *The All American War Game* (1984).

American Football is not so much a sport as a way of strife. It might be best described as Rugby League with knobs on, or feinting by numbers.

Doug Ibbotson, British sportswriter. *Sporting Scenes* (1980).

American football makes rugby look like a Tupperware party.

Sue Lawley (1946–), British radio and television presenter, 1985.

You have to play this game like somebody just hit your mother with a two-by-four.

Dan Birdwell (1940–), American football player.

Football combines the two worst things about America: it is violence punctuated by committee meetings.

George F. Will (1941–), US journalist. Quoted in the *International Herald Tribune*, 7 May 1990.

See also LAST WORDS; SUPER BOWL; TACKLES; VIOLENCE.

Anglers

There are two types of fisherman – those who fish for sport and those who fish for fish.

Anonymous.

As no man is born an artist, so no man is born an angler.

Izaak Walton (1593–1683), English writer. *The Compleat Angler*,
'Epistle to the Reader' (1653).

Angling is somewhat like poetry, men are to be born so.

Izaak Walton (1593–1683), English writer. *The Compleat Angler* (1653).

No life, my honest scholar, no life so happy and so pleasant as the life of a well-governed angler; for when the lawyer is swallowed up with business, and the statesman is preventing or contriving plots, then we sit on cowslip-banks, hear the birds sing, and possess ourselves in as much quietness as these silver streams, which we now see glide so quietly by us.

Izaak Walton (1593–1683), English writer. *The Compleat Angler* (1653).

Every man, deep down, is a fisherman.

Stephen Leacock (1869–1944), Canadian humorist.

The fish is the hunter, the angler is the hunted.

Richard Waddington, British writer. *Catching Salmon* (1978).

The formal term for a collection of fishermen is an exaggeration of anglers.

Henry Beard, US humorist. *An Angler's Dictionary* (1983).

An angler is a man who spends his rainy days sitting around on the muddy banks of rivers doing nothing because his wife won't let him do it at home.

The *Irish News*.

Angling

Fishing is the sport of drowning worms.

Saying.

The gods do not deduct from man's allotted span the hours spent in fishing.

Babylonian proverb.

The best fish swim near the bottom.

English proverb.

The salmon is the most stately fish that any man may angle to in fresh water.

Dame Juliana Berners (*fl.*1450s), English prioress. *Treatyse perteynynge to Hawkynge, Huntynge, Fyshynge, and Coote Armiris* (*c.*1479).

The pleasant'st angling is to see the fish
Cut with her golden oars the silver stream,
And greedily devour the treacherous bait.

William Shakespeare (1564–1616), English playwright and poet.
Much Ado About Nothing (c.1598).

You must lose a fly to catch a trout.

George Herbert (1593–1633), English poet.

Angling may be said to be so like the mathematics, that it can never be fully learnt.

Izaak Walton (1593–1683), English writer. *The Compleat Angler*,
'Epistle to the Reader' (1653).

It is worthy the Knowledge and practice of a wise man.

Izaak Walton (1593–1683), English writer. *The Compleat Angler* (1653).

Sir Henry Wotton ... was also a most dear lover, and a frequent practiser of the art of angling; of which he would say, 'it was an employment for his idle time ... a rest to his mind, a cheerer of his spirits, a diverter of sadness, a calmer of unquiet thoughts, a moderator of passions, a procurer of contentedness; and that it begat habits of peace and patience in those that professed and practised it.'

Izaak Walton (1593–1683), English writer. *The Compleat Angler* (1653).

We may say of angling as Dr Boteler said of strawberries, 'Doubtless God could have made a better berry, but doubtless God never did.'

Izaak Walton (1593–1683), English writer. *The Compleat Angler* (1653).

Let the blessing of St Peter's Master be ... upon all that are lovers of virtue; and dare trust in His providence; and be quiet; and go a-Angling.

Izaak Walton (1593–1683), English writer. *The Compleat Angler* (1653).

Fly fishing may be a very pleasant amusement; but angling or float fishing I can only compare to a stick and a string, with a worm at one end and a fool at the other.

Samuel Johnson (1709–84), British lexicographer. Attributed in
Hawker's *Instructions to Young Sportsmen* (1859). Also credited to
Jonathan Swift.

There is no use in your walking five miles to fish when you can depend on being just as unsuccessful near home.

Mark Twain (1835–1910), US writer.

It always was the biggest fish I caught that got away.

Eugene Field (1850–95), US poet.

Fishing is a delusion entirely surrounded by liars in old clothes.

Don Marquis (1878–1937), US novelist, playwright and poet.

It is to be observed that 'angling' is the name given to fishing by people who can't fish.

Stephen Leacock (1869–1944), Canadian humorist.

The charm of fishing is that it is the pursuit of what is elusive but attainable, a perpetual series of occasions for hope.

John Buchan (1875–1940), Scottish novelist.

All men are equal before a fish.

Herbert Hoover (1874–1964), US Republican politician and president, 1951.

Dr Strabismus (Whom God Preserve) of Utrecht is carrying out research work with a view to crossing salmon with mosquitos. He says it will mean a bite every time for fishermen.

Beachcomber (J.B. Morton; 1893–1979), British humorist. 'January Tail-piece', in *By the Way*.

All Americans believe that they are born fishermen. For a man to admit a distaste for fishing would be like denouncing mother-love or hating moonlight.

John Steinbeck (1902–68), US novelist, 1954.

It has always been my private conviction that any man who pits his intelligence against a fish and loses has it coming.

John Steinbeck (1902–68), US novelist.

Fishing differs from all other sports in one essential detail; it is the only sport in which the quarry has to co-operate and play its own active and willing part.

Vivian Bailey, British writer. *Come Fishing and Shooting* (1961).

Fishing is undoubtedly a form of madness but, happily for the once-bitten, there is no cure.

Sir Alec Douglas Home (1903–95), British Conservative politician
and prime minister, 1976.

A trout is a fish mainly known by hearsay. It lives on anything not included in a fisherman's equipment.

H.I. Philips, US writer. *On White or Rye*.

The commonly-accepted source of the term 'angling' is an ancient Indo-European word anka, meaning 'hook' or 'to fish with a hook', but several other words are also likely candidates, including enka (unwise expenditure or useless task), unglo (one who is tormented by insects), onku (loud or infrequent lamentation), angi (to deceive), onklo (possession by demons), and angla (love of pointless suffering).

Henry Beard, US humorist. *An Angler's Dictionary* (1983).

I won't die at a match. I might die being dragged down the river Tweed by a giant salmon, but at a football match, no.

Jack Charlton (1935–), English footballer and football manager,
prophesying his possible end in 1988.

See also ANGLERS.

Anti-blood sports

Hunting is not a proper employment for a thinking man.

Joseph Addison (1672–1719), British essayist and politician.

A man whose chief ambition is to show his bravery in hunting foxes. A term of reproach used of country gentlemen.

Samuel Johnson (1709–84), British lexicographer. Entry for
'foxhunter' in his *Dictionary* (1755).

It is very strange, and very melancholy, that the paucity of human pleasures should persuade us ever to call hunting one of them.

Samuel Johnson (1709–84), British lexicographer. Quoted in Hester
Lynch Piozzi, *Anecdotes of Johnson* (1786).

A man who can in cold blood hunt and torture a poor innocent animal, cannot feel much compassion for the distresses of his own species.
Frederick II (the Great; 1712–86), king of Prussia.

Detested sport,
That owes its pleasures to another's pain.
William Cowper (1731–1800), British poet. *The Task* (1785).

Wild animals never kill for sport. Man is the only one to whom the torture and death of his fellow-creatures is amusing in itself.
J.A. Froude (1818–94), British historian. *Oceana* (1886).

The English country gentleman galloping after a fox – the unspeakable in full pursuit of the uneatable.
Oscar Wilde (1854–1900), Irish writer and wit. *A Woman of No Importance* (1893).

I do not see why I should break my neck because a dog chooses to run after a nasty smell.
Arthur James Balfour (1848–1930), British Conservative prime minister, describing his reasons for not going fox-hunting. Quoted in Ian Malcolm, *Lord Balfour: A Memory* (1930).

No sportsman wants to kill a fox or the pheasant as I want to kill him when I see him doing it.
George Bernard Shaw (1856–1950), Irish playwright and critic.

A sportsman is a fellow who, every now and then, simply has to go out and kill something.
Stephen Leacock (1869–1944), Canadian humorist.

See also BULLFIGHTING; HUNTING; SHOOTING.

Anti-sports

The athlete's habit of body neither produces a good condition for the general purposes of civic life, nor does it encourage ordinary health and the procreation of children.
Aristotle (384–322 BC), Greek philosopher.

For bodily exercise profiteth little: but godliness is profitable unto all things.

The *Bible*, 1 Timothy 4:8.

Athletes live a life quite contrary to the precepts of hygiene, and I regard their mode of living as a regime far more favourable to illness than to health.

Galen (*c.*200 AD), Greek physician and anatomist.

Footballe, wherein nothing but beastlie furie and extreme violence; wherefore it is to be put in perpetual silence.

Edward II (1284–1327), king of England. Royal decree of 1314.

For as much as there is great noise in the city caused by hustling over large balls, from which many evils might arise; which God forbid.

Edward II (1284–1327), king of England. Royal decree of 1314.

It is statute and ordained that in na place of the Realme there be used Futeball, Golfe, or uther sik unproffitable sportes.

James IV (1473–1513), king of Scotland. Royal decree of 1491.

No foteball player be used or suffered within the City of London and the liberties thereof upon pain of imprisonment.

Elizabeth I (1533–1603), queen of England. Royal decree of 1572.

I debarre all rough and violent exercises, as the foot-ball, meeter for mameing than making able users thereof.

James I (1566–1625), king of England and Scotland (as James VI). Royal decree of 1603.

Watch against inordinate sensual delight in even the lawfullest of sports. Excess of pleasure in any such vanity doh very much corrupt and befool the mind.

Richard Baxter (1615–91), English Puritan. *A Christian Directory* (1678).

Science distinguishes a man of honour from one of those athletic brutes whom undeservedly we call heroes.

John Dryden (1631–1700), British poet and playwright.

Games played with the ball, and others of that nature, are too violent for the body, and stamp no character on the mind.

Thomas Jefferson (1743–1826), US politician and president.

I will not permit thirty men to travel four hundred miles to agitate a bag of wind.

Andrew Dickson White (1832–1918), US educationalist. His reasons,
while first President of Cornell University (1867–85), for not permitting
a Cornell football team to travel to a match in Michigan. Quoted in
D. Wallechinsky, *The People's Almanack* (1975).

The addiction to sports, therefore, in a peculiar degree marks an arrested development of man's moral nature.

Thorstein Veblen (1857–1929), US sociologist and philosopher, 1899.

Then ye returned to your trinkets; then ye contented your souls
With the flannelled fools at the wicket or the muddied oafs at the goals.

Rudyard Kipling (1865–1936), British novelist and poet.
'The Islanders' (1903).

Games are for people who can neither read nor think.

George Bernard Shaw (1856–1950), Irish playwright and critic.

I hate all sports as rabidly as a person who likes sports hates common sense.

H.L. Mencken (1880–1956), US journalist and critic.
Heathen Days (1943).

War is the only sport that is genuinely amusing. And it is the only sport that has any intelligible use.

H.L. Mencken (1880–1956), US journalist and critic.

Serious sport has nothing to do with fair play. It is bound up with hatred, jealousy, boastfulness, disregard of all rules and sadistic pleasure in witnessing violence: in other words, it is war minus the shooting ... there are quite enough real causes of trouble already, and we need not add to them by encouraging young men to kick each other on the shins amid the roars of infuriated spectators.

George Orwell (1903–50), British novelist. 'The Sporting Spirit', in
Tribune, 14 December 1945.

It is international sport that helps kick the world downhill. Started by foolish athletes, who thought it would promote understanding, it is supported today by the desire for political prestige and by the interests involved in gate monies. It is completely harmful.

E.M. Forster (1879–1970), British novelist, 1957.

I don't like this game.

Spike Milligan (1918–), British comedian. A catchphrase from the 1950s comedy series *The Goon Show*.

Organised sport is an occasion of pure waste – waste of time, energy, ingenuity, skill, and often money.

Roger Caillois (1913–78), French writer. *Men Play Games.*

I used to think the only use for it was to give small boys something else to kick besides me.

Katharine Whitehorn (1926–), British journalist, referring to sport in general in *Observations* (1970).

When it comes to sports I am not particularly interested. Generally speaking, I look upon them as dangerous and tiring activities performed by people with whom I share nothing except the right to trial by jury.

Fran Lebowitz (1950–), US humorist. In *Metropolitan Life* (1978).

Sport, as I have discovered, fosters international hostility and leads the audience, no doubt from boredom, to assault and do grievous bodily harm while watching it.

John Mortimer (1923–), British playwright, novelist and barrister. *Clinging to the Wreckage* (1982).

Queremos frijoles, no goles.
(We want beans, not goals.)

Banner waved by Mexican steelworkers during a World Cup football match in June 1986.

What principle governed the British sporting event? It appeared that, in exchange for a few pounds, you received one hour and forty-five minutes characterized by the greatest possible exposure to the worst possible weather, the greatest number of people in the smallest possible space and the greatest number of obstacles – unreliable transport, no parking, an intensely dangerous crush at the only exit, a repellent polio pond to pee into, last minute changes of the starting time – to keep you from ever attending a match again.

Bill Buford (1954–), US writer. *Among the Thugs* (1991).

Hang gliding, blast baseball, and sod cycling.
Anonymous.

See also ANTI-BLOOD SPORTS; BASEBALL-BASHERS; BOXING-BASHERS; COUCH
POTATOES; CRICKET-BASHERS; FOOTBALL-BASHERS; GOLF-BASHERS.

Appearance

I generally hit him in the face because I felt sorry for his family and thought
I would select the only place that couldn't be disfigured.
Mike Leonard, US boxer, referring to a bout against Jack Cushing in
1894. This was, incidentally, the first boxing match ever to be filmed.

He's so ugly that when he cries the tears run down the back of his head.
Muhammad Ali (Cassius Clay; 1942–), US heavyweight boxer.
Referring to Sonny Liston in 1964, the year in which Ali achieved a
famous victory over his rival.

Hair like badly-turned broccoli.
Clive James (1939–), Australian broadcaster and writer, referring to
US tennis player John McEnroe.

The face of a choirboy, the demeanour of a civil servant and the ruthlessness
of a rat catcher.
Geoffrey Boycott (1940–), English cricketer, describing his team-
mate Derek Underwood in Geoffrey Boycott, *Opening Up* (1980).

With four sisters about the house, I could never get my hands on a comb.
Marvin Hagler (1954–), US middleweight boxer, explaining why he
had a shaven head.

A 1914 biplane tied up with elastic bands trying vainly to take off.
Frank Keating (1937–), British sportswriter, describing the eccentric run-up
of the England fast bowler Bob Willis, in the *Guardian*.

Colin Montgomerie has a face like a warthog that has been stung by a wasp.
David Feherty (1958–), Northern Ireland-born golfer, referring to
the Scottish golfer Colin Montgomerie in 1992.

I know I'm no Kim Basinger, but she can't throw a javelin.
Fatima Whitbread (1961–), British javelin thrower, 1993.

He's the only player who, when he appears on TV, Daleks hide behind the sofa.

Nick Hancock (1963–), British television presenter, referring to the English footballer Peter Beardsley, who is often the butt of jokes about his supposedly unprepossessing appearance. From the BBC television show *They Think It's All Over*, 1995.

Mothers keep their photo on the mantelpiece to stop the kids going too near the fire.

Jim Neilly, Irish sports commentator. Referring to the rough appearance of the forwards of the Munster rugby union team. BBC TV, 1995.

Stephen Hendry is the only man with a face that comes with free garlic bread.

Nick Hancock (1963–), British television presenter, referring to the Scottish snooker player Stephen Hendry. From the BBC television show, *They Think It's All Over*, 1995.

One of the few men capable of looking more dishevelled at the start of a six-hour century than at the end of it.

Martin Johnson (1949–), British sportswriter, referring to England cricketer Mike Atherton in the *Daily Telegraph*, 1998.

I looked at it. I said, 'Wow, she's cute. She has a nice figure, very narrow hips, nice legs. Long, good hair.' All of a sudden I went, 'Wow, that was me.'

Andre Agassi (1970–), US tennis player, describing his reaction in 1999 when he was shown a picture of himself at the age of 16.

See also BEARDS AND MOUSTACHES; KIT; PHYSIQUE.

Archery

But this sufficeth for the declaration of shooting, whereby it is sufficiently proved that it incomparably excelleth all other exercise, pastime and solace.

Sir Thomas Elyot (1499–1546), English politician and writer. *The Castel of Helth* (1538).

Among the arts that have been carried to a high degree of perfection in this kingdom, there is no one more conspicuous than that of Archery.

Joseph Strutt (1749–1802), British writer and engraver. *The Sports and Pastimes of the People of England* (1830).

Poetry is an absolutely dead art – like taking up archery.

Sacheverell Sitwell (1897–1988), British writer and art critic, 1976.

John ARLOTT

English cricket writer and commentator (1914–91) famed for his Hampshire burr, evocative turn of phrase and deep love of the game.

Quotes about John Arlott

You're not only the best cricket commentator – far and away that; but the best sports commentator I've heard, ever; exact, enthusiastic; prejudiced; amazingly visual, authoritative and friendly.

Dylan Thomas (1914–53), Welsh poet. In a letter to John Arlott, 11 June 1947.

I hear John Arlott's voice every weekend, describing cricket matches. He sounds like Uncle Tom Cobleigh reading Neville Cardus to the Indians.

Dylan Thomas (1914–53), Welsh poet. In a letter, 11 July 1947.

Probably the most celebrated British voice after Churchill's.

Frank Keating (1937–), British sportswriter. The *Guardian*, 1991.

Quotes by John Arlott

So what we have here is a clear case of Mann's inhumanity to Mann.

Commentating in 1948 on a Test match in which the South African bowler 'Tufty' Mann was causing great difficulty for the England batsman George Mann. Quoted in the *Daily Mail*, 3 September 1980.

The umpire signals a bye with the air of a weary stork.

BBC radio commentary.

He approaches the wicket like Groucho Marx chasing a pretty waitress.

Describing an unidentified player's individual bowling action. BBC radio commentary.

My word, I know what the problems are. I've failed at everything.

From his final BBC radio broadcast in 1980, when asked if experience as a player of first-class cricket would have been a help to him as a cricket commentator and writer.

See also Denis COMPTON; CRICKET; CRICKET UMPIRES; FAST BOWLING; FRIENDLIES; W.G. GRACE; Sir Jack HOBBS; Brian JOHNSTON; Clive LLOYD; POLITICS; Viv RICHARDS; Sir Gary SOBERS; Fred TRUEMAN; VILLAGE SPORTS.

Arsenal

I well remember that as a boy, there was only one club for me – Arsenal.

Ferenc Puskas (1926–), Hungarian footballer. *Captain of Hungary* (1955).

We were boring when I played, we were boring in the Thirties and no doubt we'll be boring in the next decade. I don't mind as long as the trophies keep coming.

George Graham (1944–), Scottish footballer and manager. Referring, while manager of Arsenal in the early 1990s, to the club's long-standing reputation for playing tedious football.

At some clubs success is accidental. At Arsenal it is compulsory.

Arsène Wenger (1949–), French football manager, speaking as manager of Arsenal in 1998.

Artificial grass

I don't know. I never smoked Astroturf.

Joe Namath (1943–), American football player. His response when asked if he preferred Astroturf to grass.

If horses can't eat it, I won't play on it.

Dick Allen (1942–), US baseball player.

It'll never replace plastic.

Ray Harford (1945–), English football manager. On being shown the natural grass surface at Coventry, after his own club Luton Town had laid down an artificial pitch, 1988.

Ascot

Four-day annual horse-racing meeting, held in June at Ascot, Berkshire, and long considered a highlight of the British social calendar.

Ascot is so exclusive that it is the only race-course in the world where the horses own the people.

Art Buchwald (1925–), US writer. 'Ordeal at Ascot', in *I Chose Caviar*.

At one time a little humdrum adultery could prove a barrier to the Royal Enclosure at Ascot, but now something rather more spectacular is required, such as hijacking a Securicor van or taking too prominent a role in a sex instruction film designed for circulation in the best preparatory schools.

Roger Mortimer (1909–), British sportswriter. *The Sunday Times*, 1971.

Jumping at Ascot is like Blackpool with the tide out.

John Hislop, British sportswriter.

The Ashes

The nickname for the Test series contested at regular intervals between the cricket teams of England and Australia.

In affectionate remembrance of English cricket, which died at the Oval on 29th August, 1882. Deeply lamented by a large circle of sorrowing friends and acquaintances. RIP. NB The body will be cremated and the ashes taken to Australia.

Anonymous notice published in the *Sporting Times*, 2 September 1882, following England's humiliating defeat at the hands of Australia that year. The 'body' was the set of stumps used in the series, which were ceremonially burned and put in an urn: the origin of the name 'The Ashes'.

The aim of English Test cricket is, in fact, mainly to beat Australia.

Jim Laker (1922–86), English cricketer. *Over to Me* (1960).

A fart competing with thunder.

Graham Gooch (1953–), English cricketer, summing up England's ill-fated attempts to beat Australia in the 1990–91 Ashes Test series.

If the Poms bat first, let's tell the taxi to wait.

Banner waved by Australian cricket fans at an England–Australia match in 1995, alluding to the fact that England had failed to win an Ashes Test series since 1986–87.

See also BODYLINE.

Athletics *See* Sir Roger BANNISTER; BIATHLON; Linford CHRISTIE; David COLEMAN; DECATHLON; DISCUS; GYMNASTICS; HAMMER; JOGGING; Ben JOHNSON; Carl LEWIS; MARATHON; OLYMPIC GAMES; Jesse OWENS; POLE VAULT; RUNNING; Daley THOMPSON; TRIPLE JUMP.

Ron ATKINSON

English football manager (1939–) known affectionately as
'Big Ron' because of his extrovert personality.

Quotes about Ron Atkinson

As far as he's concerned, he is God. There's nobody big enough to tell him
what to do.

Margaret Atkinson, his wife, speaking in 1984 after revelations in
the press that her husband had been having an extra-marital affair.

They call him Big Ron Atkinson because he is a Big Spender in the transfer
market. I just call him Fat Ron.

Malcolm Allison (1927–), English football manager, 1993.

Quotes by Ron Atkinson

It's bloody tough being a legend.

Quoted in 1983.

I believe there are only a select few managers who can handle the real giant
clubs of this world. I happen to be one of them.

Quoted in 1988 after being appointed coach at Atletico Madrid. He
was sacked one month later.

I met Mick Jagger when I was playing for Oxford United and the Rolling
Stones played a concert there. Little did I know that one day he'd be almost
as famous as me.

Quoted in 1993.

Australian Rules football

Without giving offence to anyone, I may remark that it is a game which
commends itself to semi-barbarous races.

Edward Kinglake. 'The Australians at Home' (1891).

That's not football, mate, it's aerial ping-pong.

Frank Hardy (1917–94), Australian writer. *The Yarns of Billy Borker* (1965).

Australian Rules football might best be described as a game devised for
padded cells, played in the open air.

Jim Murray, US sportswriter.

· B ·

Backgammon

I always thought Backgammon was a side of bacon.

Spike Milligan (1918–), British comedian.

Badminton

To deceive to deceive to deceive is the art of badminton.

Sir George Thomas (1881–1972), British badminton administrator.
Quoted in *The Guinness Book of Badminton* (1983).

The shuttle is a prima donna.

Pat Davis (1915–), Welsh badminton coach and writer, 1983.

Seve BALLESTEROS

**Spanish golfer (Severiano Ballesteros; 1957–) loved
for his flamboyant playing style.**

Seve – the greatest thing to come out of Spain since a painting by Picasso
that made sense.

Dan Jenkins, US sportswriter.

Seve Ballesteros goes after a golf course the way a lion goes after a zebra.

Jim Murray, US sportswriter, in the *Los Angeles Times*.

Seve's got shots the rest of us don't even know.

Ben Crenshaw (1952–), US golfer.

See also CADDIES; LUCK; KIT; MEDICAL TREATMENT.

Ballooning

I have known today a magnificent intoxication. I have learnt how it feels to be a bird. I have flown. Yes I have flown. I am still astonished at it, still deeply moved.

Le *Figaro*, 1908.

Ballooning is an art, not a science, and is surely the only form of flying, or even locomotion, where one has no controls to turn left or right, accelerate or brake.

Christine Turnbull, writer. *Hot Air Ballooning* (1970).

Balls

Hail, Gutta-Percha! precious gum!
O'er Scotland's links lang may ye bum;
Some proud-pursed billies haw and hum,
And say ye'er douf at fleein';
But let them try ye fairly out,
Wi' ony balls for days about,
Your merits they will loudly tout,
And own they hae been leein'.

William Graham (1918–1986), Scottish poet, extolling the virtues of the golf ball in 1848.

The Ball no question makes of Ayes and Noes,
But Here or There as strikes the Player goes,
And He that toss'd it down into the Field;
He knows about it all – He knows – He knows!

Edward Fitzgerald (1809–83), British poet and translator. *The Rubaiyat of Omar Khayyám* (1879).

I really do not see why we should allow the Haskell to come in. It should be slaughtered at the ports. The discovery of a ball that flies considerably further would be a menace to the game of golf. It would immediately make all our holes the wrong length.

A lamentation on the arrival of the Haskell rubber-cored golf ball
printed in the *Manchester Guardian* in 1901.

The British 'Sphere of Influence' – the cricket ball.

Mr Punch's Book of Sport (1906).

For a long time we dreamed of a real leather ball, and at last my brother had one for his birthday. The feel of the leather, the stitching round it, the faint gold letters stamped upon it, the touch of the seam, the smell of it, all affected me so deeply that I still have that ache of beauty when I hold a cricket ball.

Alison Uttley (1884–1976), British writer. 'Carts and Candlesticks' (1948).

The ball is man's most disastrous invention, not excluding the wheel.

Robert Morley (1908–92), British film actor, 1965.

Golf balls are attracted to water as unerringly as the eye of a middle-aged man to a female bosom.

Michael Green (1927–), British humorist. *The Art of Coarse Golf* (1967).

I think football would become an even better game if someone could invent a ball that kicks back.

Eric Morecambe (1926–84), British comedian.

The balls used in top-class games are generally smaller than those used in others.

Paul Fussell (1924–), US historian and writer.

Without doubt, the single most important object in sport is the ball.

Andrew Bailey, sportswriter. *Future Sport* (1982).

If you think it's hard to meet new people, try picking up the wrong golf ball.

Jack Lemmon (1925–), US film actor. Quoted in *Sports Illustrated*, 9 December 1985.

I've always believed in treating the ball like a woman. Give it a cuddle, caress it a wee bit, take your time, and you'll get the required response.

Jim Baxter (1939–), Scottish footballer, 1991.

Football is like a religion to me. I worship the ball, and I treat it like a god. Too many players think of a football as something to kick. They should be taught to caress it and to treat it like a precious gem.

Pelé (Edson Arantes do Nascimento; 1940–), Brazilian footballer.

The one thing that has never changed in the history of the game is the shape of the ball.

Denis Law (1940–), Scottish footballer, referring to footballs.
Quoted in the *Sunday Times*, 18 December 1994.

Why is there only one ball for 22 players? If you gave a ball to each of them, they'd stop fighting for it.

Anonymous correspondent to an anti-World Cup web site, 1998.
'Sporting Quotes of the Year 1998', the *Daily Telegraph*,
28 December 1998.

Ball-tampering

The sympathetic indignation of certain English cricketers over alleged Pakistani ball-tampering: the unedifying in pursuit of the unbeatable.

Patrick Collins (1943–), in the *Mail on Sunday*, 1992, parodying
Oscar Wilde's 'The unspeakable in full pursuit of the uneatable'
(*see* ANTI-BLOOD SPORTS).

There is a lot of racism in this society. Where is that hatred coming from? I can show you millions of pictures of English players picking the seam. You see Australian cricketers with sun cream on their faces. They keep wiping sweat from their faces mixed with the cream and rubbing it on the ball. It is ball tampering. Scratching the ball is no bigger crime.

Imran Khan (1952–), Pakistani cricketer, responding to criticism of
alleged ball-tampering by Pakistani players in *India Today*, 1994.

The Soiled Skipper.

Daily Mirror headline, referring to allegations that England captain
Michael Atherton was guilty of ball-tampering, specifically by
rubbing the ball with dirt from his pocket, 1994.

Sir Roger BANNISTER

British middle-distance runner (1929–) who became the first man to run the mile in under four minutes, at Oxford on 6 May 1954.

I leapt at the tape like a man taking his last spring to save himself from the chasm that threatens to engulf him ... I felt like an exploded light-bulb with no will to live.

Referring to the moment he broke the 'four-minute mile' in 1954.
First Four Minutes (1955).

I sometimes think that running has given me a glimpse of the greatest freedom a man can ever know, because it results in the simultaneous liberation of both body and mind.

First Four Minutes (1955).

See also RUNNING.

Baseball

Monday, in Christian countries, the day after the baseball game.

Ambrose Bierce (1842–1914), US journalist and poet. *The Cynic's Wordbook* (1906); retitled *The Devil's Dictionary* (1911).

Baseball has the great advantage over cricket of being sooner ended. It combines the best features of that primitive form of cricket known as Tip-and-Run with those of lawn tennis, Puss-in-the-corner and Handel's Messiah.

George Bernard Shaw (1856–1950), Irish playwright and critic.

Two hours is as long as an American will wait for the close of a baseball game – or anything for that matter.

Albert G. Spalding (1850–1915), US baseball manufacturer.

America became a great nation under baseball. And began to decline the moment it took up a lot of poor substitutes.

Will Rogers (1879–1935), US humorist.

I've never seen a baseball game I didn't like.

Will Rogers (1879–1935), US humorist.

Play ball! Means something more than runs
Or pitches thudding into gloves!
Remember through the summer suns
This is the game your country loves.

Grantland Rice (1880–1954), US sportswriter and poet.

A baseball game is twice as much fun if you're seeing it on the company's time.

William Feather (1889–1981), US publisher.

England and America should scrap cricket and baseball and come up with a new game that they both can play. Like baseball, for example.

Robert Benchley (1889–1945), US humorist.

There's three things you can do in a baseball game – you can win, you can lose, or it can rain.

Charles 'Casey' Stengel (1890–1975), US baseball player and manager.

I suppose that even the most pleasurable of imaginable occupations, that of batting baseballs through the windows of the RCA Building, would pall a little as the days ran on.

James Thurber (1894–1961), US humorist and cartoonist.
'Memoirs of a Drudge' in *The Thurber Carnival* (1945).

No game in the world is as tidy and dramatically neat as baseball, with cause and effect, crime and punishment, motive and result, so cleanly defined.

Paul Gallico (1897–1976), US journalist, novelist and short-story writer.

Ballet is the fairies' baseball.

Oscar Levant (1906–72), US humorist.

All winter long I am one for whom the bell is tolling
I can arouse no interest in basketball, indoor fly casting or bowling.
The sports pages are strictly no soap
And until the cry of 'Play Ball', I mope!

Ogden Nash (1902–71), US poet and humorist. Quoted in *Sports Illustrated* (1957).

Whoever wants to know the heart and mind of America had better learn baseball.

Jacques Barzun (1907–), US educationalist. Quoted in Michael
Novak, *The Joys of Sports* (1976).

There's no skill involved. Just go up there and swing at the ball.

Joe DiMaggio (1914–99), US baseball player.

Baseball is the only game left for people. To play basketball, you have to be 7 feet 6 inches. To play football, you have to be the same width.

Bill Veeck (1914–86), US baseball manager, comparing baseball with
basketball and American football in 1975.

Baseball is a Lockean game, a kind of contract theory in ritual form, a set of atomic individuals who assent to patterns of limited co-operation in their mutual interest.

Michael Novak (1933–), US critic and philosopher, finding links
between baseball and the ideas of John Locke, the 17th-century
philosopher and social contract theorist, in *The Joys of Sports* (1976).

When I was a little boy, I wanted to be a baseball player and join the circus. With the Yankees I've accomplished both.

Graig Nettles (1944–), US baseball player, referring to the
New York Yankees.

I'd walk though hell in a gasoline suit to keep playing baseball.

Peter Rose (1941–), US baseball player. He played in a record
3562 games in a 20-year career that ended in the mid-1980s.

Baseball is the favourite American sport because it's so slow. Any idiot can follow it. And just about any idiot can play it.

Gore Vidal (1925–), US novelist.

Hating the New York Yankees is as American as apple pie, unwed mothers and cheating on your income tax.

Mike Royko (1932–1997), US journalist, 1981.

Baseball, it is said, is only a game. True. And the Grand Canyon is only a hole in Arizona. Not all holes, or games, are created equal.

George F. Will (1941–), US journalist. *Men at Work: The Craft of
Baseball* (1990).

In the great department store of life, baseball is the toy department.

Anonymous US sports commentator, quoted in the *Independent*,
28 September 1991.

Baseball is very big with my people. It figures. It's the only way we can get to shake a bat at a white man without starting a riot.

Dick Gregory (1932–), black US comedian. Quoted in
D.H. Nathan, *Baseball Quotations* (1991).

See also Henry ('Hank') AARON; BASEBALL-BASHERS; BASEBALL PLAYERS;
Lawrence ('Yogi') BERRA; Joe DiMAGGIO; Babe RUTH.

Baseball-bashers

Baseball is a game which consists of tapping a ball with a piece of wood, then running like a lunatic.

H. Dutiel.

The underprivileged people of the Americas play some strange game with a bat which looks like an overgrown rolling pin.

Fred Trueman (1931–), English cricketer.

I don't think I can be expected to take seriously any game which takes less than three days to reach its conclusion.

Tom Stoppard (Tom Straussler; 1937–), Czech-born British
playwright, comparing baseball unfavourably with cricket. 'Sports
Quotes of the Year', the *Guardian*, 24 December 1984.

Baseball players

A ball player's got to be kept hungry to become a big leaguer. That's why no boy from a rich family ever made the big leagues.

Joe DiMaggio (1914–99), US baseball player. Quoted in the *New
York Times*, 30 April 1961.

I ain't ever had a job. I just always played baseball.

Leroy 'Satchel' Paige (1906–82), US baseball player.

Baseball players are the weirdest of all. I think it's all that organ music.

Peter Gent (1943–), American football player and novelist,
referring to the organ music conventionally played over public
address systems at major US baseball games.

See also Henry ('Hank') AARON; Lawrence ('Yogi') BERRA; Joe DiMAGGIO; Babe RUTH.

Basketball

Nothing there but basketball, a game which won't be fit for people until they set the basket umbilicus-high and return the giraffes to the zoo.

Ogden Nash (1902–71), US poet and humorist.

Basketball ... is staying in after school in your underwear.

Ring Lardner (1885–1933), US humorist and writer. Quoted in
the film *Drive He Said* (1970).

The game is too long, the season is too long and the players are too long.

Jack Dolph, US basketball manager, 1973.

If Shakespeare had been in pro basketball he never would have had time to write his soliloquies. He would always have been on a plane between Phoenix and Kansas City.

Paul Westhead (1959–), US basketball coach.

See also Wilt CHAMBERLAIN; Earvin ('Magic') JOHNSON.

Beards and moustaches

Dr W.G. Grace,
Had hair all over his face.
Lord! How all the people cheered,
When a ball got lost in his beard.

E.Clerihew Bentley (1875–1956), British journalist and novelist. A
celebrated example of the 'clerihew' verse form that he invented.

Are you aware, Sir, that the last time I saw anything like that on a top-lip, the whole herd had to be destroyed.

Eric Morecambe (1926–84), British comedian, addressing the
moustachioed Australian cricketer Dennis Lillee in the 1970s.

I thought you needed designer stubble to get into the England team
these days.

Mike Gatting (1957–), English cricketer. Explaining, while on tour
with England in 1993, why he had shaved off his beard.

There is a modern fashion for designer stubble and some people believe
it to be very attractive. But it is aggravating to others and we shall be
looking at the whole question of people's facial hair.

Ted Dexter (1935–), English cricketer and cricket administrator.
Replying to criticism of the England cricket team's hirsute
appearance while on tour in India in 1993.

See also APPEARANCE; DRUG-TAKING.

David BECKHAM

**English footballer (1975–) whose prodigious talent,
fashionable good looks and marriage to Spice Girl Victoria
Adams made him a household name.**

Quotes about David Beckham

He has two feet, which a lot of players don't have nowadays.

Jimmy Hill (1928–), British television sports commentator.

It is left feet that are usually called educated; David Beckham's right
probably has an MA.

Ian Ridley, British sportswriter. *Independent on Sunday* (1995).

It is nothing out of the ordinary. David wears my knickers as well. He's
getting in touch with his feminine side.

Victoria Adams (1975–), British pop star, also known as 'Posh
Spice'. Referring, in 1999, to her fiancé's recent appearance in public
wearing a sarong.

This Gaultier-saronged, Posh Spiced, Cooled Britannia, look-at-me, what-a-
lad, loadsamoney, sex-and-shopping, fame-schooled, daytime-TV, over-
coiffed twerp, did not, of course, mean any harm.

Daily Telegraph report following David Beckham's sending-off
against Argentina after aiming a kick at at the Argentinian Diego
Simeone, which contributed to England's premature exit from the
1998 World Cup.

Without being too harsh on David, he cost us the match.

Ian Wright (1963–), English footballer, referring to Beckham's
sending-off in the 1998 World Cup. 'Quotes of the Year', the
Guardian, 24 December 1998.

10 Heroic Lions, One Stupid Boy.

Headline, the *Mirror* (1998), referring to Beckham's sending-off in
the 1998 World Cup.

Murderers have been treated better than David Beckham.

Glenn Hoddle (1957–), English footballer and manager. Referring
to press criticism of the England star after the 1998 World Cup in
My World Cup Diary (1998).

God forgives even David Beckham.

Poster on display outside Mansfield Road Baptist Church,
Nottingham in the wake of England's exit from the 1998 World Cup.

Quotes by David Beckham

The reason fans abuse me is because they are jealous.

'Quotes of the Year', the *Guardian*, 24 December 1998.

See also FAMOUS LAST WORDS.

Lawrence ('Yogi') BERRA

US baseball player and coach (1925–), celebrated as much
for his one-liners as for his success on the baseball field.

Baseball is 90% mental, the other half is physical.

Attributed.

If people don't want to come out to the ball park, nobody's going to stop 'em.

Discussing a drop in attendances at baseball matches.

He made too many wrong mistakes.

Attributed.

They wouldn't have won if we had beaten them.

Attributed.

It ain't over 'til it's over.

Attributed.

Always go to other people's funerals, otherwise they won't come to yours.

Attributed.

No wonder nobody comes here to eat – it's too crowded.

His response when arriving in a busy New York restaurant.

Better make it four, I don't think I can eat eight.

His reply when asked if he would like his pizza cut into four or eight pieces.

Oh, I can't do that. That's my bad side.

His response when asked by a photographer to look straight at the camera.

I really didn't say everything I said.

Attributed.

See also Joe DiMAGGIO; STREAKERS.

George BEST

Northern Ireland footballer (1946–), regarded as one of the most talented players ever to play the game.

Quotes about George Best

... doesn't smoke, drinks only occasionally and restricts his card-playing to sessions which ease the boredom of travelling.

Boy's Own Paper, cover feature of final issue, 1967.

Georgie Best, superstar,
Wears frilly knickers and a playtex bra.

Chant sung to the tune of 'Jesus Christ Superstar' in the early 1970s.

He had ice in his veins, warmth in his heart, and timing and balance in his feet.

Danny Blanchflower (1926–93), Northern Ireland footballer.

We had our problems with the wee feller, but I prefer to remember his genius.

Sir Matt Busby (1909–94), Scottish football manager.

The greatest player of my lifetime, and I include the likes of Pelé, Di Stefano, Puskas, Eusébio, Maradona, Cruyff, Matthews and Finney in that assessment.

Jimmy Greaves (1940–), English footballer.

How can you put into words what it means having George Best at Dunstable? It'll be a bigger boost for the club than having Frank Sinatra sing at half-time.

Barry Fry, English football manager, 1974.

Quotes by George Best

Most of the things I've done are my own fault, so I can't feel guilty about them.

Colemanballs (1982).

They say I slept with seven Miss Worlds, but it was only three.

Quoted in 1997.

It makes me laugh when the papers talk about 'wasted'; it makes me laugh when I see 'fallen idol' or 'fallen legend'. These people who are writing it are sitting in an office nine to five and I don't know what they earn, but I'm going out and sometimes getting paid £5,000 for an interview. And I'm thinking: who's fallen here?

Quoted in 1998.

It's a pleasure to be standing up here. It's a pleasure to be standing up.

Acceptance speech on being acclaimed 'Footballer of the Century' in 1999.

See also Eric CANTONA; Sir Bobby CHARLTON; FAME; Paul GASCOIGNE; Kevin KEEGAN; SEX; TACTICS.

Betting *See* GAMBLING.

Biathlon

In the biathlon, a Russian puts on a pair of skis, picks up a rifle, slides around in the trees, and stops every so often to shoot a West German.

Dan Jenkins, US sportswriter. *Playboy*, 1988.

Billiards

Let it alone, let's to billiards.

William Shakespeare (1564–1616), English playwright and poet.
Antony and Cleopatra (c.1606).

Up, all of us, and to Billiards.

Samuel Pepys (1633–1703), British diarist. *Diary*, 17 July 1665.

Billiards, this most genteel, cleanly and ingenious game.

Charles Cotton (1630–87), British poet, 1674.

A man who wants to play billiards must have no other ambition – billiards is all.

Edward V. Lucas (1868–1938), British novelist and poet.

It was remarked to me by the late Mr Charles Roupell ... that to play billiards well was the sign of an ill-spent youth.

Herbert Spencer (1820–1903), British philosopher. As indicated, Spencer denied being the originator of the remark with which his name became so closely associated. Another tradition has it that it was the Scottish novelist Robert Louis Stevenson who was the original author, making the observation in the billiards room at the Savile Club in London, of which he was a member in the years 1874–94. It may be a much earlier coinage, however, as a variant of it was quoted in *Noctes Ambrosianae* in March 1827. Quoted in David Duncan, *Life and Letters of Spencer* (1908).

The Billiard table is the paradise of the ball.

Alfred E. Crawley (1869–1924), British social anthropologist. *The Book of the Ball* (1913).

Bums play pool, gentlemen play billiards.

Daniel McGoorty (1901–70), US writer.

Billiards is very similar to snooker, except there are only three balls and no one watches it.

Steve Davis (1957–), British snooker player, 1988.

See also SNOOKER.

Harold 'Dickie' BIRD *See* CRICKET UMPIRES.

Biting

Norman Hunter Bites Yer Legs!

Banner waved by Leeds United fans, referring to the fierce
reputation of Leeds defender Norman Hunter (1943–).

I prefer rugby to soccer. I enjoy the violence in rugby, except when they start biting each other's ears off.

Elizabeth Taylor (1932–), British-born US film actress, 1972.

I have never knowingly bitten another player. For one thing I believe in good hygiene.

Conrad Dobler (1950–), American football player with a reputation
for rough play.

No, I'm a vegetarian.

Wali Muhammad, cruiserweight boxer, denying the suggestion that
he had bitten his opponent, James Salerno.

See also Mike TYSON; VIOLENCE.

Blood sports *See* BULLFIGHTING; HUNTING; SHOOTING.

Boat Race

Annual rowing race between eights from Oxford and
Cambridge universities, held on the River Thames in
London in late March or early April.

Oxford won, Cambridge too!

Punch report on the 1877 Boat Race, which ended in a dead heat.

Don't you think it's going to be rather wet for the horses?

Spike Milligan (1918–), British comedian. His response when told
the route used in the Oxford–Cambridge Boat Race.

The Oxford–Cambridge Boat Race would be much more attractive if the rules were changed to allow the boats to ram each other.

Miles Kington (1941–), British humorist.

See also CLASSIC COMMENTARIES; HENLEY; ROWING.

Bodybuilding

It is foolish and quite unfitting for an educated man to spend all his time on acquiring bulging muscles, a thick neck and mighty lungs. The large amounts they are compelled to eat make them dull-witted.

Seneca (4 BC– AD 65), Roman philosopher and playwright.

If nature had intended our skeletons to be visible it would have put them on the outside of our bodies.

Elmer Rice (1892–1967), US playwright.

No pain – no gain.

Anonymous slogan that was subsequently adopted as a motto throughout bodybuilding. It may have been inspired by Adlai Stevenson's 'There are no gains without pains' during his 1952 campaign for the Democratic presidential nomination.

You too can have a body like mine.

Charles Atlas (1894–1972), US bodybuilder. Advertising slogan, c.1922.

Pain means progress.

Arnold Schwarzenegger (1947–), US bodybuilder and film actor. His motto during his bodybuilding days.

Posing is a performing art.

Arnold Schwarzenegger (1947–), US bodybuilder and film actor. Quoted by Jasmine Birtles in the *Guardian*, 1975, who went on to observe 'it is difficult to respect a sport that has "posing" as part of its jargon'.

It does not befit a man to parade in front of the public flexing his muscles. They don't walk, they carry their muscled torsos proudly – self-conceited, self-important, looking like roosters on a promenade. There are very many unbalanced persons among them. Men who take anabolic steroids and men in their thirties who don't want to get married.

Sovetsky Sport, 1978, blithely ignoring the widespread use of anabolic steroids among Soviet athletes of the era.

See also DRUG-TAKING; PHYSIQUE.

Bodyline

The England cricket team's notorious 1932–33 tour of
Australia, during which Harold Larwood's aggressive 'bodyline'
bowling caused several injuries to Australian batsmen.

Bodyline bowling. In cricket, fast bowling aimed at the batsman's body
rather than the wicket. Such bowling was originally known as leg theory,
the aim being to bowl short and fast so that the batsman was obliged to use
his bat as a shield to protect his upper body and in so doing lob a catch to a
knot of expectant fielders on the leg side. In England's 1932–3 tour of
Australia the captain, Douglas Jardine, encouraged his fast bowlers, Harold
Larwood and Bill Voce, to use bodyline tactics as a counter to the threat
posed by the prodigious Australian batsman Don Bradman. The strategy
won the Ashes for England but aroused such a storm of indignation in
Australia that diplomatic relations between the two countries were almost
suspended.

The definition of 'bodyline' in *Brewer's Dictionary of Modern Phrase
and Fable* (2000).

I don't want to speak to you, Mr Warner. Of two teams out here one is
playing cricket, the other is making no effort to play the game of cricket. It
is too great a game for spoiling by the tactics that your team are adopting. I
don't approve of them and never will.

Bill Woodfull (1897–1965), Australia's captain during the 1932–33
Ashes series. His words to the England team manager, Pelham
Warner, when the latter called on the Australian dressing-room after
the Australian captain had been hit over the heart by a ball bowled
by the England fast bowler Harold Larwood during the Third Test at
Adelaide, January 1933. Quoted in Bruce Harris, *Jardine Justified*
(1933).

Bodyline bowling has assumed such proportions as to menace the best
interests of the game, making protection of the body by the batsmen the
main consideration. This is causing intensely bitter feeling between the
players as well as injury. In our opinion it is unsportsmanlike. Unless
stopped at once, it is likely to upset the friendly relationships existing
between Australia and England.

Cable sent to the MCC by the outraged Australian Cricket Board in
1933. The MCC replied with their own cable, deploring the
complaint and denying the England bowlers were at fault.

Could anything be more tactless than this blunt and clumsy challenge? Accuse any Englishman of being impolite, dishonest, even immoral, and he may hold in his anger. Accuse him of being unsportsmanlike, and you wound his deepest susceptibilities.

Bruce Harris English cricketer, in *Jardine Justified* (1933). His
reaction to the Australian Cricket Board's accusation.

I never bowled to injure a man. Frighten them, intimidate them – yes.

Harold Larwood (1904–95), English cricketer.

The term is meaningless. What is bodyline?

Douglas Jardine (1900–58), English cricketer, speaking as captain of
the England touring team.

Don't give the bastard a drink – let him die of thirst.

Heckling from the crowd directed at Douglas Jardine during the
Bodyline tour of 1932–33.

Don't swat the flies, Jardine, they're the only friends you've got in Australia.

Jeer from Australian fans at a match during the infamous Bodyline tour.

All Australians are an uneducated and unruly mob.

Douglas Jardine (1900–58), English cricketer, reacting to the
behaviour of Australian fans during the 1932–33 tour.

He is a queer fellow. When he sees a cricket ground with an Australian on it, he goes mad.

Sir Pelham Warner (1873–1963), Trinidadian-born English cricketer.
Letter to the governor of South Australia, 1934.

Body-line was not an incident, it was not an accident, it was not a temporary aberration. It was the violence and ferocity of our age expressing itself in cricket.

C.L.R. James (1901–89), Trinidadian historian and cricket writer.
Beyond a Boundary (1963).

Bodyline was devised to stifle Bradman's batting genius. They said I was a 'killer with the ball', without taking into account that Bradman, with the bat, was the greatest killer of all.

Harold Larwood (1904–95), English cricketer, 1965.

Is someone had produced a batting helmet during the Bodyline series, I would certainly have worn it.

Sir Donald Bradman (1908–), Australian cricketer.

See also THE ASHES; CRICKET; CRICKET TOURS.

Björn BORG

Swedish tennis player (1956–) whose cool, efficient technique made him the dominant player of the late 1970s, with a record five consecutive Wimbledon victories.

They should send Borg away to another planet. We play tennis. He plays something else.

Ilie Nastase (1946–), Romanian tennis player.

Like a Volvo, Borg is rugged, has good after-sales service, and is very dull.

Clive James (1939–), Australian writer and broadcaster, in the *Observer*, 29 June 1980.

Björn Borg looks like a hunchbacked, jut-bottomed version of Lizabeth Scott, impersonating a bearded Apache.

Clive James (1939–), Australian writer and broadcaster, comparing Borg to the blonde US leading lady of the 1940s.

See also COURAGE.

Ian BOTHAM

English cricketer (1955–) whose aggressive stroke-making and tireless swing bowling established him as one of the best all-rounders of his generation.

Quotes about Ian Botham

First the convicts, then the rabbits and now Botham.

Banner waved by Australian fans at an England–Australia Test match in 1978.

The most overrated player I've seen.

Harold Larwood (1904–95), English cricketer, 1983.

The first rock-and-roll cricketer.

Sir Len Hutton (1916–90), English cricketer, 1986.

As a Pom, he'd make a great Aussie.

Jeff Thomson (1950–), pays Botham the ultimate compliment.
Thommo Declares (1986).

To his credit he does not appear to harbour a grudge, despite a pen-portrait I adumbrated for the *Daily Express*, describing him as 'in no way inhibited by a capacity to over-intellectualize'.

Frances Edmonds, English writer and novelist. *Another Bloody Tour* (1986).

Bonny Botham, my oh me
Hit the ball at ten to three
Didn't come down 'til after tea.

Jeff Cloves, poet and writer, reflecting on Botham's
prodigious hitting.

A Test match without Ian Botham is like a horror film without Boris Karloff.

Fred Trueman (1931–), English cricketer, 1989.

Botham's idea of team spirit and motivation was to squirt a water pistol at someone and then go and get pissed.

Ray Illingworth (1932–), English cricketer, arguing against Botham's
inclusion as a morale booster for the England team in 1995.

The Indians kept calling him 'Iron Bottom', but he wasn't – not after all that fackin' curry.

John Emburey (1952–), Middlesex and England cricketer. Botham
had recently returned from a successful tour of India. Quoted in
Simon Hughes, *A Lot of Hard Yakka* (1997).

Quotes by Ian Botham

I have never thought life was a dress rehearsal. I once saw an advert on Australian television which said 'Life: be in it.'

Announcing his retirement in 1993.

See also ADVICE; AGE; ALCOHOL; COUNTY CRICKET; CRICKET TOURS; CRICKET UMPIRES; DRUG-TAKING; FAME; INJURIES; OFFICIALS; WALKING.

Bowls

Naught can rival bowles for sport save a good ale and a comely wench.
Anonymous.

There is more to bowls than the mere playing of it.
Anonymous.

There is plenty of time to win this game, and to thrash the Spaniards too.
Francis Drake (1540–96), English admiral. His alleged response,
while playing bowls on Plymouth Hoe on 20 July 1588, to the news
that the Spanish Armada invasion fleet had been sighted. In fact, he
knew from the state of the tides that there was no hurry to set sail
against the enemy. Quoted in the *Dictionary of National Biography*.

Nay sometimes, like to a bowl upon a subtle ground, I have tumbled past
the throw.
William Shakespeare (1564–1616), British poet and playwright.
Coriolanus (*c.*1607).

A bowling green is a place where three things are thrown away besides the
bowls – time, money and curses.
John Earle (1601–65), English writer, 1628.

To cure the mind's wrong bias, spleen
Some recommend the bowling green.
Matthew Green (1696–1737), English poet. *The Spleen* (1737).

It is a very quiet game and calculated rather for the steady old gentleman
than for his racketty son.
British Rural Sports, 1861.

Bowling is a sober game. The ruffianism of football, the effeminacy of
tennis, the manliness of cricket and the buoyancy of baseball give way to a
stateliness and gracefulness not met in no other sport.
Bowling Magazine, 1908.

Bowls is the only perfect recreation and the only pure game so far invented
by man! At what other sport do men persevere so resolutely to achieve just
nothing?
George T. Burrows, British sports journalist, 1915.

Bowling looks so simple; you only throw one thing at another.

John W. Fisher, British bowls player and writer, 1948.

A game of remorse and unpredictability; a game of skill and a game of chance; a game of joy and a game of frustration; a game of dry throats and sweaty palms.

Ronnie Harper, British writer, 1979.

It is like a street-fighter conforming to the Marquis of Queensberry rules.

Tony Allcock (1955–), British bowls champion, referring, in 1986,
to the appearance of Crown Green bowls players in Lawn bowls
tournaments.

Bowls is a young man's game which old men can play.

David Bryant (1931–), British bowls player.

See also David BRYANT; POLITICS.

Boxers

The conscientious boxer I say, is at once well behaved, a good fellow, a gentleman in nature, and a credit to his country.

Georges Carpentier (1894–1975), French light-heavyweight
boxer, nicknamed 'The Orchid Man'. *My Methods or Boxing as a
Fine Art* (1914).

While Spider McCoy manages a number of fighters, he never gets excited about anything but a heavyweight, and this is the way all fight managers are. A fight manager may have a lightweight champion of the world, but he will get more heated up about some sausage who scarcely knows how to hold his hands up if he is a heavyweight.

Damon Runyon (1884–1946), US author and journalist.
Take It Easy (1938).

Boxers are the most docile men in sport.

Henry Cooper (1934–), British heavyweight boxer.

All fighters are prostitutes and all promoters are pimps.

Larry Holmes (1949–), US heavyweight boxer. The *Guardian*,
24 December 1984.

'Marvelous Marvin' and 'Sugar Ray': sounds like a pillow fight between a hairdresser and an interior decorator.

Jan Murray (1917–), US comedian. Contemplating an imminent bout between US boxers Marvin Hagler and Sugar Ray Leonard in 1987, which resulted in Leonard taking Hagler's world title. Leonard called himself Sugar Ray in tribute to boxer Sugar Ray Robinson.

See also Muhammad ALI; Frank BRUNO; Jack DEMPSEY; Chris EUBANK; George FOREMAN; Joe FRAZIER; Jake LaMOTTA; Joe LOUIS; Rocky MARCIANO; Sugar Ray ROBINSON; Mike TYSON.

Boxing

To box, or not to box, that is the question,
Whether it is nobler in the mind to suffer
The stings and goadings of a well-tweak'd nose,
Or to take heart with Humphries or Mendoza.

Anonymous, 1792.

'Twas blow for blow, disputing inch for inch,
For one would not retreat, nor t'other flinch.

Lord Byron (1788–1824), British poet.

To set the cause above renown,
To love the game beyond the prize,
To honour while you strike him down,
The foe that comes with fearless eyes.

Sir Henry Newbolt (1862–1938), British poet, 1898.

I believe in having a little fight in most everything except funerals. Anything that ain't got some fighting in it is like a funeral and I don't like funerals.

John L. Sullivan (1858–1918), US heavyweight boxer.

I suggest that in all future boxing competitions, whether held at the National Sporting Club or anywhere else, the combatants should wear leather jerkins, under which bells should be concealed – electric, if possible. The boxing gloves should be of the largest size and should be plentifully smeared with chalk. For each chalk mark seen on the opponent's doublet the striker should be given a point. But if in the making of that mark he should happen to ring one of the bells, he should be instantly disqualified for unnecessary violence with the intention of effecting a knock-out and be rendered liable to an indictment for manslaughter.

Edward Marshall-Hall (1858–1929), British barrister. A fan of boxing himself, this was Marshall-Hall's witheringly sarcastic defence in a case in which a boxer stood accused of manslaughter following the death of an opponent in a bout. His victory in the case, which ended in a verdict of accidental death, did much to forestall further legal challenges to the sport on the grounds of the violence inflicted. Quoted in David Randall, *Great Sporting Eccentrics* (1985).

I have always considered that boxing really combines all the finest and highest inclinations of a man – activity, endurance, science, temper, and, last, but not least, presence of mind.

Hugh Cecil Lowther, 5th Earl of Lonsdale (1857–1944), British boxing enthusiast. Foreword in Eugene Corri, *Thirty Years a Boxing Referee* (1915).

There is nothing bellicose about boxing. It is fully in keeping with the principles of the United Nations Organisation.

Field-Marshal Bernard Montgomery, 1st Viscount Montgomery of Alamein (1887–1976), British soldier, 1948.

Hands were made for hitting people.

Mickey Duff (1929–), Polish-born British boxing manager and promoter, 1972.

Boxing is the sport to which all other sports aspire.

George Foreman (1948–), US heavyweight boxer.

A boxer never sees the big one that hits him.

George Foreman (1948–), US heavyweight boxer.

When I go into a ring I never know for certain that I'm coming back.

John Conteh (1951–), British light-heavyweight boxer.

It's just a job. Grass grows, birds fly, waves pound the sand. I beat people up.

Muhammad Ali (Cassius Clay; 1942–), US heavyweight boxer.
New York Times, 6 April 1977.

Boxing can be a cruel business and I know of no contrast so savage as that between the winner's and the loser's dressing room.

Peter Wilson, British sportswriter. *Boxing's Greatest Prize* (1982).

Because a boxer gets hurt, should they stop boxing? That would be crazy – more people die in the bath.

Muhammad Ali (Cassius Clay; 1942–), US heavyweight boxer, 1984.

You can sum up this sport in two words: You never know.

Lou Duva (1929–), US boxing trainer.

All I want to do is hit somebody in the mouth. It's a whole lot easier than working for a living.

Randall 'Tex' Cobb (1950–), US heavyweight boxer and actor.

If you screw things up in tennis, it's 15-love. If you screw up in boxing, it's your ass.

Randall 'Tex' Cobb (1950–), US heavyweight boxer and actor.

The nature of my business is to hurt people.

Mike Tyson (1966–), US heavyweight boxer.

If it's undisputed, what's all the fighting about?

George Carlin (1937–), US comedian, remarking upon a
competition for the title of 'undisputed champion' in boxing.

Nothing comes close to boxing. It should be added to the list: chocolate, champagne, sex.

Chris Eubank (1966–), British middleweight boxer.

See also BOXERS; BOXING-BASHERS; BOXING GLOVES; BOXING PROMOTERS; INJURIES; VIOLENCE.

Boxing-bashers

I have covered boxing, promoted boxing, watched it, thought about it, and after long reflection I cannot find a single thing that is good about it either from the point of view of participant or spectator.

Paul Gallico (1897–1976), US journalist, novelist and short-story
writer. Quoted in Edith Summerskill, *The Ignoble Art* (1956).

If I were a dictator, I would abolish prize fighting in my country by decree. I would scrap all rings, burn all boxing gloves and never let a youth be taught to strike another with his fist. For prize fighting and boxing are stupid, senseless, unappetising, inefficient and one hundred per cent useless.

Paul Gallico (1897–1976), US journalist, novelist and short-story writer. Quoted in Edith Summerskill, *The Ignoble Art* (1956).

Boxing is the only racket where you're almost guaranteed to end up as a bum.

Rocky Graziano (1922–90), US middleweight and welterweight boxer.

No physical activity is so vain as boxing. A man gets into the ring to attract admiration. In no sport, therefore, can you be more humiliated.

Norman Mailer (1923–), US novelist. *The Fight* (1976).

Among the boxing fraternity there is an adage – first the timing goes, then the legs, then the mind, and then the friends. That is the history of many people who thought boxing an easy way to riches.

Lord Thomas Taylor of Gryfe (1912–). Speech in the House of Lords, 1981.

I now find the whole subject of professional boxing disgusting. Except for the fighters, you're talking about human scum, nothing more.

Howard Cosell (1920–), US sports commentator. Comment made in 1982 following his decision not to commentate on any more boxing matches.

Probably the greatest of all arguments for banning boxing is the audience it attracts. No young people – all too busy learning a martial art or painting their toenails. Few blacks (outside the ring). No sentient girls, only middle-aged bits of fluff who look like Miss TV Times 1957. The *noise* that comes from their wretched throats indicates that, with a boxing crowd, brain damage is also in the head of the beholder.

Julie Burchill (1960–), British journalist. *Damaged Gods* (1986).

The stuff we deal with is life and death. I got my brain shook, my money took, and my name in the undertaker's book.

Joe Frazier (1944–), US heavyweight boxer. *The Times*, 31 December 1999.

Boxing gloves

The dumbest question I was ever asked by a sportswriter was whether I hit harder with red or white gloves. As a matter of fact, I hit harder with red.
Frank Crawford, boxer.

Perhaps boxing could be made safer if gloves were heavier.
James Pickles (1925–), British judge, 1995.

Boxing promoters

Never in the ring of human conflict have so few taken so much from so many.
Saoul Mamby (1947–), US super-lightweight boxer.

When Bob Arum pats you on the back, he's just looking for a spot to stick the knife.
Cus D'Amato (1908–1985), US boxing trainer, referring to
US boxing promoter Bob Arum.

Don't call me honest, you'll ruin me.
Jack Hurley, US boxing promoter. The title of his autobiography.

See also BOXERS; BUSINESS AND SPORT; CORRUPTION; Don KING.

Geoffrey BOYCOTT
**English cricketer (1940–) whose defensive batting
and combative character made him enemies as well as
admirers within the cricket world.**

Quotes about Geoffrey Boycott
You have done for Australian cricket what the Boston Strangler did for door-door salesmen.
Jack Birney. Telegram sent to Geoffrey Boycott after he took many
hours to score 50 runs during a match at Perth.

Boycott and controversy have shared the longest opening partnership in the game.
Terry Brindle, British sportswriter. 'Geoffrey Boycott', *Wisden
Cricketers' Almanack* (1978).

Even those who like him least are compelled to respect his utter dedication.

John Arlott (1914–91), English cricket writer and commentator.
'Geoffrey Boycott', *John Arlott's Book of Cricketers* (1979).

To offer Geoff Boycott a new contract is akin to awarding Arthur Scargill the Queen's Award for Industry.

Letter to the *Yorkshire Post*, 1984.

The saddest person who ever walked onto a cricket field.

Mollie Staines, English cricket administrator, speaking as the first
female member of the Yorkshire committee in 1984.

Geoff has only two points of view. You are either for him or against him. There is no middle ground.

Brian Close (1931–), English cricketer, 1984.

I know why he's bought a house by the sea ... so he'll be able to go for a walk on the water.

Fred Trueman (1931–), English cricketer, responding to news that
Boycott had bought a house overlooking Poole Harbour in 1997.

Quotes by Geoffrey Boycott

The only thing I'm bloody frightened of is getting out.

Quoted in 1973.

Nobody's perfect. You know what happened to the last man who was – they crucified him.

Responding to criticism of his slow scoring rate in 1979.

See also CRICKET; FAST BOWLING; The PRESS; YORKSHIRE COUNTY CRICKET CLUB.

Sir Donald BRADMAN

**Australian cricketer (1908–) acclaimed as one of the
greatest batsmen in the history of the game.**

Quotes about Sir Donald Bradman

He spoilt the game – he got too many runs.

Sir Jack Hobbs (1882–1963), English cricketer. An ironic remark,
considering that Hobbs made more first-class runs than anyone else.

Sir Donald Bradman
Would have been a very glad man
If his Test average had been .06 more
Than 99.94.

T.N.E. Smith (1914–), 'The Don' narrowly failed to establish a Test
average of 100 by getting out for a duck in his final Test appearance.

Bradman was the summing up of the Efficient Age which followed the
Golden Age. Here was brilliance safe and sure, streamlined and without
impulse. Victor Trumper was the flying bird; Bradman the aeroplane.

Sir Neville Cardus (1889–1975), British journalist and writer. In his
Autobiography (1947).

My first reaction was one of mild disappointment; he was smaller than I
had expected, chunky but not tall ... Bradman ... looked almost slight and as
he took guard it was difficult to believe that such a man of such a build
could have averaged 99.94 in all Test matches. But when he started to bat ...
ah, what a transformation – not so much a smallish man as a giant of
limited growth.

Barry Norman (1933–), British film critic, recalling watching Sir
Donald Bradman at Lord's in 1948. 'Bradman', *Quick Singles:
Memories of Summer Days and Cricket Heroes*.

He didn't appear to recognise yorkers; to him they were half-volleys.
Bouncers were simply long hops to be hooked away with a roll of the wrists
to the boundary behind square leg. Pitch short and he was immediately on
the back foot cracking the ball through mid-wicket or the covers; toss it up
and he was already three paces down the wicket, calmly deciding which
section of the crowd would have the privilege of collecting this one.

Barry Norman (1933–), British film critic, 'Bradman', *Quick Singles:
Memories of Summer Days and Cricket Heroes*.

Quotes by Sir Donald Bradman

Every ball is for me the first ball, whether my score is 0 or 200, and I never
visualize the possibility of anybody getting me out.

Attributed.

It's not easy to bat with tears in your eyes.

Explaining how he came to be bowled for a duck in his last Test innings.

See also BODYLINE; COACHING; CRICKETERS; ONE-DAY CRICKET.

Brazilian football

Brazil's football is like their inflation – 100 per cent.
Jornal da Tarde.

It's easy to beat Brazil. You just stop them getting 20 yards from your goal.
Sir Bobby Charlton (1937–), English footballer, 1970.

Brazil – You made me cry in 82, 86, 90. This time make me dance and I can die in peace.
Banner waved by Brazilian fans during the World Cup finals in 1994.
Brazil had failed to relive past World Cup glories in 1982, 1986 and
1990, but did indeed secure victory in 1994.

The Brazilians aren't as good as they used to be, or as they are now.
Kenny Dalglish (1951–), Scottish footballer and manager.

See also PELÉ; RONALDO.

Bridge

I say, let's banish bridge. Let's find some pleasant way of being miserable together.
Don Herold (1889–1966), US humorist.

I hate people who play bridge as though they were at a funeral and knew their feet were getting wet.
W. Somerset Maugham (1874–1965), British novelist and playwright, 1921.

Under an assumed name.
George S. Kaufman (1889–1961), US playwright. His reply when
asked by a bridge partner how he should have played the last (lost)
hand. Quoted in Scott Meredith, *George S. Kaufman and the
Algonquin Round Table* (1974).

A professor of anatomy once declared that there are only fourteen types of woman – young women, women who are really wonderful all things considered, and the twelve most famous women in history – and the same applies to Bridge partners. Over and above this, they are usually either so good that you lose all your self-confidence, or so bad that you lose all your money.

W.D.H. McCullough (1901–78) and '**Fougasse**' (1887–1965).
Aces Made Easy.

See also CARD GAMES; LUCK.

Frank BRUNO

British heavyweight boxer (1961–) who won the World Boxing Association (WBA) world title after defeating Oliver McCall in 1995. His genial manner made him a great favourite with the sporting public.

Quotes about Frank Bruno

Bruno still sounds like another British heavyweight, reminding us of Dorothy Parker's line: 'If all the British heavyweights were laid end to end, we wouldn't be surprised.'

Ring magazine.

Frank, you deserve a knighthood, or maybe even Lord of the Rings.

Desmond Lynam (1942–), British television sports presenter,
praising Bruno after he won the world heavyweight title.
Sportsnight, BBC TV, 1995.

Quotes by Frank Bruno

My mum said I used to fight my way out of the cot. But I can't remember. That was before my time.

Attributed.

I didn't want to go round mugging old ladies or robbing banks. So I took up boxing.

Attributed.

Know what I mean, Harry?

His catchphrase, originating in broadcast interviews with sports
commentator Harry Carpenter.

It was like a Michael Jackson concert, Pavarotti, Vera Lynn and VE-Day, all rolled into one.

On winning the world heavyweight title. BBC TV, *Sportsnight*, 1995.

See also AGE; BOXING; PREDICTIONS.

David BRYANT

British bowls player (1931–) who emerged as the dominant force in modern English bowling.

Quotes about David Bryant

The Don Bradman of bowls.

Anonymous.

Quotes by David Bryant

I'm not an athlete, more a gymnast and golfer, soldered together.

Attributed.

See also BOWLS.

Bullfighting

As for Bullfighting. After I had consented to them, I had the fullest determination never to attend them again in my life nor be where they were held.

Isabella I (1451–1504), queen of Spain, 1493.

Bull-baiting in any shape is irresistible to the Spaniard.

Richard Ford (1796–1858), British travel writer. *Handbook for Travellers in Spain* (1845).

Spain is the only country where death is the national spectacle.

Federico García Lorca (1898–1936), Spanish poet and playwright.

Bullfighting is the only art in which the artist is in danger of death and in which the degree of brilliance in the performance is left to the fighter's honour.

Ernest Hemingway (1899–1961), US novelist. *Death in the Afternoon* (1932).

Bullfighting is worthless without rivalry. But with two great bullfighters it becomes a deadly rivalry.

Ernest Hemingway (1899–1961), US novelist. *The Dangerous Summer* (1985).

Courage and grace is a formidable mixture. The only place to see it is the bullring.

Marlene Dietrich (1904–92), German-born US actress. *Marlene Dietrich's ABC* (1962).

Sir Matt BUSBY

Scottish football manager (1909–94) whose multi-talented Manchester United side ('the Busby Babes') won the English league championship in 1952, 1956, and 1957, before eight of its members were tragically killed in an air crash in Munich in 1958.

When Matt and Stan Cullis were first building their sides some of us who had been around before the war said to them, 'You're crazy. The young players today aren't any good, you're wasting your time.' But he knew what he was about.

Joe Mercer (1914–90), English football manager.

Matt Busby is a symbol of everything that is best in our national game.

Harold Wilson (1916–95), British Labour prime minister, 1978.

Matt was the eternal optimist. In 1968 he still hoped Glenn Miller was just missing.

Pat Crerand (1939–), Scottish footballer, recalling his former manager at Manchester United in 1997.

See also MANCHESTER UNITED; TACTICS.

Business and sport

Putting a fighter in the business world is like putting silk stockings on a pig.

Jack Hurley, US boxing promoter, 1961.

Baseball is too much of a sport to be called a business, and too much of a business to be called a sport.

Philip Wrigley (1894–1977), US chewing-gum manufacturer and baseball club owner.

In affectionate remembrance of International Cricket, which died at Hove, 9th May, 1977, deeply lamented by a large circle of friends and acquaintances. RIP. NB – The body will be cremated and the Ashes taken to Australia and scattered around the studio of TCN9 in Sydney – NTJCBM.

Notice published in *The Times* in 1977 by three Australian
journalists, imitating the famous Ashes notice, in response to the
efforts of Australian media tycoon Kerry Packer to establish a new
commercial cricket circuit, the so-called 'Packer Circus'.

There is no business like show business – except sports business.

William Baker. *Sports in the Western World* (1982).

Boxing is show-business with blood.

David Belasco (1859–1931), US theatre producer. Said in 1915, as
reported in Michael Parkinson, *Sporting Lives* (1993). Also
associated with British heavyweight boxer Frank Bruno (1961–),
quoted in the *Guardian*, 19 November 1991.

Scottish football: once a simple game played by semi-illiterates. Now a multi-million pound industry played by semi-illiterates.

It's Only an Excuse (1993).

It's like going into a nuclear war with bows and arrows.

Joe Kinnear (1947–), Irish football manager, comparing the
finances of his club Wimbledon with the resources of the top clubs
in the Premiership in 1997.

See also AGENTS; BOXING PROMOTERS; MONEY.

· C ·

Caddies

A caddie is someone who accompanies a golfer and didn't see the ball either.
Anonymous.

While tearing off
A game of golf
I may make a play for the caddy.
But when I do
I don't follow through
'Cause my heart belongs to Daddy.
Cole Porter (1891–1964), US composer. 'My heart belongs to
Daddy' (1938).

The only time I talk on a golf course is to my caddie. And then only to
complain when he gives me the wrong club.
Seve Ballesteros (1957–), Spanish golfer.

Real golfers, no matter what the provocation, never strike a caddie with the
driver. The sand wedge is far more effective.
Huxtable Pippey.

Canoeing

Boats are for work; canoes are for pleasure.
John Boyle O'Reilly (1844–90), Irish poet. *Ethics of Boxing and
Manly Sport* (1888).

Eric CANTONA

Volatile French footballer (1966–), unfortunately
remembered as much for his attack on a spectator in 1995
– which resulted in an eight-month suspension and a court
sentence of community service – as for his contribution to
two League and FA Cup 'doubles' with Manchester United
in the mid-1990s.

Quotes about Eric Cantona

1966 was a great year for English football. Eric was born.

Nike advertisement, 1994, coyly ignoring the fact that 1966 was
also the year England won the World Cup. Following football
superstar Cantona's suspension the following year, critics of
Manchester United's import from France took to wearing
T-shirts bearing the legend '1995 was a great year for English
football. Eric was banned.'

If a Frenchman goes on about seagulls, trawlers and sardines, he's called a
philosopher. I'd just be called a short Scottish bum talking crap.

Gordon Strachan (1957–), Scottish footballer, referring in 1995
to Cantona's somewhat mystical reflection upon the attentions
of the press.

The Sh*t Hits The Fan!

Headline in the *Daily Star* referring to the notorious incident in
which Cantona kicked a Crystal Palace fan during a match and was
consequently arrested, 1995.

I'd give all the champagne I've ever drunk to have played alongside him in
a big European match at Old Trafford.

George Best (1946–), Northern Ireland footballer, referring to
Cantona in 1997.

Quotes by Eric Cantona

I love the speed of the game here. Playing from goal to goal, keeping the
momentum going at all times. There's beauty in the game here. The
spontaneity is beautiful.

Referring to his experience of playing football in England.
La Philosophie de Cantona (1995).

When the seagulls follow a trawler, it is because they think sardines will be thrown into the sea.

Referring to the attentions he received from the press following his
appearance in court on charges of assaulting a fan during a match in
January 1995. Quoted in the *Guardian*, 30 December 1995.

The danger with games is that you can get tired of them. That's why I swapped soccer for cinema in the way a child takes up playing Cluedo when he is sick of Monopoly. But I'm still interested in football. It is like when you leave a woman and you don't cry when she goes off with someone else.

Reflecting upon his retirement from football in 1998 to begin a new
career as a film actor.

Captaincy

In nine matches out of ten, Blanchflower has the ball more than any two other players on the field – it's an expression of his tremendous ego which is just what a great captain needs.

Arthur Rowe (1906–93), English football manager, referring to
Northern Ireland footballer Danny Blanchflower (1926–93). Quoted
in Julian Holland, *Spurs – The Double* (1961).

A PR officer, agricultural consultant, psychiatrist, accountant, nursemaid and diplomat.

Doug Insole (1926–), English cricketer, defining the skills required
of a cricket captain.

Captains have to work hard to maintain a standard: they have to keep their committees happy, appease the supporters' clubs, attend all training sessions, study the opposition, make diplomatic speeches and be above reproach themselves.

J.G.B. Thomas. Quoted in *Rugby World*, 1973.

As harrowing occupations go, there can't be much to choose between the Australian cricket captaincy and social work on skid row.

Doug Ibbotson, British sports journalist. *Sporting Scenes* (1980).

You'll have the most miserable time of your life.

Brian Close (1931–), English cricketer, warning Ian Botham about
accepting the England captaincy in 1980.

It is easier for a football manager to 'play God', to read the riot act to the
players, because he doesn't have to perform himself. Sales managers don't
sell, foremen don't hump bricks. All cricket captains bat and field, and some
bowl. We receive repeated intimations of our own fallibility.

Mike Brearley (1942–), English cricketer, lamenting the lot of the
cricket captain in *The Art of Captaincy* (1985).

Captaincy is ninety per cent luck and ten per cent skill. But don't try it
without that ten per cent.

Richie Benaud (1930–), Australian cricketer and commentator.

The hallmark of a great captain is the ability to win the toss, at the right time.

Richie Benaud (1930–), Australian cricketer and commentator.
Quoted in Barry Fantoni, *Colemanballs* (1982).

Card games

I must complain the cards are ill shuffled till I have a good hand.

Jonathan Swift (1667–1745), Anglo-Irish poet and satirist.

When in doubt, win the trick.

Edmond Hoyle (1672–1769), British authority on card
games. *A Short Treatise on the Game of Whist* (1742).
Possibly an interpolation to the 1790 edition, edited by
Charles Jones.

Let spades be trumps! she said, and trumps they were.

Alexander Pope (1688–1744), British poet. *The Rape of the Lock* (1714).

I am sorry I have not learnt to play at cards. It is very useful in life: it
generates kindness, and consolidates society.

Samuel Johnson (1709–84), British lexicographer. Quoted in James
Boswell, *Tour to the Hebrides*, 11 November 1773.

With spots quadrangular of diamond form,
Ensanguined hearts, clubs typical of strife,

And spades, the emblem of untimely graves.

William Cowper (1731–1800), British poet. *The Task*, IV (1785).

'A clear fire, a clean hearth, and the rigour of the game.' This was the celebrated wish of old Sarah Battle (now with God), who, next to her devotions, loved a good game at whist.

Charles Lamb (1775–1834), British essayist. 'Mrs Battle's Opinions on Whist' *Essays of Elia*, (1823).

One should always play fairly when one has the winning cards.

Oscar Wilde (1854–1900), Irish writer and wit.

A guy who'd cheat on his wife would cheat at cards.

Texas Guinan (1884–1933), US nightclub owner.

A man's idea of a card game is war – cool, devastating and pitiless. A lady's idea of it is a combination of larceny, embezzlement and burglary.

Finlay Peter Dunne (1867–1936), US humorist.

Poker shouldn't be played in a house with women.

Tennessee Williams (1911–83), US playwright. *A Streetcar Named Desire* (1948).

Solitaire is the only thing in life that demands absolute honesty.

Hugh Wheeler (1912–). *A Little Night Music*.

See also BRIDGE; LUCK.

Sir Neville CARDUS

British journalist and writer (1889–1975) remembered for his authoritative writing on English cricket for the *Manchester Guardian*, and for his florid prose style.

It is more than a game, this cricket, it somehow holds a mirror up to English society.

English Cricket (1945).

Like the British constitution, cricket was not made: it has 'grown'.

English Cricket (1945).

To go to a cricket match for nothing but cricket is as though a man were to go into an inn for nothing but drink.

Autobiography (1947).

If anyone had told me I was one day destined to make a reputation as a writer upon cricket I should have felt hurt.

Autobiography (1947).

The first vision that comes to mind as we think of West Indies cricket is of joyful noise, a bat flailing the air, the ball whizzing here, there, everywhere, stumps flying, shining black faces and mouths laughing white-toothed, like melons.

Quoted in 1966.

But my dear chap, it's the spirit of the thing that counts. Often when I quoted a player he may not have literally said those things. But he'd have liked to.

Admitting the things he reported cricketers as saying were not
always rendered verbatim.

See also ALCOHOL; Sir Donald BRADMAN; CRICKET UMPIRES; W.G. GRACE; Sir Jack HOBBS; RULES; SCORELINES; Sir Gary SOBERS; WEATHER.

Steve **CAUTHEN**

US jockey (1962–), the only jockey to win the Kentucky,
Epsom, Irish, French and Italian Derbies.

Quotes about Steve Cauthen

They say Steve Cauthen is 18 and comes from the Bluegrass country, but I don't believe them – he's 103 and comes from another planet.

Laz Barrera (1923–), US racehorse trainer, 1978.

Quotes by Steve Cauthen

In this game, you're only as good as your last ride – just like many think horses are only as good as their last run.

Quoted in 1981.

Wilt CHAMBERLAIN

US basketball star (1936–99), nicknamed 'Wilt the Stilt'
because of his height of over seven feet tall.

Nobody roots for Goliath.

Attributing his own lack of support among fans to his giant stature, 1967.

If I were given a change of life, I'd like to see how it would be to live as a
mere six-footer.

Attributed.

Chants

Easy, easy!

Traditional chant of crowds at football games, cricket matches etc.
when it seems their own side is going to enjoy an easy victory. It had
been widely adopted throughout sport by the early 1970s, as
evidenced by the Scotland World Cup Squad single 'Easy, easy'
released in 1974.

Oggi, oggi, oggi, oi, oi, oi!

Traditional rugby chant first heard in the late 1970s, which
subsequently became a favourite of crowds at a wide range of
sporting and other occasions. Opinion is divided over its origins. One
theory links it to a warning cry uttered by thieves operating on the
Thames whenever the Thames River police approached, while
another links it to the Cornish dialect word 'oggy', a nickname for
the pasty, and explains that it was well established as a rallying cry in
that part of the world long before it was taken up elsewhere.
Variants include the chant 'Maggie, Maggie, Maggie, out, out, out!',
frequently heard at political rallies of the 1980s, when Margaret
Thatcher was prime minister.

Here we go, here we go, here we go!

Traditional football chant, heard at grounds throughout the British
Isles since the 1980s. Sung to the tune of Sousa's 'Stars and Stripes
for Ever', it was recorded by the Everton squad and released as a
single in 1985 and was subsequently heard during the World Cup
campaign in Mexico the following year.

Play up Pompey, Pompey play up.

Traditional football chant associated with fans of the English football club Portsmouth, nicknamed Pompey. Sung over and over when things are going well, in imitation of the tune of a chiming clock, the origins of the so-called 'Pompey Chimes' are obscure. The chant may have been inspired by the striking of a clock in the city's shipyards, or may otherwise constitute a garbled reference to the local beaches known as the Portsmouth Chines.

Two World Wars and one World Cup, doo-dah, doo-dah.

Traditional England fans' chant directed at rival German fans, sung to the tune 'The Camptown Races'.

You only sing when you're whaling.

Scottish football chant directed at Norwegian fans during the 1998 World Cup finals. Quoted in the *Daily Telegraph*, 'Sporting quotes of the Year 1998', 28 December 1998.

You couldn't score in a brothel.

Chant directed by Crystal Palace fans against Newcastle United after the press published allegations about the sex lives of some members of the club. 'Quotes of the Year', the *Guardian*, 24 December 1998.

See also FANS; SONGS.

Sir Bobby CHARLTON

English footballer (1937–) whose long career with Manchester United and England established him as an international football icon.

He was idolized from his twentieth year on. There has never been a more popular footballer. He was as near perfection as man and player as it is possible to be.

Sir Matt Busby (1909–94), Scottish football manager.

Bobby Charlton almost rivals Churchill as the best-known Briton of the 20th century. Britain never had a greater sporting ambassador.

Jimmy Greaves (1940–), English footballer and commentator.

I sent my son to one of his schools of excellence and he came back bald.

George Best (1946–), Northern Ireland footballer. Speaking on *The Mrs Merton Show*, BBC TV, 1996.

His reputation as a grizzlin' old miser was legendary.

Ron Atkinson (1939–), English football manager, referring to
Charlton in *Big Ron: A Different Ball Game* (1998).

See also BRAZILIAN FOOTBALL; EUROPEAN FOOTBALL; Sir Alex FERGUSON;
FOOTBALL GROUNDS; PROFESSIONALISM.

Cheating *See* GAMESMANSHIP.

Cheerleaders

We were so bad last year, the cheerleaders stayed home and phoned in
the cheers.

Pat Williams (1940–), US basketball manager, speaking as
manager of Orlando Magic in 1991.

One of the great disappointments of a football game is that the cheerleaders
never seem to get injured.

New York Tribune.

Chelsea

Chelsea are the most unusual of clubs. They have never done what every
other club was doing at the same time as every other club was doing it.

Ralph Finn, British sportswriter. *A History of Chelsea FC* (1969).

Blue is the colour,
Football is the game,
We're all together,
And winning is our aim,
So cheer us on through the wind and rain,
For Chelsea, Chelsea is our name.

'Blue is the Colour' pop song recorded by Chelsea football club in 1972.

Commodore already sponsors Tessa Sanderson, Chelsea FC and a football
team, Bayern Munich.

Computer Guardian, 1988.

I thought that coming to Chelsea was the best idea I'd ever had – that is until I saw Stamford Bridge. It was a terrible mess and a real shock. I thought to myself: 'Jesus Christ, what did I do?'

Ruud Gullit (1962–), Dutch footballer, reflecting upon his move to Chelsea as manager in 1997.

See also FOREIGN SIGNINGS; Gianfranco ZOLA.

Chess

Chess is a sea in which a gnat may drink and an elephant may bathe.

Indian proverb.

Chess is a game too troublesome for some men's braines, too testy full of anxiety, all out as bad as study; besides, it is a cholericke game, and very offensive to him that looseth the Mate.

Robert Burton (1577–1640), English writer and clergyman. *The Anatomy of Melancholy* (1652).

When a man's house is on fire, it's time to break off chess.

Thomas Fuller (1608–61), British clergyman.

For a game it is too serious, for seriousness too much of a game.

Moses Mendelsson (1729–86), German philosopher.

'Tis all a chequer board of nights and days,
Where destiny with men for pieces plays;
Hither and thither, and mates, and slays.

Edward Fitzgerald (1809–83), British poet and translator. *The Rubaiyat of Omar Khayyám* (1859).

The chess-board is the world; the pieces are the phenomena of the universe; the rules are what we call the laws of Nature. The player on the other side is hidden from us. We know that his play is always fair, just and patient. But also we know, to our cost, that he never overlooks a mistake, or makes the smallest allowance for ignorance.

Thomas H. Huxley (1825–95), British teacher and biologist. *Lay Sermons, Addresses and Reviews* (1870).

Life's too short for chess.

Henry James Byron (1834–84), British playwright and actor. *Our Boys* (1874).

Poets do not go mad; but chess-players do.

G.K. Chesterton (1874–1936), British novelist and poet.
Orthodoxy (1908).

Chess is the gymnasium of the mind.

Vladimir Ilyich Lenin (1870–1924), Russian revolutionary
and politician.

Chess is a foolish expedient for making idle people believe they are doing
something clever, when they are only wasting their time.

George Bernard Shaw (1856–1950), Irish playwright and critic.

It is impossible to win gracefully at chess. No man has yet said 'Mate!'
in a voice which failed to sound to his opponent bitter, boastful and
malicious.

A.A. Milne (1882–1956), British writer. *Not That It Matters* (1919).

Chess can be described as the movement of pieces eating one another.

Marcel Duchamp (1887–1968), French artist.

As elaborate a waste of human intelligence as you can find outside an
advertising agency.

Raymond Chandler (1888–1959), US novelist.

Chess is seldom found above the upper-middle class; it's too hard.

Paul Fussell (1924–), US historian and writer.

There are far, far more permissible moves in a chess game than there are
electrons in the universe.

Durrell Huff, writer and statistician 1959.

A game to subdue the turbulent spirit, or to worry a tranquil mind.

William Hartston (1947–), British chess writer. *The Kings of Chess*.

Chess is ruthless: you've got to be prepared to kill people.

Nigel Short (1965–), British chess player. Quoted in the *Observer*,
11 August 1991.

See also Bobby FISCHER; WOMEN IN SPORT.

Linford CHRISTIE

British sprinter (1960–) whose victory in the 1993 World Championships 100 metres made him the first track athlete ever to hold World, Olympic, European, and Commonwealth titles simultaneously.

There's nothing new you can say about Linford Christie – except, he's slow and has got a small penis.

Nick Hancock (1963–), British television presenter. Referring ironically to the revealing figure-hugging cycle shorts favoured by Christie. *They Think It's All Over*, BBC TV, 1995.

Linford Christie: the generously-beloined sprint supremo.

Punch magazine.

Classic commentaries

I can't see who's in the lead but it's either Oxford or Cambridge.

John Snagge (1904–96), British sports commentator. Said during his commentary on the 1949 University Boat Race after the engine of the boat in which he was following the race broke down. Quoted in C. Dodd, *Oxford and Cambridge Boat Race* (1983).

Yorkshire were 232 all out. Hutton ill. No! I'm sorry, Hutton 111.

John Snagge (1904–96), British sports commentator. Extract of BBC Radio commentary.

There are people on the pitch ... they think it's all over ... it is now!

Kenneth Wolstenholme (1920–), British football commentator. His commentary during the last moments of the 1966 Wembley World Cup Final, when England were leading West Germany by three goals to two. Wolstenholme's comment was prompted by the appearance on the pitch of England fans who believed the match to be over. As he was speaking, the English forward Geoff Hurst scored a fourth goal for England, hence Wolstenholme's 'it is now!'. *They Think It's All Over* subsequently provided the title for an irreverent BBC TV sports quiz show broadcast from the 1990s.

Up and under.

Eddie Waring (1909–86), British television sports commentator. His catchphrase, describing a rugby league tactic that involves a player kicking the ball high in the air and then running forward to get below it and catch it.

Oh, I say!

Dan Maskell (1908–92), British tennis commentator. His catchphrase.

This is Cunis at the Vauxhall End. Cunis – a funny sort of name. Neither one thing nor the other.

Alan Gibson (1923–), English cricket commentator, 1969.

It's obviously a great occasion for all the players. It's a moment they will always forget.

Ray Hudson, describing the presentation of the England and New Zealand cricket teams to the Queen at Lord's in 1969.

And now over to ringside, where Harry Commentator is your carpenter.

Anonymous BBC TV announcer, introducing commentator Harry Carpenter.

Every time he opens his legs he shows his class.

Ron Pickering (1931–91), British television commentator, referring to Cuban runner Alberto Juantorena during the 1976 Montreal Olympics.

The athletes here in Edmonton are beginning to open wide their legs and show their form.

Chris Brasher (1928–), British middle-distance runner. Extract of race commentary, 1976.

Ah! Isn't that nice, the wife of the Cambridge President is kissing the cox of the Oxford crew.

Harry Carpenter (1925–), British television sports commentator. Extract of commentary on the 1977 Oxford–Cambridge Boat Race.

For those of you watching in black-and-white, Spurs are in the all-yellow strip.

John Motson (1945–), British television sports commentator, 1978.

He's going for the pink, and for those of you with black-and-white sets, the yellow is behind the blue.

Ted Lowe (1920–), British television snooker commentator. Extract of BBC TV snooker commentary.

Fred Davis, the doyen of snooker, now 67 years of age and too old to get his leg over, prefers to use his left hand.

Ted Lowe (1920–), British television snooker commentator. Extract of BBC TV snooker commentary.

The crowd are literally electrified and glued to their seats.

Ted Lowe (1920–), British television snooker commentator. Extract of BBC TV snooker commentary, 1980.

We are the best in the world. We have beaten England. Lord Nelson ... Lord Beaverbrook ... Sir Winston Churchill ... Sir Anthony Eden ... Clement Attlee ... Henry Cooper ... Lady Diana. We have beaten them all. Maggie Thatcher, can you hear me? Maggie Thatcher, your boys took a helluva beating. Norway have beaten England at football!

Borge Lillelien, Norwegian sports commentator. His reaction when supposedly humble Norway unexpectedly beat supposedly mighty England 2–1 in a crucial 1981 World Cup tie.

And there's the unmistakable figure of Joe Mercer ... or is it Lester Piggott?

Brough Scott (1942–), British television horse racing commentator. Extract of television broadcast, ITV, 1981.

Quarante-deux seconds ... that's about forty-two seconds.

Stuart Hall, British television athletics commentator.

After a goalless first half, the score at half-time is 0–0.

Brian Moore (1932–), British football commentator.

And Ritchie has now scored 11 goals, exactly double the number he scored last season.

Alan Parry (1948–), British sports commentator.

And there'll be more football in a moment, but first we've got the highlights of the Scottish League Cup Final.

Gary Newbon (1945–), British television sports presenter.

Chesterfield 1, Chester 1. Another score draw there in that local derby.

Des Lynam (1942–), British television sports presenter. *Grandstand*, BBC TV.

The only thing that Norwich didn't get was the goal that they finally got.

Jimmy Greaves (1940–), English footballer and commentator.

There's been a colour clash: both teams are wearing white.

John Motson (1945–), British football commentator. Quoted in
Ned Sherrin, *Cutting Edge* (1984).

He didn't quite manage to get his leg over.

Jonathan Agnew (1960–), British radio cricket commentator,
referring to an incident in which batsman Ian Botham accidentally
collided with his own wicket after turning suddenly and failing to
step over the bails. Agnew's unintentional gaffe led to fellow-
commentator Brian Johnston collapsing in helpless laughter, one of
radio sport's most cherished moments.

Hi folks! I'm Gerry Gross.

Jerry Coleman (1924–), US baseball manager and announcer,
introducing himself with the name of another sports announcer
on a San Diego radio programme.

Last night's homer was Willie Stargell's 399th home run, leaving him one
shy of 500.

Jerry Coleman (1924–), US baseball manager and announcer.

Houston has its largest crowd of the night here this evening.

Jerry Coleman (1924–), US baseball manager and announcer.

It's a hot night at Madison Square Gardens, and at ringside I see several
ladies in gownless evening straps.

Jimmy Powers (1903–95), US radio sports commentator. Extract of
boxing match commentary.

Glenn Hoddle hasn't been the Hoddle we know. Neither has Bryan Robson.

Ron Greenwood (1921–), English football manager. Extract of
match commentary, in which neither Hoddle nor Robson were
distinguishing themselves.

Every time he gets the ball he moves around like a banana-shaped umbrella
to cut the park off.

Alex Murphy (1939–), British rugby commentator.

Zola Budd: so small, so waif-like, you literally can't see her. But there she is.

Alan Parry (1948–), British sports commentator.

England were beaten in the sense that they lost.

Dickie Davies (1933–), British television sports commentator.

And now for the goals from Carrow Road, where the game ended 0–0.

Elton Welsby, British football commentator.

Australia 602 for 6 dec., England 20 for 3. And in the fifth Test, victory is possibly slipping away from England.

Steve Rider (1950–), British television sports presenter.

I wouldn't be surprised if this game went all the way to the finish.

Ian St John (1938–), Scottish footballer and commentator.

They've picked their heads up off the ground, and they now have a lot to carry on their shoulders.

Ron Atkinson (1939–), English football manager.

Lee Sharpe has got dynamite in his shorts.

Stuart Hall, British sports commentator, referring to
the then Manchester United footballer.

These two horses have met five times this season, and they've beaten each other on each occasion.

Jimmy Linley, British television sports commentator. BBC television.

The racecourse is as level as a billiard ball.

John Francome (1952–), British jockey. *Racing*, Channel 4
television, 1995.

Apart from their goals, Norway haven't scored.

Terry Venables (1943–), English footballer and manager. Extract
of match commentary.

Chile have three options – they could win or they could lose.

Kevin Keegan (1951–), English footballer and manager.

Leicester 0, Wimbledon 1, Football minus 1.

Alan Green (1952–), British football commentator. Referring in the
late 1990s to an alleged decline in quality in Premier League games.

Hagi could open a tin of beans with his left foot.

Ray Clemence (1948–), English footballer. Referring to the
Romanian footballer Gheorghe Hagi, nicknamed the 'Maradona of
the Carpathians'.

He's chanced his arm with his left foot.

Trevor Brooking (1948–), English footballer and commentator.

England now have three fresh men, with three fresh legs.

Jimmy Hill (1928–), British television football commentator.

The match will be shown on Match of the Day this evening. If you don't
want to know the result, look away now as we show you Tony Adams
lifting the trophy for Arsenal.

Steve Rider (1950–), British television sports presenter.

We've just seen the teams and they both look like they've come here
to play football.

Frank Clark (1943–), English football manager. Extract of BBC
Radio 5 broadcast on the 1998 FA Cup Final. 'Sporting Quotes of
the Year', the *Daily Telegraph*, 28 December 1998.

The Croatians don't play well without the ball.

Barry Venison (1964–), English footballer and sports commentator.

There are the boys, their balls between their legs.

Amanda Redington, British television presenter. Extract of football
commentary, GMTV.

See also ACTION REPLAYS; John ARLOTT; David COLEMAN; COMMENTATING;
COMMENTATORS; GAFFES; Brian JOHNSTON; MIXED METAPHORS; PREDICTIONS;
SPORTING SIMILES; TELEVISION; Murray WALKER.

Clichés

The harder they are, the heavier they fall.

Bob Fitzsimmons (1862–1917), light heavyweight and heavyweight
boxer. Said just before a bout with James Jeffries in San Francisco, 9
June 1899: he lost. Quoted in the *Brooklyn Daily* Eagle on 11
August 1900 and now associated primarily with Fitzsimmons,
although much the same thought (more commonly rendered today

as 'The bigger they come, the harder they fall' or sometimes as 'The bigger they are, the further they have to fall') had been voiced by others over preceding years, as far back indeed as the 15th century.

We was robbed!

Joe Jacobs (1896–1940), US boxing manager. His reaction as manager of Max Schmeling after the latter unexpectedly lost his heavyweight title to Jack Sharkey on 21 June 1932. His complaint – often rendered as 'we wuz robbed' – echoed Jack Dempsey's 'I was robbed of the championship' when he was defeated in controversial circumstances by Gene Tunney in 1927: in this earlier fight Dempsey was slow to retreat to his corner after knocking down Tunney and consequently the countdown began a full six seconds late, allowing Tunney time to regain his feet. This lament has long since become a cliché mouthed by countless defeated participants throughout the world of sport. Quoted in Peter Heller, *In This Corner* (1975).

When the going gets tough, the tough get going.

Knute Rockne (1888–1931), Norwegian-born American football coach.

Over the moon.

Football cliché much repeated by players and managers expressing their delight at some recent success and later vilified, alongside 'sick as a parrot', as an example of formulaic 'football speak'. It was heard with increasing regularity from the late 1970s, although the earliest discoverable instance of it in a footballing context goes back to 1962, when England manager Sir Alf Ramsey was reported saying 'I feel like jumping over the moon'. In non-sporting usage, the phrase appears to go back at least as far as the middle of the 19th century, appearing for instance in the published diary of May, Lady Cavendish in her entry for 7 February 1857. It may have been inspired originally by the nursery rhyme 'Hey diddle diddle, the cat and the fiddle; the cow jumped over the moon', dating from around 1765.

Sick as a parrot.

Anonymous. This notorious football cliché, signifying extreme disappointment, was taken up throughout the football world around 1978 but opinion is divided over its origins. One suggestion claims it was originally 'sick as a pierrot', a reference to the melancholy Pierrot of 18th-century French theatrical tradition, although an almost identical phrase also appears in the works of the 17th-century British playwright Aphra Behn. Its emergence in the 1970s was undoubtedly influenced by the popularity of a contemporary comedy sketch about a dead parrot performed by the British television comedy team Monty

Python's Flying Circus. A link has also been suggested with the parrot disease psittacosis, which is communicable to man and which was blamed for several deaths in the early 1970s.

The opera ain't over till the fat lady sings.

Dan Cook (1926–), US baseball commentator. Uttered during a television commentary in April 1978 and quoted in the *Washington Post*, 11 June 1978. Sometimes incorrectly ascribed to Washington Bullets coach Dick Motta, one of the first of countless sports figures in many disciplines to adopt it to suggest that while a game is still in progress there is still hope of a reversal in a player's or team's fortunes. The origins of the cliché lie in the lengthy Wagner opera *Siegfried*, the end of which is signalled by the appearance of Brunnhilde, traditionally played by a substantially-proportioned soprano.

Most of my clichés aren't original.

Chuck Knox (1932–), American football coach.

Nobody I've ever played with has said 'Sick as a parrot' when I've asked them how they were. But thrust a microphone in front of them, and it all comes out, 'It was a game of two halves', 'We'll take each match as it comes', 'The boy done good.' We have caught it from them – we're as sick as a commentator.

Gary Lineker (1960–), English footballer and commentator 1990.

It's a funny old game but all credit to the Iran lads, they gave 110 per cent.

Savo Milosevic (1973–), Yugoslav footballer, demonstrating his mastery of English football cliché during the 1998 World Cup finals.

See also COMMENTATING.

Climbing

Hasty climbers have sudden falls.

German proverb.

Great things are done when men and mountains meet;
This is not done by jostling in the street.

William Blake (1757–1827), British poet, engraver and visionary, 1808.

Do nothing in haste, look well to each step, and from the beginning think what may be the end.

Edward Whymper (1840–1911), British mountaineer. *Scrambles Amongst the Alps* (1871).

Truly it may be said that the outside of a mountain is good for the inside of a man.

George Wherry. *Alpine Notes and the Climbing Foot* (1896).

To climb with a friend is a pleasure; to climb alone is an education.

Count Henry Russell (b.1834). Quoted in Walter Larden, *Recollections of an Old Mountaineer* (1910).

Because it is there.

George Leigh Mallory (1886–1924), British mountaineer. This most famous of all quotations associated with climbing was apparently first uttered by Mallory in the course of a US lecture tour in reply to questions about his motivation for wishing to climb Everest. It has been suggested that he may have been inspired by recollection of a comment made to him at Cambridge in 1911 by A.C. Benson, who urged him to read Carlyle's life of John Sterling, a book he described as important simply 'by being there'. Alternatively, it may have been put into his mouth by a reporter called Benson writing in the *New York Times* on 18 March 1923. The quotation subsequently became linked with Sir Edmund Hillary, the eventual conqueror of Everest in 1953, who like many other climbers adopted it as his own justification from time to time. Mallory himself disappeared on an Everest expedition in 1924. His body was eventually located a little way below the peak in 1999, when speculation was renewed as to the possibility of his having actually reached the top, though this was considered unlikely by Mallory's son.

Mountaineering is a game second only to the greatest and best of man's games – life.

George Ingle Finch (1888–1970), British mountaineer and writer. *The Making of a Mountaineer* (1924).

The Japanese ... have a saying that there are two kinds of fool: those who have never climbed Mount Fuji, and those who have climbed it more than once.

John Morris (1895–1980), British writer and traveller. *Traveller from Tokyo* (1943).

We knocked the bastard off!

Sir Edmund Hillary (1919–), New Zealand mountaineer. These,
apparently, were the words with which Hillary greeted his fellow
climbers on descending from the summit of Everest in company with
Nepalese Sherpa Tenzing Norgay in June 1953, although some
sources have Tenzing himself saying 'We done the bugger!'
According to his own account of this epic moment, described in
Nothing Venture, Nothing Win (1975), fellow-climber George
Lowe's matter-of-fact response was 'Thought you must have!'

Nobody climbs mountains for scientific reasons. Science is used to raise money for the expeditions, but you really climb for the hell of it.

Sir Edmund Hillary (1919–), New Zealand mountaineer.

The mountains were there and so was I.

Maurice Herzog (1919–), French mountaineer and engineer,
explaining why he became a mountaineer. Quoted in *Annapurna:
Conquest of the First 8000-metre Peak* (1952).

We climb mountains because we like it.

Sir John Hunt (1910–), British mountaineer. *The Ascent of Everest*
(1953).

Climb every mountain, ford every burn,
Suffer a thrombosis, end up in an urn.

Arthur Marshall (1910–89), British journalist and writer. Parody of
the Rodgers and Hammerstein song 'Climb every mountain' from
the musical *The Sound of Music* (1959).

Ballet in a vertical idiom.

John Cleare, British photographer, writer and mountaineer. His definition of
rock-climbing. *Mountaineering* (1980).

The hills are the opponents with whom we compete, not other climbers.

Geoffrey Winthrop Young (1876–1958), writer. Quoted in Sidney
Spencer, *The Lonsdale Library*.

Mount Everest is very easy to climb, only just a little too high.

André Roch (1906–), Swiss climber.

Brian CLOUGH

English football manager (1935–) renowned for his outspoken manner, and for his feat of taking two clubs (Derby County and Nottingham Forest) from the former English second division to the old first division championship.

Quotes about Brian Clough

He's a kind of Rolls-Royce communist.

Malcolm Allison (1927–), English football manager, 1973.

Quotes by Brian Clough

Say nowt, win it, then – talk your head off.

Describing his approach to football management.

I shout my opinion. I yell my contempt. I mean every word of it. But when you talk like that you are a target. I've got to be a winner or they'll cut me to shreds.

Referring to his uneasy relationship with the sports press.

It doesn't matter if the players like you or dislike you. It's when they respect you that they play for you.

Attributed.

I don't drop players. I make changes.

Attributed.

See also COACHING; CORRUPTION; HOOLIGANISM; INTELLIGENCE; RETIREMENT; VANITY; YORKSHIRE COUNTY CRICKET CLUB.

Coaches

A football coach is a person who is willing to lay down your life for the good of the team.

Anonymous.

A good coach needs a patient wife, a loyal dog and a great quarterback, but not necessarily in that order.

Bud Grant (1927–), American football coach.

There are only two kinds of coach – those who have been fired and those who will be fired.

Ken Loeffler (1902–), US basketball coach.

If caring for a person is based on yelling and screaming, then he loves us very much.

Terry Nelson (1951–), Cincinnati Bearcats forward, referring to Cincinnati Bearcats coach Bob Huggins.

At least our relationship lasted longer than either of Nick's two marriages.

David Leadbetter (1955–), British golf coach. Commenting upon his dismissal as coach to Nick Faldo after 13 years. 'Sports Quotes of the Year 1998', *Daily Telegraph*, 28 December 1998.

See also COACHING; FOOTBALL MANAGEMENT; FOOTBALL MANAGERS; TRAINING.

Coaching

Coaching is 80% kidology.

Anonymous. Quoted by Dr N. Whitehead in *Conditioning for Sport* (1975).

You can't put in what God left out.

Sam Mussabini (1867–1927), British athletics coach. He was coach to Harold Abrahams, the runner whose rivalry with Eric Liddell at the 1924 Olympics provided the basis of the popular 1981 movie *Chariots of Fire*.

A coach who suppresses natural instincts may find that he has lifted a poor player to a mediocre one but has reduced a potential genius to the rank and file.

Sir Donald Bradman (1908–), Australian cricketer, 1967.

I was never coached; I was never told how to hold a bat.

Sir Donald Bradman (1908–), Australian cricketer.

The best and fastest way to learn a sport is to watch and imitate a champion.

Jean-Claude Killy (1944–), French skier.

There is a syndrome in sports called 'paralysis by analysis'.

Arthur Ashe (1943–93), US tennis player. *Scholastic Coach*,
September 1983.

Coaching is for kids. If a player can't trap a ball and pass it by the time he's in the team, he shouldn't be there in the first place. I told Roy McFarland to go and get his bloody hair cut – that's coaching at this level.

Brian Clough (1935–), English footballer and football manager.
Clough: The Autobiography (1994).

Professional coaching is a man trying to get you to keep your legs together when other men have spent a lifetime trying to get them wide apart.

Rachael Heyhoe-Flint (1939–), English cricketer.

See also COACHES; FOOTBALL MANAGEMENT; TRAINING.

David COLEMAN
Perennial British television sports commentator
(1926–) famed for his many gaffes on air.

Quotes about David Coleman
Just by being so madly keen, he helps you get things in proportion. Anything that matters so much to David Coleman, you realise doesn't matter so much at all!

Clive James (1939–), Australian broadcaster and writer. In the
Observer, 1978.

Quotes by David Coleman
For those of you watching who haven't television sets, live commentary is on Radio Two.

Extract of television commentary.

Don't tell those coming in now the result of that fantastic match. Now let's have another look at Italy's winning goal.

Extract of television commentary.

The Italians are hoping for an Italian victory.

Extract of television commentary.

If that had gone in, it would have been a goal.

Extract of television commentary.

One of the great unknown champions, because very little is known about him.

Extract of television commentary.

They came through absolutely together ... with Allan Wells in first place.

Extract of television commentary.

Bradford, who had gone up from 200 metres to 400, found it hard going for the last 100 metres and was always going backwards.

Extract of television commentary.

There is Brendan Foster, by himself, with twenty thousand people.

Extract of television commentary.

That's the fastest time ever run – but it's not as fast as the world record.

Extract of television commentary.

She's not Ben Johnson, but then who is?

Extract of television commentary.

I hope the Romanian doesn't get through, because I can't pronounce her bloody name.

Said when he mistakenly thought he was off air during an Olympic Games broadcast.

Comebacks

There are certain things you can't get back, like the elastic in your socks.

Eddie Futch (1912–), US boxing trainer, referring to comebacks by ageing boxers.

Sportsmen are always trying to make comebacks; it is part of the rhythm of every sporting year. Perhaps they cannot stand the drabness of living in the shadow of their own youth. Always they believe it is possible to find within themselves one more last hurrah.

Simon Barnes (1951–), British sportswriter.

A boxer makes a comeback for one or two reasons: either he's broke or he needs the money.

Alan Minter (1951–), British boxer. Quoted in Barry Fantoni,
Colemanballs 5 (1990).

Commentating

There are two professions that one can be hired at with little experience. One is prostitution. The other is sportscasting. Too frequently, they become the same.

Howard Cosell (1920–), US sports commentator.

Plainly no way has yet been found to stop long-jump commentaries sounding like naughty stories after lights-out in the dorm – 'Ooooh! It's enormous. It was so long!'

Russell Davies (1946–), British writer and broadcaster, *The Sunday Times*.

Commentating isn't as simple as it sounds.

Ted Lowe (1920–), British television snooker commentator. BBC TV.

Conjugate the verb 'done great': I done great. He done great. We done great. They done great. The boy Lineker done great.

Letter in the *Guardian*, responding to the ungrammatical World Cup commentaries of Emlyn Hughes and Mike Channon, 1986.

It's not going to be old farts talking about cakes.

Talk Radio spokesman, promising a new approach to radio cricket commentary, 1999.

See also ACTION REPLAYS; CLASSIC COMMENTARIES; GAFFES; MIXED METAPHORS; PREDICTIONS; SPORTING SIMILES; TELEVISION.

Commentators

The Russians have a weapon that can wipe out two hundred eighty thousand Americans. That puts them exactly ten years behind Howard Cosell.

Red Smith (1905–82), US sportswriter, referring to US sports commentator Howard Cosell (1920–).

In one year I travelled 450,000 miles by air. That's about 18 and a half times around the world or once around Howard Cosell's head.

Jackie Stewart (1939–), Scottish racing driver, referring to US sports
commentator Howard Cosell (1920–).

His voice could peel the skin off a potato.

Norman Chad, US journalist, referring to US basketball commentator
Dick Vitale.

There's a simple recipe about this sports business. If you're a sporting star, you're a sporting star. If you don't quite make it, you become a coach. If you can't coach, you become a journalist. If you can't spell, you introduce *Grandstand* on a Saturday afternoon.

Des Lynam (1942–), British television sports presenter, for many
years *Grandstand*'s presenter.

Had he been at Balaclava he would have kept pace with the Charge of the Light Brigade in precise order and described the riders' injuries before they hit the ground.

Hugh McIlvanney, British sportswriter, referring to BBC television
horse-racing commentator Peter O'Sullevan. The *Observer*, 1977.

See also John ARLOTT; David COLEMAN; COMMENTATING; Jimmy GREAVES; Brian JOHNSTON; Gary LINEKER; Murray WALKER.

Denis COMPTON

English cricketer and footballer (1918–97) nicknamed 'The Brylcreem Boy', who played for his country with distinction in both sports.

Denis Compton was the only player to call his partner for a run and wish him good luck at the same time.

John Warr (1927–), English cricketer, recalling the sometimes
hair-raising experience of batting with Compton at Middlesex,
Compton having a predilection for calling for quick runs.

Recorded centuries leave no trace,
On memory of that timeless grace.

John Arlott (1914–91), English cricket writer and commentator.

To watch Denis Compton play cricket on a good day was to know what joy was. I could have been in Hong Kong, but I think I made the right choice.

John Major (1943–), British Conservative prime minister, speaking at Compton's memorial service in 1997. He opted to attend the service rather than the handover of Hong Kong to China.

Confidence

Besides pride, loyalty, discipline, heart, and mind, confidence is the key to all the locks.

Joe Paterno (1926–), American football coach.

I am a great golfer. I just haven't played the game yet.

Muhammad Ali (Cassius Clay; 1942–), US heavyweight boxer.

Confidence is a very fragile thing.

Joe Montana (1956–), American football player.

It didn't demoralize us, but it moralized them.

Dick Greenwood (1941–), England rugby union coach. He was referring to a costly error made during a match between England and Wales. Quoted in the *Guardian*, 24 December 1985.

And I honestly believe that we can go all the way to Wembley ... unless somebody knocks us out.

Dave Bassett (1944–), English football manager, speaking as manager of Wimbledon in the 1980s.

You've got to believe that you're going to win and I believe that we'll win the World Cup until the final whistle blows and we're knocked out.

Peter Shilton (1949–), English footballer. Quoted during England's 1986 World Cup campaign, which ended in the notorious 'hand of God' quarter-final against Argentina.

There's no such thing as lack of confidence. You either have it or you don't.

Rob Andrew (1963–), English rugby union player.

I must admit when I came here I thought we were certs to finish bottom. Now I am very optimistic and I think we'll finish second bottom.

Barry Fry (1945–), English football manager, reflecting in 1993 upon his move to Southend.

The new manager has given us unbelievable belief.

Paul Merson (1968–), English footballer, refererring to his new
manager at Arsenal, Arsène Wenger, in 1996.

See also Muhammad ALI; FAMOUS LAST WORDS; VANITY; WILLPOWER.

Jimmy CONNORS

**US tennis player (1952–), well known for his ebullient
behaviour on court and for his habit of grunting as his
despatched his powerful two-handed backhand. He won
the men's singles at Wimbledon in 1974 and 1982.**

Quotes about Jimmy Connors

Jimmy Connors is loud, aggressive and with the face and hairstyle of a
medieval varlet; he personifies a generation which tips its hat to no man.

Ian Wooldridge (1932–), British sportswriter.

Quotes by Jimmy Connors

I don't know that my behaviour has improved that much with age. They
just found someone worse.

Quoted in 1984.

Corruption

Say it ain't so, Joe.

Anonymous young fan addressing US baseball star 'Shoeless Joe'
Jackson (1887–1951) during the notorious 'Black Sox' scandal of
1919. Jackson had been accused of accepting bribes to throw the
1919 World Series and with seven other players ended up being
barred from the game for life, although he always protested he was
innocent of the charges.

They went down the list of every known charge conceivable to man:
racketeering, skimming, kickback, ticket scalping, fixing fights, pre-
ordaining fights, vitiating officials, corrupting judges, all the way down to
laundering money. Everything, but the Lindbergh baby.

Don King (1932–), US boxing promoter, describing how his affairs
were examined by the FBI. The 'Lindbergh baby' was a notorious
murder case of 1932, in which the infant son of aviator Charles
Lindbergh was kidnapped and murdered.

Sure the fight was fixed. I fixed it with a right hand.

George Foreman (1948–), US heavyweight boxer. Quoted in
the *Sunday Times*, 18 December 1994, after knocking out
Michael Moorer.

The only bung I knew went into a barrel of beer.

Brian Clough (1935–), English football manager, denying any
knowledge of 'bungs' (or bribes) in football in 1997.

There are no bungs in football, only presents.

Eric Hall (1937–), English football agent. His reaction to the furore
that surrounded allegations implicating Arsenal manager George
Graham in a 'bungs' scandal involving illicit bribes. 'Quotes of the
Year', the *Guardian*, 24 December 1998.

Couch potatoes

The only athletic sport I ever mastered was backgammon.

Douglas Jerrold (1803–57), British playwright. Quoted in Walter
Jerrold, *Douglas Jerrold* (1914).

I have never taken any exercise, except sleeping and resting, and I never
intend to take any. Exercise is loathsome.

Mark Twain (1835–1910), US writer.

I take my only exercise acting as pallbearer at the funerals of my friends
who exercise regularly.

Mark Twain (1835–1910), US writer. Attributed in James Munson,
The Sayings of Mark Twain (1992).

I am pushing sixty. That is enough exercise for me.

Mark Twain (1835–1910), US writer. Attributed in James Munson,
The Sayings of Mark Twain (1992).

I'm afraid I play no outdoor games at all, except dominoes. I have
sometimes played dominoes outside a French café.

Oscar Wilde (1854–1900), Irish writer and wit. Quoted in
Gelett Burgess, 'A Talk with Mr Oscar Wilde' in *The Sketch*,
9 January 1895.

Exercise! The only possible form of exercise is to talk, not to walk.

Oscar Wilde (1854–1900), Irish writer and wit. Interview
in *The Sketch*.

At what time does the dissipation of energy begin?

Lord Kelvin (1824–1907), British physicist. His response when his
wife suggested an afternoon excursion. Quoted in Alexander
Fleming, *Memories of a Scientific Life*.

Exercise is bunk. If you are healthy, you don't need it: if you are sick, you shouldn't take it.

Henry Ford (1863–1947), US industrialist. Attributed.

The need for exercise is a modern superstition, invented by people who ate too much, and had nothing to think about.

George Santayana (1863–1952), Spanish philosopher,
poet and novelist.

Whenever I feel like exercise, I lie down until the feeling passes.

Robert M. Hutchins (1899–1977), US educator. Attributed in
P. McEvoy, *Young Man Looking Backwards* (1938).

Exercise? I get it on the golf course. When I see my friends collapse, I run for the paramedics.

Red Skelton (1910–97), US comedian.

The only exercise I get is when I take the studs out of one shirt and put them in another.

Ring Lardner (1885–1933), US humorist and writer.

My idea of exercise is a good brisk sit.

Phyllis Diller (1917–), US comedienne.

I consider exercise vulgar. It makes people smell.

Alec Yuill Thornton, US writer.

Bewdy Newk!

Australian slogan, more correctly 'Beautiful shot, Newcombe!',
dating from the late 1970s. It referred to Australian tennis player
John Newcombe (1944–) and featured originally in a television
campaign designed to encourage armchair sports fans to participate

more actively in healthy exercise, depicting an overweight
Newcombe follower called Norm cheering on his hero as he watches
a match on the television screen.

I believe every human has a finite number of heart-beats. I don't intend to waste any of mine running around doing exercises.

Neil Armstrong (1930–), US astronaut.

I'm Jewish. I don't work out. If God had wanted us to bend over he'd've put diamonds on the floor.

Joan Rivers (Joan Alexandra Molinsky; 1933–), US comedienne.

I bought all those Jane Fonda videos. I love to sit and eat cookies and watch 'em.

Dolly Parton (1946–), US singer.

I never did like working out – it bears the same relationship to real sport as masturbation does to real sex.

David Lodge (1935–), British novelist. *Therapy* (1995).

See also ANTI-SPORTS; EXERCISE; TELEVISION.

County cricket

The most famous cricketers are too big to play county cricket.

Ian Botham (1955–), English cricketer, 1980s.

You can't consider yourself a county cricketer until you've eaten half a ton of lettuce.

Sir Gary Sobers (1936–), West Indian cricketer, referring to the
standard fare dished up to players in English county cricket.

Our cricket is too gentle – all of it.

Alec Stewart (1963–), English cricketer, 1994.

As preparation for a Test match, the domestic game is the equivalent of training for the Olympic marathon by taking the dog for a walk.

Martin Johnson (1949–), British sportswriter. Quoted in the *Independent*,
1995.

This softness comes from playing county cricket, which is all very matey and lovey-dovey. We're all mates out there and it's about a few cups of tea and maybe a Pimm's or two afterwards. The gap between that cosy little world and Test cricket is immense. The Aussies, even in their grade cricket, are abusing you and rucking you. Our club cricket, in comparison, is like a social gathering.

Nasser Hussain (1968–), English cricketer, attempting to explain why England lost the Ashes against Australia in 1997.

The worry, the pain, the torment, the heartless comments and unexpected disappointments, the love–hate relationship and the hard *yakka*, is *all* worth it. Worth it for the buzz, the achievement, the satisfaction, the camaraderie, the outdoor life, the public support, the ounce of fame and the abiding fascination of the game itself.

Simon Hughes (1959–), Middlesex cricketer and cricket writer, on being a county cricketer. *A Lot of Hard Yakka* (1997).

See also CRICKETERS; YORKSHIRE COUNTY CRICKET CLUB.

Courage

I can't see my man, your Highness. I am blind. But not beat, only place me before him and he shall yet not gain the day.

Jack Broughton (1704–89), British bareknuckle boxer. He was addressing his backer, the Duke of Cumberland, when, during a championship bout in 1750, he was temporarily blinded by blows from his opponent. After losing the bout he retired to become a boxing coach to the nobility and is remembered as the 'Father of Boxing'. Quoted in David Randall, *Great Sporting Eccentrics* (1985).

It asks more steadiness, self-control, ay, and manly courage, than any other exercise. You must take as well as give – eye to eye, toe to toe, and arm to arm.

Sir Robert Peel (1788–1850), British Conservative politician, referring to boxing. Quoted by John Boyle O'Reilly in *Ethics of Boxing and Manly Sport* (1888).

At least I can get in someone's way.

Dan Dempsey, Australian rugby league player. His explanation as he returned to the field against England in 1932 after suffering a broken arm earlier in the match.

There's no substitute for guts.

Paul 'Bear' Bryant (1913–83), American football coach.

You learn you can do your best even when it's hard, even when you're tired and maybe hurting a little bit. It feels good to show some courage.

Joe Namath (1943–), American football player.

I've been knocked down more than any heavyweight champion in history, but I consider that a compliment, because I must have got up more than any heavyweight champion.

Floyd Patterson (1935–), US heavyweight boxer, 1972.

If you're afraid of losing, then you daren't win.

Björn Borg (1956–), Swedish tennis player.

You must be strong in March, when the fish are down.

Gianluca Vialli (1964–), Italian footballer. 'Quotes of the Year', the *Guardian*, 24 December 1998.

See also CONFIDENCE; NERVES; WILLPOWER.

Cricket

The youths at cricks did play
Throughout the merry day.

Joseph of Exeter (*fl. c.*1190), English poet. Possibly an early reference to the game of cricket. Quoted in Ivor Brown, *A Book of England* (1958).

A sport in which contenders drive a ball with sticks or bats in opposition to each other.

Samuel Johnson (1709–84), British lexicographer. His definition of cricket.

Hail Cricket! glorious, manly, British game!
First of all Sports! be first alike in fame!

James Love (James Dance; 1722–74), British actor and writer. 'Cricket: An Heroic Poem' (1744).

Who would think that a little bit of leather, and two pieces of wood, had such a delightful and delighting power!

Mary Russell Mitford (1787–1855), British novelist and playwright.
Our Village (1824–32).

It's more than a game. It's an institution.

Thomas Hughes (1822–96), British novelist. *Tom Brown's Schooldays* (1856).

If the wild bowler thinks he bowls
Or if the batsman thinks he's bowled,
They know not, poor misguided souls,
They too shall perish unconsoled.
I am the batsman and the bat,
I am the bowler and the ball,
The umpire, the pavilion cat,
The roller, pitch, and stumps and all.

Andrew Lang (1844–1912), Scottish writer. 'Brahma'.

I do love cricket – it's so very English.

Sarah Bernhardt (1844–1923), French actress. Said while watching a game of football in Manchester. Quoted in R. Buckle, *Nijinsky*.

It is surely the loveliest scene in England and the most disarming sound. From the ranks of the unseen dead for ever passing along our country lanes, the Englishman falls out for a moment to look over the gate of the cricket field and smile.

J.M. Barrie (1860–1937), Scottish novelist and playwright.

It is little I repair to the matches of the Southron folk,
Though my own red roses there may blow;
It is little I repair to the matches of the Southron folk,
Though the red roses crest the caps, I know.
For the field is full of shades as I near the shadowy coast,
And a ghostly batsman plays to the bowling of a ghost,
And I look through my tears on a soundless-clapping host
As the run-stealers flicker to and fro,
To and fro: –
O my Hornby and my Barlow long ago!

Francis Thompson (1859–1907), British poet, explaining to his

friends why he no longer came to Lord's because of the sad
memories it evoked of long-gone friends he used to watch there.
'At Lord's' (1907).

Casting a ball at three straight sticks and defending the same with a fourth.

Rudyard Kipling (1865–1936) British novelist and poet, defining cricket.

Cricket is certainly one of the most powerful links that keep our Empire together. It is one of the greatest contributions which the British people have made to the cause of humanity.

Prince Ranjitsinhji (1872–1933), Indian cricketer.

To some people cricket is a circus show upon which they may or may not find it worthwhile to spend sixpence; to others it is a pleasant means of livelihood; to others a physical fine art full of plot, interest and enlivened by difficulties; to others, in some sort, it is a cult and a philosophy.

C.B. Fry (1872–1956), English cricketer, footballer and athlete.
Foreword to D.L.A. Jephson, *A Few Overs* (1913).

The fellows were practising long shies and bowling lobs and slow twisters. In the soft grey silence he could hear the bump of the balls: and from here and from there through the quiet air the sound of the cricket bats: pick, pack, pock, puck: like drops of water in a fountain falling softly in the brimming bowl.

James Joyce (1882–1941), Irish writer. *A Portrait of the Artist as a Young Man* (1916).

Heavenly weather. If life was always like that. Cricket weather. Sit around under sunshades. Over after over. Out. They can't play it here. Still, Captain Buller broke a window in Kildare Street Club with a slog to square leg.

James Joyce (1882–1941), Irish writer. Passage reportedly inspired by an incident in which W.G. Grace managed a similar feat while batting at Dublin's College Park in the 1870s. *Ulysses* (1922).

But what care I? It's the game that calls me –
Simply to be on the field of play;
How can it matter what fate befalls me,
With ten good fellows and one good day!

A.A. Milne (1882–1956), British writer.

Novelty is the one quality required for Christmas games ... If a game is novel it is enough. To the manager of a toy department the continued vogue of cricket must be very bewildering.

A.A. Milne (1882–1956), British writer.

Cricket to us was more than play,
It was a worship in the summer sun.

Edmund Blunden (1896–1974), British poet. 'Pride of the Village'.

Cricket is the greatest game that the wit of man has yet devised.

Sir Pelham Warner (1873–1963), Trinidadian-born English cricketer.

The very word 'cricket' has become a synonym for all that is true and honest. To say 'that is not cricket' implies something underhand, something not in keeping with the best ideals.

Sir Pelham Warner (1873–1963), Trinidadian-born English cricketer.

In the manner in which soccer is the great way up for the children from the economic sumps of Brazil, so cricket was the great way out of Australian cultural ignominy. No Australian had written *Paradise Lost*, but Bradman had made a hundred before lunch at Lord's.

Thomas Kenneally (1879–1954), Australian politician.

We may be a small race, but there's divinity in our cricket.

Thomas Kenneally (1879–1954), Australian politician.

Since cricket became brighter, a man of taste can only go to an empty ground and regret the past.

C.P. Snow (1905–80), British novelist and physicist, 1932.

First-class cricket is a subtle as well as a strenuous game. It is a thing of leisure, albeit of leisure today not easily found or arranged; a three-act play, not a slapstick turn.

R.C. Robertson-Glasgow (1901–65), English cricketer. *Wisden Cricketers' Almanack*, 1945.

Of course it's frightfully dull! That's the whole point! Any game can be exciting – football, dirt track racing, roulette ... To go to cricket to be thrilled is as stupid as to go to a Chekhov play in search of melodrama.

Terence Rattigan (1911–77), British playwright. Spoken by Robert Morley's character, Alexander Whitehead in the film *The Final Test* (1953), about a famous cricketer's last game.

Cricket, like the novel, is great when it presents men in the round, when it shows the salty quality of human nature.

John Arlott (1914–91), English cricket writer and commentator, 1953.

When's the game itself going to begin?

Groucho Marx (Julius Henry Marx; 1895–1977), US film comedian. Said while watching a cricket match at Lord's.

Foreigners suspect that cricket is some form of English lunacy. They will never understand there is a method in this English madness. It is what keeps them sane.

André Drucker (1909–), writer.

Cricket is first and foremost a dramatic spectacle. It belongs with the theatre, ballet, opera and the dance.

C.L.R. James (1901–89), Trinidadian historian and cricket writer. *Beyond a Boundary* (1963).

Cricket – a game which the English, not being a spiritual people, have invented in order to give themselves some conception of eternity.

Lord Mancroft (1914–), British peer. 'Scorecard', *Sports Illustrated*, 11 November 1963.

With a thorough knowledge of the Bible, Shakespeare and Wisden you cannot go far wrong.

Arthur Waugh, father of the novelist Evelyn Waugh. Quoted in Evelyn Waugh, *A Little Learning* (1964). Wisden is *Wisden Cricketers' Almanack*, published every year since 1864.

Watching cricket is habit-forming, it can become habitual,
It's a kind of long-lasting white-robed ritual.
And until recently it's been a male prerogative,
Played by big hairy bowlers and blacksmiths who were slogative.

Gavin Ewart (1916–), poet. *Not Quite Cricket.*

Cricket shares with Cleopatra the charm of infinite variety.

J.M. Kilburn, British sportswriter. *Overthrows: A Book of Cricket* (1975).

There is a widely held and quite erroneously held belief that cricket is just another game.

Prince Philip, Duke of Edinburgh (1921–), Greek-born consort of
Queen Elizabeth II. 'The Pleasures of Cricket', in *Wisden Cricketers'*
Almanack (1975).

Any detached observer has reluctantly to admit that most of what passes for top-level cricket today is the wrong kind of cricket played by the wrong kind of cricketer to titillate the wrong kind of spectator.

H.A. Harris, British writer, in *Sport in Britain: Its Origins and*
Development (1975).

Most games are skin-deep, but cricket goes to the bone.

John Arlott (1914–91), English cricket writer and commentator.
Arlott and Trueman on Cricket (1977).

Cricket is a game of the most terrifying stresses with more luck about it than any other game I know. They call it a team game, but in fact it is the loneliest game of all.

John Arlott (1914–91), British journalist and cricket commentator.
Another Word from Arlott.

I have always imagined cricket as a game invented by roughnecks in a moment of idleness by casually throwing an unexploded bomb at one another. The game was observed by some officer with a twisted and ingenious mind who devoted his life to inventing impossible rules for it.

Peter Ustinov (1921–), British actor and playwright.

There is no essential discrepancy between the game's time-honoured virtues and the world we live in. It is a matter of creatively adapting the form in order to preserve the content. So far much valuable time has been wasted on quibbling over what 'isn't cricket', and not much has been devoted to what cricket should become.

Imran Khan (1952–), Pakistani cricketer. *All Round View* (1988).

Cricket remains for me the game of games, the sanspareil, the great metaphor, the best marriage ever devised of mind and body ... For me it remains the Proust of pastimes, the subtlest and most poetic, the most past-and-present; whose beauty can lie equally in days, in a whole, or in one tiny phrase, a blinding split second.

John Fowles (1926–), British novelist. 'Vain Memories', in *Quick Singles*.

Cricket? It civilizes people and creates good gentlemen. I want everyone to play cricket in Zimbabwe. I want ours to be a nation of gentlemen.

Robert Mugabe (1924–), Zimbabwean president.

I want to play cricket, it doesn't seem to matter if you win or lose.

Meat Loaf (Marvin Lee Aday; 1948–), US rock star.

How can we interrupt such a noble activity as cricket?

Marc Joando, French court president, responding to the news that
Geoffrey Boycott would not be attending court to answer charges
that he had assaulted his former girlfriend, owing to his
commitments as a cricket commentator, 1998.

See also John ARLOTT; THE ASHES; BALLS; BALL-TAMPERING; BODYLINE;
COUNTY CRICKET; CRICKET-BASHERS; CRICKET BATS; CRICKETERS; CRICKET
PITCHES; CRICKET TOURS; CRICKET UMPIRES; FAST BOWLING; LEG SPIN
BOWLING; MARYLEBONE CRICKET CLUB; ONE-DAY CRICKET; PHILOSOPHY;
PLAYING THE GAME; POLITICS; RULES; SEX; VILLAGE SPORTS; YORKSHIRE
COUNTY CRICKET CLUB.

Cricket-bashers

I never was a boy, never played at cricket; it is better to let Nature take her course.

John Stuart Mill (1806–73), British philosopher. In his
Autobiography (1867).

It requires one to assume such indecent postures.

Oscar Wilde (1854–1900), Irish writer and wit, explaining why he
did not play cricket.

Personally, I have always looked on cricket as organized loafing.

William Temple (1881–1944), British educationist and clergyman. He
was addressing parents as headmaster of Repton School, Derbyshire, in
about 1914. Quoted in Michael Parkinson, *Sporting Lives* (1993).

Oh God, if there be cricket in heaven, let there also be rain.

Sir Alec Douglas Home (1903–95), British Conservative prime
minister. 'Prayer of a Cricketer's Wife'.

I have seen cricket, and I know it isn't true.

Danny Kaye (1913–87), US entertainer.

Cricket is the only game that you can actually put on weight when playing.

Tommy Docherty (1928–), Scottish football manager. Piccadilly
Radio, 1990.

Cricket is baseball on valium.

Robin Williams (1952–), US comedian.

See also ANTI-SPORTS.

Cricket bats

That bat that you were kind enough to send,
Seems (for as yet I have not tried it) good:
And if there's anything on earth can mend
My wretched play, it is that piece of wood.

Henry Manning (1808–92), British Roman Catholic churchman.
Poem sent in thanks to William Wordsworth's nephew Charles in
return for the gift of a cricket bat, 1826.

From the very earliest days I can recall, I have loved the feel of a cricket bat.

Sir Len Hutton (1916–90), English cricketer. *Cricket* (1961).

How much simpler it is to swat a fly with a rolled-up newspaper than with
a telephone directory.

Denis Compton (1918–97), English cricketer, recommending the use
of lighter bats in *Cricket and All That* (1978).

A cricket bat is an instrument that looks like a baseball bat run over by a
steam-roller.

Canadian newspaper article.

See also BALLS.

Cricketers

A cricketer's life is a life of splendid freedom, healthy effort, endless variety, and delightful fellowship.

W.G. Grace (1848–1915), English cricketer.

Batsmen are the darlings of the committees; bowlers are cricket's labourers.

Sir Donald Bradman (1908–), Australian cricketer.

Tha knows one thing I learned about cricket: tha can't put in what God left out. Tha sees two kinds of cricketers, them that uses a bat as if they are shovelling muck and them that plays proper, and like as not God showed both of 'em how to play.

Wilfred Rhodes (1877–1973), English cricketer. Quoted in Michael
Parkinson, *Cricket Mad* (1969).

Cricketer: a creature very nearly as stupid as a dog.

Bernard Levin (1928–), British journalist and author in *The Times*, 1965.

I have often thought of how much better a life I would have had, what a better man I would have been, how much healthier an existence I would have led, if I had been a cricketer.

Sir Laurence Olivier (1907–89), British actor.

The truest of all axioms about cricket is that the game is as good as those who play it.

E.W. Swanton (1907–2000), British sportswriter. *Sort of a Cricket
Person* (1972).

The vast majority of county cricketers have two topics of conversation: 'Me and My Cricket', or, as a high day and holiday variant, 'My Cricket and Me'.

Frances Edmonds, British writer, novelist and wife of England
cricketer Phil Edmonds, 1994.

See also Ian BOTHAM; Geoffrey BOYCOTT; Sir Donald BRADMAN; Denis COMPTON;
COUNTY CRICKET; David GOWER; W.G. GRACE; Sir Richard HADLEE;
Walter ('Wally') HAMMOND; Sir Jack HOBBS; Sir Len HUTTON; Brian LARA;
Dennis LILLEE; Clive LLOYD; Viv RICHARDS; Sir Gary SOBERS; Jeff THOMSON;
Fred TRUEMAN; WOMEN IN SPORT.

Cricket pitches

The wicket reminded me of a middle-aged gentleman's head of hair when the middle-aged gentleman, to conceal the baldness of his crown, applies a pair of wet brushes to some favourite long locks and brushes them across the top of his head.

Fred 'Old Buffer' Gale (1823–1904), British writer, 1868.

It is that cricket field that, in all the sharp and bitter moments of life as they come to me now, gives me a sense of wholesome proportion: 'At least I am not playing cricket!'

John Cowper Powys (1872–1963), British novelist and essayist.

Drinking the best tea in the world in an empty cricket ground – that, I think, is the final pleasure left to man.

C.P. Snow (1905–80), British novelist and physicist, 1932.

Pitches are like wives, you can never tell how they're going to turn out.

Sir Len Hutton (1916–90), English cricketer, 1954.

It is a remarkable fact that every time a side has a bad innings it is the wicket that is blamed – never the player.

The *Groundsman* magazine, 1958.

The Port Elizabeth ground is more of a circle than an oval. It's long and square.

Trevor Bailey (1923–), British sports commentator. BBC radio, 1995.

If there's no room in heaven when I die, I'll accept a West Indian cricket ground.

Simon Hughes (1959–), Middlesex cricketer and cricket writer.
A Lot of Hard Yakka (1997).

See also LORD'S CRICKET GROUND.

Cricket tours

A cricket tour in Australia would be a most delightful period in one's life if one was deaf.

Harold Larwood (1904–95), English cricketer, reflecting upon the

barbed comments of Australian fans that were directed at England
cricketers during the infamous 'bodyline' tour of 1932–33, in
Bodyline (1933).

When you come back from touring Australia, you almost feel like you've
been to Vietnam.

Glenn Turner (1947–), New Zealand-born cricketer, 1983.

The sort of place everyone should send his mother-in-law for a month, all
expenses paid.

Ian Botham (1955–), English cricketer, referring to Pakistan during
a BBC radio interview in March 1984. This unguarded comment
subsequently earned him a £1000 fine from the Test and County
Cricket Board.

Up, breakfast, stretch, practise, play, bathe, bar, steak, bed. Same company,
day in, day out.

Ian Botham (1955–), English cricketer, describing the routine while
on tour with England in Ian Botham and Peter Roebuck, *It Sort of
Clicks* (1986).

I'm probably best out of touring. Nobody seems to smile any more.

Ian Botham (1955–), English cricketer, reflecting in 1991 upon
England's recent tour of Australia.

Being the manager of a touring team is rather like being in charge of a
cemetery – lots of people underneath you, but no one listening.

Wes Hall (1937–), West Indian cricketer, 1995.

See also BODYLINE.

Cricket umpires

Shall I never storm or swear,
Just because the umpire's fair?
If he will not favour me,
What care I how fair he be?

Edmund B.V. Christian (1864–1938), British solicitor and poet.

The umpire at cricket is like the geyser in the bathroom; we cannot do
without it, yet we notice it only when it is out of order.

Sir Neville Cardus (1889–1975), British journalist and writer.

It is rather suitable for umpires to dress like dentists, since one of their tasks is to draw stumps.

John Arlott (1914–91), English cricket writer and commentator.

I want to stress again one aspect of the game which is most important. *Never argue with an umpire.*

Ian Botham (1955–), English cricketer. *Ian Botham on Cricket* (1980).

A dirty look is the only acceptable expression of dissent, and we don't even like that.

Anonymous cricket umpire, quoted in 'Inside Track', the *Sunday Times*, 22 August 1982.

He arrived on earth from the Planet Looney to become the best and fairest of all umpires. Great bloke, completely bonkers.

Ian Botham (1955–), English cricketer, referring in *Botham: My Autobiography* (1994) to the legendary cricket umpire Harold 'Dickie' Bird (1933–).

Umpire Harold Bird, having a wonderful time, signalling everything in the world, including stopping traffic coming on from behind.

John Arlott (1914–91), English cricket writer and commentator, referring to umpire Harold 'Dickie' Bird (1933–).

What are the butchers for?

Pauline Chase (1885–1962), US actress. On attending her first game of cricket.

Croquet

Praise the sports of the land
And water, each one –
The bath by the beach, or the yacht on the sea –
But of all the sweet pleasures
Known under the sun;
A good game of Croquet's the sweetest to me.

Thomas Mayne Reid (1818–83), Anglo-Irish novelist, 1863.

My doctor forbids me to play, unless I win.

Alexander Woollcott (1887–1943), US critic, writer and actor.
Reflecting upon the competitive pressures of the game.

It is no game for the soft of sinew and the gentle of spirit. The higher and dirtier croquet-player can use the guile of a cobra and the inhumanity of a boa constrictor. Then, the general physique of a stevedore comes in handy, too.

Alexander Woollcott (1887–1943), US critic, writer and actor.

The clunk of the ball against mallet is a lovely sound, just like ice cubes in a gin and tonic.

The *Sunday Times*, 1987.

Cross-country *See* RUNNING.

Curling

Frae Maidenkirk to John O'Groats
Nae curlers like the clergy.

Scottish proverb.

To curle on the ice, does greatly please,
Being a manly Scottish exercise;
It clears the Brains, stirs up the Native Heat,
And gives a gallant appetite for Meat.

Alex Penecuik (1652–1722), Scottish poet, 1715.

When winter muffles up his cloak,
And binds the mire like a rock,
Then to the loch,
The Curlers flock.

Robert Burns (1759–96), Scottish poet.

Curling lifts the spirit and captivates the mind.

Robin Welsh. *Beginner's Guide to Curling* (1969).

Competitive housework.

Anonymous commentator.

Cycling

Whoop la, out of the way
We come with lightning speed,
There's nothing like the rattling gait
Of the flying velocipede.

Anonymous.

The first race probably took place as soon as the second bicycle was completed.

J. Else, writer. 'The A–Z of Cycling' in *Cycling a New Deal – Report of a Conference Held at Nottingham*, 24 November 1978.

Any cyclist will confirm that in hilly country the slope is always steeper the side you are going up. This is one of the great mysteries of Nature.

Philippa Gregory (1954–). Quoted in the *Guardian*, 12 October 1985.

See also DRUG-TAKING; MOTOR CYCLING.

· D ·

Kenny DALGLISH

Scottish footballer and manager (1951–). 'King Kenny' won 102 caps for Scotland and nine League championship medals, two FA Cups and four European Cups as a player and manager with Liverpool in the years 1977–90.

I never saw anyone in this country to touch him. I can think of only two who could go ahead of him – Pelé and possibly Cruyff.

Graeme Souness (1953–), Scottish footballer and manager, 1988.

He wasn't a bad player really, you know, average.

Paul Dalglish, son of Kenny Dalglish. 'Quotes of the Year', the *Guardian*, 24 December 1998.

Kenny Dalglish has about as much personality as a tennis racquet.

Mick Channon (1948–), English footballer and racehorse trainer.

See also BRAZILIAN FOOTBALL; FOOTBALL MANAGEMENT; MARRIAGE; TRAGEDIES.

Darts

There's only one word for that – magic darts!

Tony Green, British television sports commentator.

I was watching Sumo wrestling on the television for two hours before I realised it was darts.

Hattie Hayridge, British comedienne, 1989.

Steve DAVIS

British snooker player (1957–), who won recognition as the finest player of the 1980s.

I suppose the charisma bypass operation was a big disappointment in my life.

Reflecting upon press criticism of his 'boring' personality.

Frame and fortune.

Title of his autobiography.

See also BILLIARDS; SEX; SNOOKER.

Death

Old golfers never die – they simply lose their drive.

Anonymous.

Impossible to come today. Please put corpse on ice.

E.M. Grace (1841–1911), English cricketer and coroner, elder brother of W.G. Grace. Telegram sent in reply when his presence was requested at an inquest, threatening to curtail his appearance in a cricket match. Quoted in A.A. Thomson, *The Great Cricketer* (1957).

At his funeral in Omaha he filled the church to capacity. He was a draw right to the finish.

Jack Hurley, US boxing promoter. Following the funeral of US boxer Vince Foster in 1949.

Even when you're dead you shouldn't lie down and let yourself be buried.

Gordon Lee (1934–), English football manager. Quoted on losing the post of manager of Everton in 1981.

Sadly, the immortal Jackie Milburn died recently.

Cliff Morgan (1930–), Welsh rugby player and sports broadcaster, 1988.

We have the naïve expectation that when we go, we won't be leaving any loose ends lying around ... It's all nonsense, of course, and football fans contemplating their own mortality know that it is all nonsense. There will be hundreds of loose ends. Maybe we will die the night before our team appears at Wembley, or the day after a European Cup first-leg match, or in the middle of a promotion campaign or a relegation battle, and there is every prospect, according to many theories about the afterlife, that we will not be able to discover the eventual outcome. The whole *point* about death, metaphorically speaking, is that it is almost bound to occur before the major trophies have been awarded.

Nick Hornby (1957–), British writer and novelist. *Fever Pitch* (1992).

Through football we're trying to show that Colombia is about more than cocaine, violence, terrorism and death.

Francisco Maturana (1949–), Colombian national football coach.
Quoted shortly before the 1994 World Cup finals, which were
subsequently marred by the assassination of the Colombian centre-
back Andres Escobar, murdered by vengeful fans after the defeated
squad returned home.

See also EPITAPHS; LAST WORDS; TRAGEDIES.

Decathlon

The decathlon is nine Mickey Mouse events and the 1500 metres.

Steve Ovett (1955–), British middle-distance runner.

Behind every good decathlete, there's a good doctor.

Bill Toomey (1939–), US decathlete.

See also Daley THOMPSON.

Defeat

You can't win them all.

Proverb.

It signifies nothing to play well and lose.

Thomas Fuller (1654–1734), British physician and writer.
Gnomologia (1732).

I should of stood in bed.

Joe Jacobs (1896–1940), US boxing manager. His response, having left his sick bed to place a bet on one of the sides in the 1935 World Baseball Series in Detroit, only to see his team lose. Quoted in John Lardner, *Strong Cigars* (1951).

Every man's got to figure to get beat some time.

Joe Louis (1914–81), US heavyweight boxer.

I'd rather be a poor winner than any kind of loser.

George S. Kaufman (1889–1961), US humorist and playwright.

Show me a good loser and I'll show you an idiot.

Leo Durocher (1906–91), US baseball manager, 1950.

Most games are lost, not won.

Charles 'Casey' Stengel (1890–1975), US baseball player and manager.

You gotta lose 'em some time. When you do, lose 'em right.

Charles 'Casey' Stengel (1890–1975), US baseball player and manager.

Without losers, where would the winners be?

Charles 'Casey' Stengel (1890–1975), US baseball player and manager.

Even the push button elevators don't stop for me now.

Sonny Liston (1932–71), US heavyweight boxer. Quoted in 1965, after he had lost the heavyweight title to Cassius Clay.

Sometimes you wake up in the morning and wish your parents had never met.

Bill Fitch (1934–), US basketball coach.

Success is important but defeats are valuable.

C.M. Jones (1912–), British journalist. *Bowls: How to Become a Champion* (1972).

If we lose I go home, crawl in bed, and suck my thumb.

Buddy Ryan (1934–), US baseball coach.

If you can accept defeat and open your pay envelope without feeling guilty, you're stealing.

George Allen (1922–90), American football coach.

It's easy to do anything in victory. It's in defeat that a man reveals himself.

Floyd Patterson (1935–), US heavyweight boxer.

The sooner we get rid of losing, the happier everyone will be.

Philip Roth (1933–), US novelist. *The Great American Novel*
(1986).

I consider this defeat to be the mother of future victories.

Antonio Oliveira (1952–), Portuguese football manager, looking on
the bright side after Portugal lost to the Republic of Ireland in 1995.

I've just been given a video recording of the game, and I'm going to tape *Neighbours* over it.

Harry Redknapp (1947–), English football manager. As manager
of West Ham, following a disappointing goalless draw against
Southampton, 1995.

If I were an England player I'd be hiding in my room this morning.

John Mitchell (1963–), New Zealand-born England assistant
rugby union coach, responding to England's record 76–0 defeat by
Australia in 1998. 'Sporting Quotes of the Year 1998', the *Daily
Telegraph*, 28 December 1998.

You can do yourself an injury thinking about the various ways of losing a cricket match.

David Lloyd (1947–), England cricket team coach. Quoted after
losing to South Africa in cricket's World Cup in *The Times*, 31
December 1999.

See also LOSING STREAKS; RUNNERS-UP; VICTORY; WINNING STREAKS.

Jack DEMPSEY

US heavyweight boxer (1895–1983), nicknamed the 'Manassa Mauler' after his Colorado birthplace, who became world champion in 1919.

Quotes about Jack Dempsey

The champion, Jess Willard, had about as much chance in this fight as a dish-faced chimpanzee in a beauty contest.

Arthur 'Bugs' Baer (1876–1969), US sportswriter, referring to Dempsey's victory over Willard to win the world heavyweight title in 1919.

Jack Dempsey hits like an epileptic pile-driver.

Harry C. Witwert, US sportswriter.

Quotes by Jack Dempsey

Tall men come down to my height when I hit 'em in the body.

Defying the suggestion that his diminutive height was a disadvantage in the ring.

Honey, I forgot to duck.

Addressing his wife after defeat against world heavyweight championship challenger Gene Tunney on 23 September 1926. The phrase enjoyed renewed exposure in 1981 when US President Ronald Reagan borrowed it after being wounded in an attempted assassination attempt.

See also CLICHÉS; MONEY; TECHNIQUE.

The Derby

Annual horse-racing event, long considered the most prestigious prize in thoroughbred racing, held at Epsom racecourse in Surrey, in June.

The blue ribbon of the turf.

Benjamin Disraeli (1804–81), British Conservative prime minister and novelist, referring to the Epsom Derby. *Lord George Bentinck: a Political Biography* (1852).

Why all the fuss? After all, the Derby is just another race.

Lester Piggott (1935–), British jockey, on winning the Derby in 1954, at the age of 18.

You've got no chance with a race like the Derby – the bastards are all trying.
Anonymous stable lad, 1979.

Dice

The devil invented dice.
St Augustine (354–430), Numidian-born churchman and religious writer.

Death and dice level all distinctions.
Samuel Foote (1720–77), British actor and playwright.

And once or twice,
To throw the dice
Is a gentleman's game.
Oscar Wilde (1854–1900), Irish writer and wit.

See also GAMBLING.

Dieting

If you come to think of it, you never see deer, dogs and rabbits worrying about their menus and yet they run much faster than humans.
Emil Zatopek (1922–), Czech athlete and middle-distance runner.

I can't even spell 'diet'.
Gareth Edwards (1947–), Welsh rugby player, 1984.

Avoid any diet that discourages the use of hot fudge.
Don Kardong (1949–), runner.

I can't see how one kebab can be the difference between beating one or three men or running from box to box or scoring a goal. Bloody hell, in Scotland I had haggis and won the double!
Paul Gascoigne (1967–), English footballer, refuting media criticism
of his indulgence in fatty foods prior to the 1998 World Cup
campaign in which he hoped to (but did not) participate.

See also FOOD.

Joe DiMAGGIO

US baseball player (1914–99), variously nicknamed 'Joltin'
Joe' and the 'Yankee Clipper', remembered today as much
for his brief marriage (1954) to film star Marilyn Monroe as
for his achievements on the baseball field.

Quotes about Joe DiMaggio

I don't know if it's good for baseball but it sure beats the hell out of
rooming with Phil Rizzuto!

Lawrence 'Yogi' Berra (1925–), US baseball player, responding to
the recent marriage of DiMaggio and Monroe. 1954.

Quotes by Joe DiMaggio

It's no fun being married to an electric light.

Referring to his wife, actress Marilyn Monroe. When the marriage
broke up, humorist Oscar Levant observed 'It proves that no man
can be a success in two national pastimes.'

I remember a reporter asking for a quote, and I didn't know what a quote
was. I thought it was some kind of drink.

Attributed.

Discus

I don't think the discus will ever attract any interest until they let us start
throwing them at one another.

Al Oerter (1936–), US discus thrower.

See also TECHNIQUE.

Diving *See* SWIMMING.

Tommy DOCHERTY

Scottish football manager (1928–), nicknamed 'Doc' and
renowned for his flamboyant personality and management
of numerous football clubs.

Quotes about Tommy Docherty

Who would have guessed that behind that arrogant Scots bastard image
there lay an arrogant Scots bastard.

Mike Ticher, British sportswriter. *When Saturday Comes*, 1986.

Quotes by Tommy Docherty

Preston? They're one of my old clubs. But then most of them are. I've had more clubs than Jack Nicklaus.

Referring, in 1979, to his wide experience as a manager, having
worked as manager of Chelsea, Rotherham United, Queen's Park
Rangers (twice), Aston Villa, Porto, Hull City, Manchester United,
Derby County, Sydney Olympic, Preston North End, South
Melbourne, Wolverhampton Wanderers and Altrincham.

The ideal board of directors should be made up of three men – two dead and the other dying.

A typically robust view of the people to whom, ostensibly at least,
he owed his living.

I talk a lot. On any subject. Which is always football.

Acknowledging his reputation for garrulity.

See also CRICKET-BASHERS; DRUG-TAKING; FOOTBALL CLUB OWNERS; Paul GASCOIGNE; INCOMPETENCE; INTELLIGENCE; MANCHESTER CITY; MANCHESTER UNITED; MONEY; POLITICS; The PRESS; TACTICS.

Dog-racing *See* GREYHOUND RACING.

Drag-racing

If horse racing is the sport of kings, then drag racing must be the sport of queens.

Bert R. Sugar, US sports journalist.

Drug-taking

Without the use of drugs our athletes are like drivers of a racing car with one gear less than their rivals.

Harvey Smith (1938–), British showjumper, 1967.

Drugs are very much a part of professional sports today, but when you think about it, golf is the only sport where the players aren't penalized for being on grass.

Bob Hope (1903–), US comedian.

Death is the final penalty, but the life of a sportsman on drugs is a perpetual living penalty because he is offending against himself.

Chris Brasher (1928–), British middle-distance runner, 1978.

After the match an official asked for two of my players to take a dope test. I offered him the referee.

Tommy Docherty (1928–), Scottish football manager, 1985.

The fact is that I have, at various times in the past, smoked pot. I had been with a group of people who had been doing it and I went along with it. On other occasions I have smoked simply in order to relax – to get off the sometimes fearful treadmill of being an international celebrity.

Ian Botham (1955–), English cricketer, admitting his use of dope in the *Mail on Sunday* in 1986.

You have to be suspicious when you line up against girls with moustaches.

Maree Holland, Australian athlete, 1988.

If cocaine were helium, the NBA would float away.

Art Rust, US basketball player.

It is like being told Pavarotti has been using someone else's voice.

Vicente Modahl, husband of British runner Diane Modahl: his reaction in 1994 to allegations that his wife had used a banned drug.

They should save money and check for those who are negative.

Mark Sturgeon, British sports journalist: his comment after Canadian snowboarder Ross Rebagliati had tested positive for marijuana at the Winter Olympics. The *Daily Telegraph*, 'Sporting Quotes of the Year', 28 December 1998.

We think the riders deserve to arrive at the Paris finish on a high note.

Jean-Marie Leblanc, French director of the Tour de France. Quoted towards the end of the 1998 Tour de France, which was badly disrupted by drugs scandals implicating several riders.

There is no doping in cyling.

Laurent Jalabert (1968–), French cyclist, attempting against the odds to mend the tarnished image of international cycling in 1999. Quoted in *The Times*, 31 December 1999.

I hear of athletes on EPO being woken in the night to walk around so the blood does not solidify and bring on heart attacks while they sleep. They take rat poison to thin the blood. This isn't sport as I want to know it.

David Hemery (1934–), British athletics administrator, speaking as president of UK Athletics. Quoted in *The Times*, 31 December 1999. EPO is an abbreviation for the performance-enhancing drug erythropoietin.

See also BODYBUILDING; Ben JOHNSON; Diego MARADONA.

·E·

Education

I quit school in the sixth grade because of pneumonia. Not because I had it, but because I couldn't spell it.

Rocky Graziano (1922–90), US middleweight and welterweight boxer.

I say get an education. Become an electrician, a mechanic, a doctor, a lawyer – anything but a fighter. In this trade, it's the managers that make the money and last the longest.

Muhammad Ali (Cassius Clay; 1942–), US heavyweight boxer.

This job is better than I could get if I used my college degree, which, at this point, I can't remember what it was in.

Bob Golic (1962–), American football player, speaking as a graduate
of Notre Dame.

We say 'educated left foot' ... of course, there are many players with educated right foots.

Ron Jones, British sports commentator. Radio 5 Live.

See also INTELLIGENCE; LITERATURE AND SPORT; SCHOOL SPORTS.

Epitaphs

Sacred to the memory of
Captain Anthony Wedgewood
Accidentally shot by his gamekeeper

Whilst out shooting
'Well done thou good and faithful servant.'

Anonymous.

Here lies, bowl'd out by Death's unerring ball,
A cricketer renowned, by name John Small;
But though his name was small, yet great was his fame,
For nobly did he play the 'noble game'.
His life was like his innings – long and good;
Full ninety summers had Death withstood,
At length the ninetieth winter came – when (Fate
Not leaving him one solitary mate)
This last of Hambledonians, old John Small,
Gave up his bat and ball – his leather, wax and all.

Pierce Egan (1772–1849), British journalist. *Pierce Egan's Book of Sports* (1832).

He died at last, from forty-seven
Tumblers of punch he drank one even';
Overthrown by punch, unharmed by fist,
He died, unbeaten pugilist.

Anonymous epitaph on the celebrated 19th-century bare-knuckle champion Dan Donnelly.

Spirits of well-shot woodcock, partridge, snipe
Flutter and bear him up the Norfolk sky.

John Betjeman (1906–84), British poet. Epitaph for King George V, a noted sportsman who was particularly fond of shooting. 'Death of King George V', in *Continual Dew* (1937).

First Innings
Abdul Aziz retired hurt 0

Second Innings
Abdul Aziz did not bat, dead 0

Entries in the scorebook for the Quaid-I-Azam Trophy cricket final held in Karachi in 1959, during which a player named Abdul Aziz died after being struck by the ball.

You can stop counting, I'm not getting up.

Jim Watt (1948–), Scottish lightweight boxer. His suggestion for a boxer's epitaph.

Equestrianism *See* HORSE RACING.

Equipment *See* BALLS; BOXING GLOVES; CRICKET BATS; KIT.

Chris EUBANK

British middleweight boxer (1966–) whose much-lampooned pseudo-cultured manner and professed dislike of boxing did not prevent him taking the WBO title from fellow-Briton Nigel Benn in 1990.

Quotes about Chris Eubank

Chris Eubank lost his recent comeback fight on points ... the main one being that he's a total git.

Nick Hancock (1963–), British television presenter. BBC TV, *They Think It's All Over*, 1995.

Quotes by Chris Eubank

On what?

His response when asked if he would write an autobiography, 1995.

See also BOXING; MONEY.

European football

The European Cup is 17 pounds of silver and is worth its weight in gold.

Brian Moore (1932–), British television sports commentator. ITV.

Germany are probably, arguably, undisputed champions of Europe.

Bryan Hamilton (1946–), Northern Ireland football manager.

They know on the Continent that European football without the English is like a hot dog without the mustard.

Sir Bobby Charlton (1937–), English footballer, referring in 1988 to the ban then in place preventing English teams playing in Europe, following the Heysel Stadium disaster.

It was like being in a foreign country.

Ian Rush (1961–), Welsh footballer, reflecting on his experiences as a player in Italy.

Someone asked me last week if I missed the Villa. I said 'No, I live in one.'

David Platt (1966–), English footballer. Quoted in 1991 following
his transfer from Aston Villa to the Italian football club Bari.

I'd like to play for an Italian club, like Barcelona.

Mark Draper (1970–), English footballer.

In England, football's just like rugby. All the balls go flying through the air
or you're kicked into the stand. They never think of keeping the ball and
trying to play.

Richard Witschge (1969–), Dutch footballer, comparing, in 1996, his
experience of football with Blackburn Rovers with football on the Continent.

English football is the most fun to watch because they take risks and make
a lot of mistakes. As a fan and a spectator I really love it. But as a coach I
don't feel good about it at all. When I played I always loved to go out
against English teams because they always gave you the ball back if you
lost it. They still do.

Johann Cruyff (1947–), Dutch footballer, comparing English
football with the Continental style of play in 1998.

Sometimes now, when I watch continental games on television, I'm a bit
bored. I'm thinking: 'Where is the intensity?'

Arsène Wenger (1949–), French footballer manager, speaking as
manager of Arsenal in 1998.

See also FOREIGN SIGNINGS; GERMAN FOOTBALL; ITALIAN FOOTBALL.

Excuses

It's the ground; it's too far away.

W.G. Grace (1848–1915), English cricketer, explaining why he had
failed to stop a ball while fielding.

We have lost a couple of games at home which we probably wouldn't have
lost a couple of years ago, and not because of the talent level, just because of
the inexperience of the building.

Jerry Krause (1936–), US basketball manager, referring to a
recent loss of form suffered by the Chicago Bulls after their
installation in the new United Center.

The day you take complete responsibility for yourself, the day you stop making any excuses, that's the day you start to the top.

O.J. Simpson (1947–), American football player.

It was like an alien abduction out there. Someone invaded his body and turned him into the greatest volleyer in the universe.

Jim Courier (1970–), US tennis player, explaining why he had lost so heavily to an inspired Tim Henman during the 1999 Wimbledon championship.

Exercise

He that in his studies wholly applies himself to labour and exercise, and neglects meditation, loses his time; and he that only applies himself to meditation, and neglects labour and exercise, only wanders and loses himself.

Confucius (551–497 BC), Chinese philosopher.

Lack of activity destroys the good condition of every human being, while movement and methodical physical exercise save it and preserve it.

Plato (429–347 BC), Greek philosopher. Quoted in Charles A. Bucher, *Foundations of Physical Education* (1964).

It is exercise alone that supports the spirits and keeps the mind in vigour.

Cicero (106–43 BC), Roman orator and statesman. Quoted in John Boyle O'Reilly, *Ethics of Boxing and Manly Sport* (1888).

The rich advantage of good exercise.

William Shakespeare (1564–1616), English playwright and poet. *King John* (c.1594).

So long as nature will bear up this exercise, so long I daily vow to use it.

William Shakespeare (1564–1616), English playwright and poet. *The Winter's Tale* (1611).

As men
Do walk a mile, women should take an hour,
After supper. 'Tis their exercise.

Francis Beaumont (1584–1616) and **John Fletcher** (1579–1625), English playwrights. *Philaster* (1609).

Better to hunt in fields, for health unbought,
Than fee the doctor for a nauseous draught,
The wise, for cure, on exercise depend;
God never made his work for man to mend.

John Dryden (1631–1700), English poet and playwright. 'Epistle to
John Driden of Chesterton'.

I take the true definition exercise to be labour without weariness.

Samuel Johnson (1709–84), British lexicographer.

Of exercises, swimming's best,
Strengthens the heart and the chest,
And all their fleshy parts confirms.
Extends and stretches legs and arms.

Dr E. Baynard. *Health* (1764).

There is a necessity for a regulating discipline of exercise that, whilst
evoking the human energies, will not suffer them to be wasted.

Thomas de Quincey (1785–1859), British essayist and critic.

It is very important for a man who wishes to have a good season to take
regular exercise.

Prince Ranjitsinhji (1872–1933), Indian cricketer.

Physical fitness is not only one of the most important keys to a healthy
body, it is the basis of dynamic and creative intellectual activity. The
relationship between the soundness of the body and the activities of the
mind is subtle and complex. Much is not yet understood. But we do know
what the Greeks knew: that intelligence and skill can only function at the
peak of their capacity when the body is healthy and strong; that hardy
spirits and tough minds usually inhabit sound gods.

John F. Kennedy (1917–63), US president.

Any workout which does not involve a certain minimum of danger or
responsibility does not improve the body – it just wears it out.

Norman Mailer (1923–), US novelist.

Fitness has to be fun. If it is not play, there will no fitness. Play, you see, is the process. Fitness is merely the product.

Dr George Sheehan (1918–93), US cardiologist.

I've got ten pairs of training shoes. One for every day of the week.

Samantha Fox (1966–), British model and pop singer.

See also ANTI-SPORTS; COUCH POTATOES; HEALTH; JOGGING.

·F·

Fair play *See* SPORTSMANSHIP.

Fame

Always give an autograph when somebody asks you. You never can tell. In baseball, anything can happen.

Tommy Lasorda (1927–), US baseball manager.

I might go to Alcoholics Anonymous, but I think it'd be difficult for me to be anonymous.

George Best (1946–), Northern Ireland footballer, 1980.

I don't want to be a star. Stars get blamed too much.

Enos Cabell (1949–), US baseball player.

Being a celebrity is like being raped, and there's absolutely nothing a player can do about it.

John McEnroe (1959–), US tennis player.

When you're on the way up there are plenty of people climbing over each other to buy you drinks, but when things start going wrong, more often than not, you drink alone.

Ian Botham (1955–), English cricketer. *Botham: My Autobiography* (1994).

I must be the only person who could actually get less publicity by becoming manager of England.

Terry Venables (1943–), English football manager, reflecting upon
his appointment as manager of England in 1994, in the wake of
persistent media interest over the years in his business interests.

The only thing that endures is character. Fame and wealth – all that is
illusion. All that endures is character.

O.J. Simpson (1947–), American football player. Quoted in the
Guardian, 30 December 1995, after his acquittal for the murder of
his wife and her lover.

Famous last words

I make so bold to say that I don't believe that in the future history of the
world any such feat will be performed by anybody else.

The mayor of Dover, hailing the achievement of Captain Matthew
Webb in swimming the English Channel in 1875. Some 2000
swimmers have since repeated his feat.

The man who has made the mile record is W.G. George. His time was 4
minutes 12.75 seconds and the probability is that this record will never
be broken.

Harry Andrews, British athletics coach, referring in 1903 to the
record time for the mile set by Walter George in 1886. In 1999
Hicham El Guerrouj of Morocco reduced the record to a new low of
3 minutes 43.13 seconds.

If there's a goal now, I'll eat my hat!

Tommy Woodruffe, British radio commentator. Extract of
commentary of the 1938 FA Cup Final. A goal was subsequently
scored and Woodruffe was obliged to do as he had promised.

I'll moider da bum!

Tony 'Two-Ton' Galento, boxer. Referring to his upcoming bout with
Joe Louis in 1939, which he lost – although another tradition gives
this as his reply when asked what he thought of William
Shakespeare.

The difference between me and the other athletes who go to the Olympics
is that they go to compete and I go to win.

David Bedford (1949–), British athlete, looking forward to victory in the
10,000 metres at the 1972 Munich Olympic Games. He came sixth.

If the West Indies are on top, they're magnificent. If they are down, they grovel. I intend to make them grovel.

Tony Grieg (1946–), English cricketer, speaking as England captain
in 1976 prior to a Test series that the West Indies won 3–0.

If we dig in and show our character, we can get a result. It'll be backs to the wall, but it's like that with Wimbledon. We've won at places like Manchester United and Liverpool. If Wimbledon can do that, there's no reason why Wales can't do it against Holland.

Vinny Jones (1965–), Welsh footballer, speaking before Wales
played the Netherlands in 1996: Wales lost 7–1.

After tonight England v Argentina will be remembered for what a player did with his feet.

Adidas advertisement, featuring David Beckham, during the
World Cup finals of 1998. The slogan deliberately evoked the
'hand of God' match in the 1986 World Cup campaign in which
England had fallen victim to Argentina as a result of what Diego
Maradona did with his hand. The 1998 match was indeed
remembered for what Beckham did with his feet: he was sent
off for kicking his Argentinian opponent Diego Simeone and
thus contributed greatly to England's exit from the competition.
'Sporting Quotes of the Year 1998', *Daily Telegraph*,
28 December 1998.

There's only one team going to win this now and that's England.

Kevin Keegan (1951–), English footballer and manager. Extract
of ITV television commentary on a World Cup game between
England and Romania in 1998: Romania scored a minute later
and won the game 2–1. 'Sporting Quotes of the Year 1998',
Daily Telegraph, 28 December 1998.

The only crises I can remember were Suez and the Bay of Pigs, when I thought my life might end because of a nuclear war.

Roy Hodgson (1947–), English football manager, denying talk
of a crisis at his club Blackburn Rovers: he was sacked shortly
afterwards. 'Sports Quotes of the Year 1998', *Daily Telegraph*,
28 December 1998.

I am more pumped up than ever for what lies ahead. I want another championship and we have a chance.

Damon Hill (1960–), British racing driver. Quoted on the unveiling

of his new Jordan Formula One car in 1999: he retired at the end of
the year after a thoroughly disappointing season. *The Times*,
31 December 1999.

I'm not interested in the England job, so I hope no one's had a bet on me.

Kevin Keegan (1951–), English footballer and manager. Quoted a
week before accepting the post of England coach in 1999.

See also LAST WORDS; RETIREMENT.

Juan Manuel FANGIO

**Argentinian racing driver (1911–95) who won the Formula
One championship a record five times in the 1950s.**

Quotes about Juan Manuel Fangio

The best classroom of all times was about two car lengths behind Juan
Manuel Fangio.

Stirling Moss (1929–), British racing driver.

Quotes by Juan Manuel Fangio

Never think of your car as a cold machine, but as a hotblooded horse.

Quoted in 1958.

In my day it was 75% car and mechanics, 25% driver and luck. Today it is
95% car. A driver can emerge in a good new car, become world champion
and a year later disappear to the back of the queue. Driving skill hardly
counts any more.

Quoted in 1983.

Fans

There's only two things that concern them – bread and games.

Juvenal (*c*.55–*c*.140 AD), Roman satirist, referring to the interests of
the contemporary population of Rome. Often quoted as 'bread and
circuses'. *Satirae*, X.

Onlookers have a clearer view of the game than the players.

Sir Richard Livingstone (1880–1960), British scholar.

One of the chief duties of the fan is to engage in arguments with the man behind him. This department of the game has been allowed to run down fearfully.

Robert Benchley (1889–1945), US humorist. Quoted in Ralph S. Graben, *The Baseball Reader* (1951).

Eighteen men play a game and eighteen thousand watch them, and yet those who play are the only ones who have any official direction in the matter of rules and regulations. The eighteen thousand are allowed to run wild.

Robert Benchley (1889–1945), US humorist.

Oh, he's football crazy, he's football mad
And the football it has robbed him o' the wee bit sense he had.
And it would take a dozen skivvies, his clothes to wash and scrub,
Since our Jock became a member of that terrible football club.

Jimmy McGregor, Scottish singer. 'Football Crazy' (1960).

We are inclined that if we watch a football game or baseball game, we have taken part in it.

John F. Kennedy (1917–63), US president, 1961.

Baseball without fans is like Jayne Mansfield without a sweater.

Richard Nixon (1913–94), US president, referring to the US filmstar and sex symbol Jayne Mansfield, who became known as the 'Sweater Girl' through photographs of her wearing figure-hugging jumpers.

Most people are in a factory from nine till five. Their job may be to turn out 263 little circles. At the end of the week they're three short and somebody has a go at them. On Saturday afternoons they deserve something to go and shout about.

Rodney Marsh (1944–), English footballer, 1969.

It's a funny kind of month, October. For the really keen cricket fan it's when you discover that your wife left you in May.

Denis Norden (1922–), British humorist. Quoted in *She* magazine, October 1977.

We do have the greatest fans in the world, but I've never seen a fan score a goal.

Jock Stein (1922–85), Scottish football manager, 1982.

A shrieking, whistling, fire-cracking mass of bias.

David Lacey (1938–), British sportswriter, referring to the supporters
of the Italian football club Roma in the *Guardian*, 27 April 1984.

Three cheers for Spurs!
They beat Stoke!
Glad I'm a football fan.
Glad I'm a bloke.

Wendy Cope (1945–), British poet. *Roger Bear's Football Poems*.

To be an intelligent fan is to participate in something. It is an activity, a
form of appreciating that is good for the individual's soul, and hence for
society.

George F. Will (1941–), US journalist. Introduction, *Men at Work:
The Craft of Baseball* (1990).

English crowds are like sherry. West Indian crowds are like rum. Australian
crowds are like Foster's.

Peter Roebuck (1956–), English cricketer, describing cricket
spectators around the world in *Tangled up in White* (1990).

The natural state of the football fan is bitter disappointment, no matter what
the score.

Nick Hornby (1957–), British writer and novelist. *Fever Pitch* (1992).

There must be many fathers around the country who have experienced the
cruellest, most crushing rejection of all: their children have ended up
supporting the wrong team.

Nick Hornby (1957–), British writer and novelist. *Fever Pitch* (1992).

Be tolerant of those who describe a sporting moment as their best ever. We
do not lack imagination, nor have we had sad and barren lives; it is just that
real life is paler, duller, and contains less potential for unexpected delirium.

Nick Hornby (1957–), British writer and novelist. *Fever Pitch* (1992).

Keep the television down low. When you see a great goal, keep your
emotions under control. Don't shout loudly or applaud. You must especially
guard against accidents happening because of lack of sleep.

Editorial, *People's Daily of China*. Advice aimed at football fans
during the World Cup finals in 1994.

It says on my birth certificate that I was born in the borough of West Bromwich, in the district of West Bromwich. I said all right, all right, I'll support the bloody Albion – there's no need to twist my arm.

Frank Skinner (1957–), British comedian, 1995.

Every thousandth person created, God unhinges their heads, scoops out their brains and then issues them to a football club (as supporters).

Mike Bateson, English football club administrator, 1996.

The fans who give me stick are the sort of people who still point at aeroplanes.

Ian Wright (1963–), English footballer, 1997.

If you're dealing with the English all you need is beer and good toilets.

Anonymous French bar owner's advice on keeping English fans from
causing trouble during the 1998 World Cup finals in France.
'Sporting Quotes of the Year 1998', *Daily Telegraph*, 1998.

English people go to matches as a form of psychoanalysis – they turn up, have a good shout and then go home. That goes for everybody, bankers in their Rolls-Royces and ordinary working people too. You'll see them all letting rip with a mouthful.

Emmanuel Petit (1970–), French footballer, speaking as a player
with Arsenal in 1999.

See also CHANTS; OBSESSION; SONGS.

Fast bowling

The difference between a fast bowler and a good fast bowler is not extra muscle but extra brains.

Fred Trueman (1931–), English cricketer. *Freddie Trueman's Book
of Cricket* (1964).

Ashes to ashes, dust to dust –
If Thomson don't get ya, Lillee must.

Sydney Telegraph, cartoon caption, 1975. A reference to the Australian
fast bowlers Jeff Thomson and Dennis Lillee and their dominance over
England's batsmen during the 1974–75 Ashes series.

There's no batsman on earth who goes out to meet Dennis Lillee and Jeff Thomson with a smile on his face.

Clive Lloyd (1944–), West Indian cricketer, 1975.

There is no more savagely moving sight than to be part of a crowd watching a fast bowler – better still, a pair of fast bowlers – knocking down wickets. When the pitch is fast, or 'green' – preferably both – and batsman are being tumbled out, the temper of the crowd becomes almost primitive. Each time a wicket falls, the killer howl goes up.

John Arlott (1914–91), English cricket writer and commentator.
Preface to David Frith, *The Fast Men* (1975).

Fast bowlers are bully boys. They dish it out but they can't take it.

Brian Close (1931–), English cricketer.

To have some idea what it's like, stand in the outside lane of a motorway, get your mate to drive his car at you at 95 mph and wait until he's 12 yards away, before you decide which way to jump.

Geoffrey Boycott (1940–), English cricketer, describing how a
batsman feels when facing a fast bowler, 1989.

The sight of Imran tearing fearsomely down the hill and the baying of the excited crowd made me realize for the first time that adrenaline was sometimes brown.

Simon Hughes (1959–), Middlesex cricketer and writer, on a Gillette
Cup semi-final against Sussex in 1980. *A Lot of Hard Yakka* (1997).

See also BODYLINE; Sir Richard HADLEE; HARD MEN; Dennis LILLEE; PHYSIQUE;
Jeff THOMSON; Fred TRUEMAN.

Fencing

Fencing is like playing chess with a sword in your hand.

Valentina Sidorova, Soviet fencer. *Sport in the USSR*, October 1978.

Experienced fencers occasionally spend a few minutes giving pointers to beginners.

Albert Manley, British fencer and writer. *Complete Fencing* (1979).

Sir Alex **FERGUSON**

**Scottish football manager (1941–) under whose
management from 1986 Manchester United emerged
as the dominant side in English football.**

He's so greedy for success that when his grandkids beat him at cards, he
sends them to bed without any supper.

Gary Pallister (1965–), English footballer, referring to his manager
at Manchester United in 1997.

In the early days we used to call the boss the Hairdryer because he would
come right up to your face and scream at you.

Gary Pallister (1965–), English footballer, 1997.

A magical manager, the greatest motivator there has ever been.

Sir Bobby Charlton (1937–), English footballer, 1999.

See also FOOTBALL; Ryan GIGGS; Paul INCE; ITALIAN FOOTBALL.

Tom **FINNEY**

**English footballer (1921–), nicknamed the 'Preston
Plumber', who became the first man to be named
Footballer of the Year in two English seasons (1954
and 1957).**

Finney would have been great in any team, in any match and in any age –
even if he had been wearing an overcoat ... he had the opposition so
frightened that they'd have a man marking him when they were warming
up before the kick-off.

Bill Shankly (1919–81), Scottish football manager.

Tom Finney was the first gentleman of football.

Jimmy Greaves (1940–), English footballer and commentator.

Bobby FISCHER

US chess player (1943–) who reigned as world champion
1972–75, in the process gaining a reputation for an
unpredictable and temperamental manner.

Quotes about Bobby Fischer

Bobby Fischer is a chess phenomenon, it is true, but is also a social illiterate, a political simpleton, a cultural ignoramus, and an emotional baby.

Mary Kenny (1944–), US journalist.

Quotes by Bobby Fischer

Chess is better than romance.

Attributed.

Chess is like war. The object is to crush the other man's mind. I like to see them squirm.

Attributed.

Food

I don't mind what you call me as long as you don't call me late for lunch.

William 'Fatty' Foulke (1874–1916), English goalkeeper, 1901.

Baseball players who are first into the dining room are usually last in the statistics.

Jimmy Cannon (1910–73), US sportswriter.

Breakfast of champions.

US advertising slogan used to promote sales of Wheaties
breakfast cereal since around 1950. Among the sports stars to
claim they owed their greatness to Wheaties was Dodgers
baseball star Jackie Robinson.

The breakfast of champions is not cereal, it's the opposition.

Nick Seitz (1939–), US writer.

I had to be fast, otherwise there was nothing left to eat on the dinner table.

Wilma Rudolph (1940–), US runner, attributing her speed to the
fact that she grew up in a family with 22 children.

The champagne's all right, but the blackcurrant jam tastes of fish.

Derek Randall (1951–), English cricketer. His reaction on being
treated to champagne and caviar during a tour of India in 1976.

Every night I tell myself, 'I'm going to dream about my girl, I'm going to
dream about my girl.' But it's always ham hocks.

Nate Newton (1961–), American football player. A star with the
Dallas Cowboys, he weighed in at 320 pounds.

The most famous recipe in racing is the one for Lester Piggott's breakfast – a
cough and a copy of *The Sporting Life*.

Simon Barnes (1951–), British sportswriter.

I told the caddie I wanted a sand wedge and he brought me a ham on rye.

Chi Chi Rodrigues (1935–), Puerto Rican golfer.

Without ice cream, there would be darkness and chaos.

Don Kardong (1949–), runner.

What's really dreadful is the diet in Britain. The whole day you drink tea
with milk and coffee with milk and cakes. If you had a fantasy world of
what you shouldn't eat in sport, it's what you eat here.

Arsène Wenger (1949–), French football manager, speaking as
manager of Arsenal in 1997.

Lunchtime saw the same feeding frenzy as at breakfast. Then, at 4.10 p.m. at
most grounds, plates of Hovis suddenly arrived, usually containing
processed ham or that funny fish paste out of a jar, along with chocolate
mini-rolls, Bakewell tarts and those cakes covered in stringy bits of coconut.
The players, led by Gatting, attacked this offering like hyenas, tearing the
meat from the bread, and less than sixty seconds later the tea tray was just a
mass of discarded crusts and wrappers. You'd never eat this kind of thing in
mid-afternoon at home.

Simon Hughes (1959–), Middlesex cricketer and cricket writer,
describing tea time on the county cricket circuit. *A Lot of Hard
Yakka* (1997).

See also DIETING; George FOREMAN.

Football *See* AMERICAN FOOTBALL; AUSTRALIAN RULES FOOTBALL;
BRAZILIAN FOOTBALL; FOOTBALL (ASSOCIATION); GERMAN FOOTBALL; ITALIAN
FOOTBALL.

Football (Association)

One rolls along a football to his foes.

Geoffrey Chaucer (1343–1400), English poet.

The sturdy plowman, lustie, strong and bold,
Overcometh the winter with driving the footeball,
Forgetting labour and many a grievous fall.

Alexander Barclay (1475–1552), Scottish poet, 1508.

Up and by coach to Sir Ph. Warwickes, the street being full of footballs, it being a great frost.

Samuel Pepys (1633–1703), British diarist. The frosty condition of
the roads that year led to a reduction in the movement of traffic and
thus made football possible. *Diary*, 2 January 1665.

Then strip lads and to it, though sharp be the weather,
And if, by mischance, you should happen to fall,
There are worse things in life than a tumble on the heather,
And life is itself but a game of football.

Sir Walter Scott (1771–1832), Scottish novelist and poet.

Football, in itself, is a grand game for developing a lad physically and also morally, for he learns to play with good temper and unselfishness, to play in his place and 'play the game', and these are the best of training for any game of life. But it is a vicious game when it draws crowds of lads away from playing the game themselves to be merely onlookers at a few paid performers.

Lord Baden-Powell (1857–1941), British founder of the Boy Scouts.
Scouting for Boys (1908).

The one passion in my life has been football – the most exhilarating game I know, and the strongest protest against selfishness, without sermonizing, that was ever put before a thoughtful people.

John Goodall (1863–1942), English footballer. Quoted in Andrew
Ward and Anton Rippon, *The Derby County Story* (1983).

A man who had missed the last home match of 't' United' had to enter social life on tiptoe in Bruddersford.

J.B. Priestley (1894–1984), British playwright and novelist.
The Good Companions (1928).

To say that these men paid their shillings to watch twenty-two hirelings kick a ball is merely to say that a violin is wood and catgut, that *Hamlet* is so much paper and ink. For a shilling Bruddersford United AFC offered you Conflict and Art ...

J.B. Priestley (1894–1984), British playwright and novelist. *The Good Companions* (1928).

If this can be termed the century of the common man, then soccer, of all sports, is surely his game ... In a world haunted by the hydrogen and napalm bomb, the football field is a place where sanity and hope are still left unmolested.

Stanley Rous (1895–1986), English football administrator, 1952.
Quoted in Bryon Butler, *The Official History of the Football Association* (1986).

When more people are talking soccer topics from one Saturday to the next instead of 'H' bombs, wars and politics, the country will be a better place to live in.

Henry Adamson. FA News: *The Official Journal of the Football Association*, 1962.

Five days shalt thou labour, as the Bible says. The seventh day is the Lord thy God's. The sixth day is for football.

Anthony Burgess (1917–94), British novelist.

The point about football in Britain is that it's not just a sport people take to, like cricket or tennis or running long distances. It is inherent in the people. It is built into the urban psyche, as much a common experience to our children as are uncles and schools. It is not a phenomenon; it is an everyday matter. There is more eccentricity in deliberately disregarding it than in devoting a life to it. It has more significance in the national character than theatre has.

Arthur Hopcraft (1932–), British writer. Introduction, *The Football Man* (1968).

The great fallacy is that the game is first and last about winning. It's nothing of the kind. The game is about glory. It's about doing things in style, with a flourish, about going out and beating the other lot, not waiting for them to die of boredom.

Danny Blanchflower (1926–93), Northern Ireland footballer. Quoted in Hunter Davis, *The Glory Game* (1972).

The beauty has gone out of football ... it has lost its poetry, its artistic gentleness.

Alfredo Di Stefano (1926–), Argentinian footballer. Quoted by
Matt D'Arcy in the *Manchester Evening News*, 13 September 1972.

Soccer in England is a grey game, played on grey days, by grey people.

Rodney Marsh (1944–), English footballer. Speaking on US
television, having been recruited by the US soccer team the Tampa
Bay Rowdies, in 1979.

Football's football; if it weren't the case it wouldn't be the game it was.

Garth Crooks (1958–), English footballer.

If there wasn't such a thing as football, we'd all be frustrated footballers.

Mick Lyons (1951–), English footballer. *Colemanballs* (1982).

Football's a game of skill ... we kicked them a bit and they kicked us a bit.

Graham Roberts (1959–), English footballer.

Football is the opera of the people.

Stafford Heginbotham (1934–1995), English football official,
speaking as chairman of Bradford City in 1985.

Football is a simple game. The hard part is making it look simple.

Ron Greenwood (1921–), English football manager.

Football's about ninety minutes on the day; it's about tomorrows really.

Glenn Hoddle (1957–), English footballer and manager.

Football is a sport with a great future behind it.

Julie Burchill (1960–), British journalist. *Damaged Gods* (1986).

Football today would certainly not be the same if it had not existed.

Elton Welsby, British television sports commentator. ITV.

Football will always be laddish ... at the end of the day, football means not having to go to Asda on Saturday.

From the *Guardian*, 1995.

A sport where the players actually enjoy getting hit in the head by a ball.

Soccer advertisement published on behalf of the New York/New
Jersey MetroStars Major League Soccer team, 1997.

Football and cookery are the two most important subjects in the country.

Delia Smith (1941–), British cookery writer, speaking in her
capacity as a director of Norwich City in 1997.

The hardest part is what do you find to replace football – because there isn't anything.

Kevin Keegan (1951–), English footballer and manager, speaking as
chief operating officer of Fulham in 1998.

Football? Bloody hell!

Sir Alex Ferguson (1941–), Scottish football manager. His reaction
after his team Manchester United's sensational last-minute victory in
the 1999 European Cup final 'Those Things They Said',
Independent, 31 December 1999.

See also ANTI-SPORTS; ARSENAL; BALLS; BRAZILIAN FOOTBALL; BUSINESS AND
SPORT; CHANTS; CHELSEA; COACHING; EUROPEAN FOOTBALL; FANS;
FOOTBALL-BASHERS; FOOTBALL CLUB OWNERS; FOOTBALL GROUNDS;
FOOTBALL MANAGEMENT; FOOTBALL MANAGERS; FOOTBALL PLAYERS;
FOOTBALL REFEREES; FOREIGN SIGNINGS; FRIENDLIES; GAMESMANSHIP;
GERMAN FOOTBALL; GOALKEEPERS; HARD MEN; HOOLIGANISM; ITALIAN
FOOTBALL; KIT; LEEDS UNITED; LIVERPOOL; MANCHESTER CITY; MANCHESTER
UNITED; MONEY; THE 'OLD' FIRM; PENALTIES; PENALTY SHOOT-OUTS; RULES;
SEXISM IN SPORT; SONGS; TACTICS; TRAGEDIES; TRANSFERS; VIOLENCE;
WEMBLEY; WOMEN IN SPORT; WORLD CUP.

Football-bashers

You base foot-ball player!

William Shakespeare (1564–1616), English playwright and poet.
King Lear (1605).

Me thinks I am stopt by one of your heroic games, call'd football, which I
conceive not very conveniently civil in the streets, especially in such
irregular and narrow roads as Crooked Lane.

Sir William Davenant (1606–68), English poet and playwright.

Football is all very well as a game for rough girls, but is hardly suitable for delicate boys.

Oscar Wilde (1854–1900), Irish writer and wit. Quoted in Alvin Redman, *The Epigrams of Oscar Wilde* (1952).

I loathed the game, and since I could see no pleasure or usefulness in it, it was very difficult for me to show courage at it. Football, it seemed to me, is not really played for the pleasure of kicking a ball about, but is a species of fighting.

George Orwell (1903–50), British novelist. *Such, Such Were the Joys.*

Soccer is a game in which everyone does a lot of running around. Twenty-one guys stand around and one guy does a tap dance with the ball. It's about as exciting as Tristan and Isolde.

Jim Murray, US sportswriter, in the Los Angeles *Times*, 1967.

The rest of the world loves soccer. Surely we must be missing something. Uh, isn't that what the Russians told us about communism? There's a good reason why you don't care about soccer – it's because you are an American and hating soccer is more American than mom's apple pie, driving a pick-up and spending Saturday afternoon channel-surfing with the remote control.

Tom Weir, US sportswriter in *USA Today*.

Soccer is to sport what athlete's foot is to injuries.

Tom Weir, US sportswriter in *USA Today*.

All that proves is that most of the world is too poor to build bowling alleys, golf courses, tennis courts and baseball fields. There's hundreds of millions of poor people out there who still ain't got indoor plumbing, but that don't mean there's something great about an outhouse. Soccer is boring. I've never seen a more boring sport.

Mike Royko (1932–97), US journalist, writing on the subject of soccer's worldwide popularity in the *Detroit Free Press*, 1994.

Football club owners

Robert Maxwell has just bought Brighton and Hove Albion, and he's furious to find it is only one club.

Tommy Docherty (1928–), Scottish football manager, 1988.

He said he was right behind me, so I told him I'd rather have him in front where I could see him.

Tommy Docherty (1928–), Scottish football manager, referring to
Aston Villa chairman Doug Ellis.

If I fail, I'll stand up and be counted – let some other brain surgeon take over.

Alan Sugar (1947–), British businessman, speaking as chairman of
Tottenham Hotspur in 1996.

I've been chairman of a football club. I know how to lose.

Elton John (1947–), British pop singer, speaking as a former
chairman of Watford prior to the 1996 Oscar ceremony.

If anyone asks whether they should become a chairman, I'd tell them to give it a miss. If I had known the magnitude of my task beforehand, I'd have told myself, 'Hey, do you really need all this?'

Francis Lee (1944–), English footballer and manager, speaking as
chairman of Manchester City in 1996.

I have spent some time with some tough cookies over the years, Mrs Thatcher and Saddam Hussein to name but two. But when it comes to ruthlessness in defence of his own interests, Ken Bates leaves them all behind.

David Mellor (1949–), British Conservative politician and radio
sports commentator, referring, in 1997, to the owner of Chelsea
football club, Ken Bates.

The first thing I will do is negotiate a pay rise, give myself a ten-year contract – and then sack myself.

Graham Turner, English football manager, on becoming owner-
manager of Hereford United, 1997.

I've had enough. As soon as I get home I'm gonna buy that club. I'm gonna walk in and say, 'you ... fuck off; you ... fuck off; you ... fuck off; you ... make me a cup of tea.'

Noel Gallagher (1967–), British rock star, voicing his exasperation
with the disappointing performance of his favourite football club,
Manchester City, in 1998, the year in which the team was relegated
to the English Second Division. 'Sporting Quotes of the Year 1998',
Daily Telegraph, 28 December 1998.

It's a bit ironic that when nobody will let me have a passport, it's left to me to save the England team.

Mohamed Al-Fayed (1933–), Egyptian-born businessman and owner of Fulham football club, referring in 1999 to the government's steadfast refusal to grant him UK citizenship despite his gesture in allowing Fulham coach Kevin Keegan to take over managerial responsibility for the England team.

Football grounds

Old Trafford is the 'Theatre of Dreams'.

Sir Bobby Charlton (1937–), English footballer. The 'Theatre of Dreams' is now an established nickname for the ground, the home of Manchester United.

Blimey, the ground looks a bit different to Watford. Where's the dog track?

Luther Blissett (1958–), English footballer, on seeing Milan's San Siro Stadium in 1983.

Hampden Park is the only ground which looks the same in black and white as it does in colour.

David Lacey (1938–), British sportswriter, in the *Guardian*, 1987.

Many supporters say they wouldn't stand for all-seater stadiums.

Guy Michelmore (1919–), British television broadcaster. *Colemanballs 5* (1990).

White Hart Lane is a great place. The only thing wrong is the seats face the pitch.

Les Dawson (1934–93), British comedian, referring to White Hart Lane, the home of Tottenham Hotspur, in 1991.

See also WEMBLEY.

Football management

All a manager has to do is keep eleven players happy – the eleven in the reserves. The first team are happy because they are in the first team.

Rodney Marsh (1944–), English footballer, 1979.

I think I have the best job in the country.

Bobby Robson (1933–), English football manager, speaking as manager of England in 1985.

It's an incestuous business. It's the only one I know where unqualified people are hired, allowed to spend £20 million, fail miserably, toddle off to play golf for six months, walk straight back into another job, and fail again.

Paul Fairclough, English football manager.

His management style seems to be based on the chaos theory.

Mark McGhee (1968–), English football manager, referring to the management style of his colleague Barry Fry in 1996.

It seems you can get sacked for farting in the wrong direction at the moment.

Joe Kinnear (1947–), Irish football manager. His response to news of Kenny Dalglish's controversial sacking as manager of Newcastle in 1998. 'Sporting Quotes of the Year 1998', *Daily Telegraph*, 28 December 1998.

I'm an assistant, an advisor, a consultant – which usually means you get paid a lot of money for doing bugger all.

John McGovern (1949–), English football manager, reflecting upon the role of assistant manager, 1999.

See also COACHES; COACHING.

Football managers

Football is a simple game made unnecessarily complicated by managers.

Anonymous.

You're not a real manager unless you've been sacked.

Malcolm Allison (1927–), English football manager.

Who wants to be a football manager? Well, people like me who are too old to play, too poor to be a director and too much in love with the game to be an agent.

Steve Coppell (1955–), English footballer and manager, 1993.

There's only two types of manager. Those who've been sacked and those who will be sacked in the future.

Howard Wilkinson (1943–), English football manager, 1995.

As a manager, you always have a gun to your head. It's a question of whether there is a bullet in the barrel.

Kevin Keegan (1951–), English footballer and manager, 1995.

My brother always said you'd have to be mad to be a football manager. What other job is there where your entire livelihood depends on 11 daft lads?

Francis Lee (1944–), English football club chairman, speaking as chairman of Manchester City following the dismissal of Alan Ball in 1996.

If I told my wife I was considering a career as a manager, she'd say: 'Sign this then. Don't worry, it's only a divorce. Au revoir.

David Ginola (1967–), French footballer, 1997.

You have to be a masochist to be an international manager.

Arsène Wenger (1949–), French football manager, speaking as manager of Arsenal in 1998.

See also Ron ATKINSON; Sir Matt BUSBY; Brian CLOUGH; Kenny DALGLISH; Tommy DOCHERTY; Sir Alex FERGUSON; Glenn HODDLE; Kevin KEEGAN; Sir Alf RAMSEY; Bill SHANKLY; Graham TAYLOR.

Football players

What they say about footballers being ignorant is rubbish. I spoke to a couple yesterday and they are quite intelligent.

Raquel Welch (1940–), US film actress.

Footballers are only interested in drinking, clothes and the size of their willies.

Karren Brady (1969–), English football official, speaking as managing director of Birmingham City, 1994.

Dreams, I reckon, constitute roughly 75 per cent of the make-up of any true football man.

Ron Atkinson (1939–), English football manager. *Big Ron: A Different Ball Game* (1998).

See also AMERICAN FOOTBALL; David BECKHAM; George BEST; Eric CANTONA; Sir Bobby CHARLTON; Dennis COMPTON; Kenny DALGLISH; Tom FINNEY; Paul GASCOIGNE; Ryan GIGGS; David GINOLA; Jimmy GREAVES; Glen HODDLE;

Sir Geoff HURST; Paul INCE; Vinny JONES; Kevin KEEGAN; Gary LINEKER; Diego MARADONA; Sir Stanley MATTHEWS; Bobby MOORE; Michael OWEN; PELÉ; Sir Alf RAMSEY; RONALDO; Bill SHANKLY; Alan SHEARER; Gianfranco ZOLA.

Football referees

To regulate the game, to earn expenses and a guinea fee!
Yes! There is great attraction in the name of Referee.

Anonymous. Referring specifically to football referees, 1893.

I never comment on referees and I'm not going to break the habit of a lifetime for that prat.

Ron Atkinson (1939–), English football manager. Quoted after a game in which the referee made several dubious decisions, 1979.

It's like a toaster, that shirt pocket. Every time there's a tackle, up pops a yellow card.

Kevin Keegan (1951–), English football manager. Extract of ITV football commentary, remarking upon the zeal of French referee Joel Quiniou during a 1994 World Cup game between the USA and Brazil.

In all fairness, the referee had a complete cerebral failure.

Rick Holden (1964–), English footballer, referring to a controversial match between Oldham and Southend in 1995.

I know where he should have put this flag up, and he'd have got plenty of help.

Ron Atkinson (1939–), English football manager, referring to a linesman who made a disputed decision during a game between Coventry and Chelsea in 1996.

The referee was amusing. Here they either shoot you down with a machine-gun or don't blow their whistle at all.

Gianluca Vialli (1964–), Italian footballer, commenting upon his first taste of Premier League football in England in 1996.

The referee was booking everyone. I thought he was filling in his Lottery numbers.

Ian Wright (1963–), English footballer, speaking as an Arsenal striker in 1996.

You cannot assault a referee. He stands between the game and chaos.

Tony Banks (1943–), British sports minister. 'Quotes of the Year', the *Guardian*, 24 December 1998.

If that was a penalty, I'll plait sawdust.

Ron Atkinson (1939–), English football manager, questioning a referee's decision in a game between his own side Sheffield Wednesday and Chelsea in 1998.

I was sorely provoked.

Melvin Sylvester (1956–), English football referee. Quoted after he sent himself off for punching a player. 'Quotes of the Year', the *Guardian*, 24 December 1998.

Foreign signings

There are so many Latino ball-players, we're going to have to get a Latin instructor up here.

Phil Rizzuto (1949–), US baseball player. From a baseball television commentary.

Apparently Man City are hoping to exploit fully the Bosman ruling in order to play 11 Germans. That way they can go down with all Hans.

Martin Thorpe, British journalist, referring to the 'Bosman ruling', which eased restrictions on the signing of players from other countries, in the *Guardian*, 1996.

When I first heard about Viagra, I thought it was a new player Chelsea had just signed.

Tony Banks (1943–), British sports minister, referring in 1998 to the prevalence of foreign players in the Chelsea side.

I hope Tony Adams is playing because he's the only name I know. All these Viallis, Vieiras and Viagras.

Sir Jack Hayward (1923–), English football club chairman, remarking upon the number of foreign players taking part in a match between his own club, Wolverhampton Wanderers, and Arsenal, 1999.

It always seems to be pitch dark by 3.30 pm in Blackburn. There is no language school, nor is there a fitness centre. And if you want to go shopping, there is nothing to buy. When I see the way people live up here, I realise how lucky I am.

Stephane Henchoz (1974–), Swiss footballer, reflecting upon life in northern England following his move to Blackburn Rovers, 1999.

See also TRANSFERS.

George FOREMAN

US heavyweight boxer (1948–) who reigned as world champion 1973–74 and returned to reclaim the heavyweight title in 1994.

Quotes about George Foreman

There seems only one way to beat George Foreman: shell him for three days and then send the infantry in.

Hugh McIlvanney, British sportswriter, 1974.

When George goes into a restaurant, he doesn't ask for a menu. He asks for an estimate.

Lou Duva (1929–), US boxing trainer, referring to the legendary appetite of George Foreman.

Some people say George is fit as a fiddle, but I think he looks more like a cello.

Lou Duva (1929–), US boxing trainer, referring to George Foreman during one of his comebacks, in 1990, by which time he was into his 40s.

Quotes by George Foreman

Depends on how far my refrigerator is.

His response when asked how far he liked to run when training.

I want to keep fighting because it is the only thing that keeps me out of the hamburger joints. If I don't fight, I'll eat this planet.

Quoted in *The Times*, 17 January 1990.

See also BOXING; CORRUPTION; MONEY; Mike TYSON.

Form

I'm hitting the driver so good, I gotta dial the operator for long distance after I hit it.

Lee Trevino (1939–), US golfer. 'What They Are Saying', *New York Times*, 21 May 1978.

I'm playing like Tarzan and scoring like Jane.

Chi Chi Rodrigues (1935–), Puerto Rican golfer.

Form is temporary. Class is permanent.

Slogan on a T-shirt worn by English cricketer Ian Botham in 1990.

Form is just like a bird that passes by. Sometimes you have it all the time around you, sometimes it just flies away and you don't know what the reason is.

Ruud Gullit (1962–), Dutch footballer and manager.

Formula One

It is like balancing an egg on a spoon while shooting the rapids.

Graham Hill (1929–75), British racing driver, describing Formula One motor racing.

As for the accidents and tragedy – the circus goes on. There is no room for tears.

François Cevert (1944–73), French racing driver. Said in 1973, the day before he was killed in his Formula One racing car.

In my sport the quick are too often listed among the dead.

Jackie Stewart (1939–), Scottish racing driver, 1973.

The crashes people remember, but drivers remember the near misses.

Mario Andretti (1940–), US racing driver.

My biggest concern during a race is getting bored. The biggest thing I have to combat is falling asleep while going around and around.

Mario Andretti (1940–), US racing driver.

Motor racing's less of a sport these days than a commercial break doing 150 mph.

Peter Dunne in the *Independent on Sunday*, 1992.

My dad once said that you meet a much nicer class of person there, but I'm not sure.

Damon Hill (1960–), British racing driver, recalling the words of his father, racing driver Graham Hill, about starting races from the back of the grid, 1993.

I thought the last two rolls were unnecessary. I'd got the message by then.

Martin Brundle (1959–), British racing driver, describing his horrendous crash in the 1996 Australian Grand Prix, in the course of which his Jordan car somersaulted several times. Miraculously, he emerged unscathed.

Less girls, more technology.

Jody Schekter (1950–), South African racing driver. His reply when asked to summarize the changes in Formula One since his day. 'Motor Racing Quotes of the Year', in the *Daily Telegraph*, 23 December 1997.

See also Juan Manuel FANGIO; Stirling MOSS; MOTOR RACING; Alain PROST; Michael SCHUMACHER; Ayrton SENNA; Murray WALKER.

Joe FRAZIER

US heavyweight boxer (1944–), nicknamed 'Smokin' Joe', who was WBA world heavyweight champion from 1970 to 1973 before losing the classic 'Thrilla in Manila' against Muhammad Ali in 1975.

Quotes about Joe Frazier

Joe's gonna come out smokin',
And I won't be jokin'.
I'm gonna be a peckin' and a pokin',
Pouring water on his smokin'.
This might shock and amaze ya,
But Ali will destroy Joe Frazier!

Muhammad Ali (Cassius Clay; 1942–), US heavyweight boxer. Quoted in 1971, shortly before his first fight with Frazier, which resulted in Ali's defeat.

Frazier is so ugly that he should donate his face to the US Bureau of Wild Life.

Muhammad Ali (Cassius Clay; 1942–), US heavyweight boxer.
'Sports Quotes of the Year', the *Guardian*, 23 December 1972.

Quotes by Joe Frazier

I don't want to knock my opponent out. I want to hit him, stay away, and watch him hurt. I want his heart.

Attributed.

See also BOXING-BASHERS.

Friendlies

The struggle between defence and attack – the basic contest in football – is really, and always, the chief interest in any football: that is why a 'friendly' match never quite rings true.

John Arlott (1914–91), English cricket writer and commentator. Quoted
in A.H. Fabian and Geoffrey Green, *Association Football* (1960).

Pavarotti is not judged by how he sings in the shower. People wait until he gets on the stage.

Frank Rijkaard (1962–), Dutch football manager. His warning
against pundits drawing conclusions from warm-up friendlies before
a big game. Quoted in *The Times*, 9 October 1999.

·G·

Gaffes

All right, line up alphabetically according to your height.

Charles 'Casey' Stengel (1890–1975), US baseball player and
manager, addressing his squad of players.

You guys pair off in groups of three, then line up in a circle.

Bill Peterson (1964–), American football coach.

Sure there have been injuries and deaths in boxing, but none of them
serious.

Alan Minter (1951–), British boxer.

G'day, howya going?

Dennis Lillee (1949–), Australian cricketer. His greeting on being
introduced to Queen Elizabeth II at Lord's in 1972.

All the Leeds United team are 100% behind the manager, but I can't speak
for the rest of the squad.

Brian Greenhoff (1953–), English footballer, 1980.

I felt a lump in my mouth as the ball went in.

Terry Venables (1943–), English footballer and manager.

I owe a lot to my parents, especially to my mother and father.

Greg Norman (1955–), Australian golfer.

I only hope people will come along in peace and enjoy a good fight.

Mickey Duff (1929–), Polish-born British boxing manager and
promoter. BBC radio, 1988.

We didn't underestimate them. They were a lot better than we thought.

Bobby Robson (1933–), English football manager, speaking as
manager of England following a match with Cameroon in the 1990
World Cup finals. 'Sports Quotes of the Year', the *Guardian*,
24 December 1990.

Willie Carson, riding his 180th winner of the season, spent the last two
furlongs looking over one shoulder then another, even between his legs, but
there was nothing there to worry him.

Sporting Life.

Multi-millionaire sex king Paul Raymond wants to buy Watford, the
English First Division's bottom club.

Gulf Daily News.

I can't really remember the names of the clubs that we went to.

Shaquille O'Neal (1972–), American football player. His
response when asked whether he had visited the Parthenon
in Greece while on tour.

Brentford Reserves were involved in a nine-goal thriller when they beat
Orient 4–3.

Ealing Gazette.

They used to be a bit like Arsenal, winning by one goal to nil – or even less.

Nasser Hussain (1968–), English cricketer, referring to Leeds United
on Channel 5 television.

See also CLASSIC COMMENTARIES; David COLEMAN; MIXED METAPHORS;
Murray WALKER.

Gambling

A racehorse is an animal that can take several thousand people for a ride at
the same time.

Anonymous.

A very smart lady named Cookie
Said, 'I like to mix business with nookie.
Before every race
I go home to my place
And curl up with a very good bookie.'
Anonymous.

Gamesters and racehorses never last long.
George Herbert (1593–1633), English poet.

Gaming is a principle inherent in human beings.
Edmund Burke (1729–97), Irish-born statesman and writer, 1780.

Man is a gaming animal. He must always be trying to get the better in something or other.
Charles Lamb (1775–1834), British essayist. In 'Mrs Battle's Opinions on Whist', *Essays of Elia* (1823).

Never back anything as can talk.
Fred Swindell (*fl.*19th century), British bookmaker. His own policy was to accept bets on horses only.

Betting is the manure to which the enormous crop of horse-races and race-horse breeding in this and other countries is to a large extent due.
Richard Blackmore (1825–1900), British novelist. *The Jockey Club and its Founders* (1891).

The only man who makes money following the races is one who does it with a broom and a shovel.
Elbert Hubbard (1856–1915), US humorist.

In betting on races, there are two elements that are never lacking – hope as hope, and an incomplete recollection of the past.
Edward V. Lucas (1868–1938), British novelist and poet.

Horse sense is a good judgement which keeps horses from betting on people.
W.C. Fields (1879–1946), US comedian. Quoted on the Sam Ervin record album *Senator Sam at Home* (1974).

Remember – Lady Godiva put all she had on a horse.
W.C. Fields (1879–1946), US comedian.

'You are snatching a hard guy when you snatch Bookie Bob. A very hard guy, indeed. In fact,' I say, 'I hear the softest thing about him is his front teeth.'

Damon Runyon (1884–1946), US author and journalist.
From 'The Snatching of Bookie Bob', *Collier's Magazine*,
26 September 1931.

The race is not always to the swift nor the battle to the strong, but that's the way to bet.

Damon Runyon (1884–1946), US author and journalist. The
biblical reference is to *Ecclesiastes* 9:11.

During the between-war years the football pools did more than any one thing to make life bearable for the unemployed.

George Orwell (1903–50), British novelist.

I backed the right horse, but the wrong horse went and won.

H.A. Jones and **H. Herman**, US writers.

I got a horse right here,
The name is Paul Revere,
And here's a guy that says if the weather's clear,
Can do, can do, this guy says the horse can do.

Frank Loesser (1910–69), US composer. 'Fugue for
Tinhorns' (1950).

My immediate reward for increasing the tax on bookmaking was major vilification. It was confidently asserted in the bookmakers' circles that my mother and father met only once and then for a very brief period.

George Wigg (1900–83), British Labour politician. His recollection of
decisions made in 1972, when he was chairman of the British
Betting Levy Board.

It's one thing to ask your bank manager for an overdraft to buy 500 begonias for the borders in Haslemere, but quite another to seek financial succour to avail oneself of some of the 5–2 they're offering on Isle de Bourbon for the St Leger.

Jeffrey Bernard (1932–97), British journalist. Quoted in 'Sports
Quotes of the Year', the *Guardian*, 23 December 1978.

In most betting shops you will see three windows marked 'Bet Here', but only one window with the legend 'Pay Out'.

Jeffrey Bernard (1932–97), British journalist.

I met with an accident on the way to the track; I arrived safely.

Joe E. Lewis (1926–), US comedian.

The time has come, the Walrus said, to talk of football pools.
Of fixture lists and copyright, of clever men and fools.

Percy Rudd, British writer, *News Chronicle*.

The lower classes are such fools,
They waste their money on the pools.
I bet, of course, but that's misleading.
One must encourage bloodstock breeding.

Bernard Fergusson (1911–80), British writer.

Gamesmanship

The billiard sharp whom any one catches,
His doom's extremely hard –
He's made to dwell,
In a dungeon cell,
On a spot that's always barred.
And there he plays extravagant matches,
In fitless finger stalls,
On a cloth untrue,
With a twisted cue,
And elliptical billiard balls.

William S. Gilbert (1836–1911), British dramatist and lyricist.

In football it is widely acknowledged that if both sides agree to cheat, cheating is fair.

C.B. Fry (1872–1956), English cricketer, footballer and athlete, 1911.

The tradition of baseball always has been agreeably free of chivalry. The rule is 'Do anything you can get away with.'

Heywood Broun (1888–1939), US humorist.

There is no reason why the infield should not try to put the batter off his stride at the critical moment, by neatly-timed disparagements of his wife's fidelity and his mother's respectability.

George Bernard Shaw (1856–1950), Irish playwright and critic, referring to baseball.

I shall never forget my mother's horror and my father's cry of joy when, for the first time in my life, I said angrily to my father, 'That's not the hand I dealt you, Dad.'

Beachcomber (J.B. Morton; 1893–1979), British humorist.
The Best of Beachcomber.

What are we out at the park for? I'd trip my mother. I'll help her, brush her off, tell her I'm sorry. But mother don't make it to third.

Leo Durocher (1906–91), US baseball manager.

Though your game is hardly the best
You can fray your opponent's nerves
By methodically bouncing the ball
At least ten times before your serves.

Arnold J. Zarett.

Gamesmanship or The Art of Winning Games Without Actually Cheating.

Stephen Potter (1900–69), British writer. Book title.

We're having a philosophical discussion about the yob ethics of professional footballers.

Tom Stoppard (1937–), Czech-born British playwright. *Professional Foul* (1978).

It was an act of cowardice and I consider it appropriate that the Australian team were wearing yellow.

Robert Muldoon (1921–92), New Zealand prime minister, 1981. His reaction to Australian bowler Trevor Chappell's decision to bowl an underarm delivery as the last ball of a one-day international against New Zealand at Melbourne, with the batsman needing six to win.

If you're up against a girl with big boobs, bring her to the net and make her hit backhand volleys.

Billie Jean King (1943–), US tennis player. *Billie Jean King* (1982).

I was thinking that if I hit his nuts, maybe he would serve like a woman.

Thomas Muster (1967–), German tennis player, describing his
tactics against the Canadian-born Briton Greg Rusedski, renowned
for his fast serves. 'Sports Quotes of the Year 1998', *Daily
Telegraph*, 28 December 1998.

See also BALL-TAMPERING; PLAYING THE GAME.

Paul GASCOIGNE

**English footballer (1967–), affectionately known as 'Gazza'.
Gazza's career as a creative midfielder player with England and
clubs in England, Italy and Scotland was blighted by injury and
by media interest in his activities off the pitch.**

Quotes about Paul Gascoigne

He is accused of being arrogant, unable to cope with the press and a boozer.
Sounds like he's got a chance to me.

George Best (1946–), Northern Ireland footballer.

Comparing Gascoigne to Pelé is like comparing Rolf Harris to Rembrandt.

Rodney Marsh (1944–), English footballer.

He has the brain-power of an iron filing.

Marcus Berkman, journalist. *Punch* magazine, 1992.

Gazza is no longer a fat, drunken imbecile ... he is in fact a football genius.

A rather hollow apology for earlier stories printed by the
Daily Mirror in 1996.

He's a fantastic player when he isn't drunk.

Brian Laudrup (1969–), Danish footballer, referring to his team-
mate at Rangers in 1997.

He's a disgrace... 30 going on six.

Tommy Docherty (1928–), Scottish football manager, 1997.

When God gave him this enormous footballing talent he took his brain out
at the same time to equal it up.

Tony Banks (1943–), British sports minister, 1997.

There's nobody more serious than Gazza when he's got his committed head on.

Bryan Robson (1957–), English footballer. 'Quotes of the Year', the *Guardian*, 24
December 1998.

Quotes by Paul Gascoigne

I don't like being on my own because you think a lot and I don't like to
think a lot.

Gazza's Coming Home, Channel Four documentary, 1996.

I'm out of the squad, dad. Cancel the holiday to France.

Breaking the news to his father of his failure to win a place in the
1998 England World Cup squad. 'Sporting Quotes of the Year', the
Daily Telegraph, 28 December 1998.

What people don't understand is that underneath I'm just an ordinary bloke
from Newcastle. I'd much prefer to go to a working men's club, have a pint,
play dominoes or a game of cards than go to flash parties or film premières.

Quoted in the wake of his omission from the 1998 England World
Cup squad.

See also ALCOHOL; DIETING; FOOD; INJURIES; ITALIAN FOOTBALL; PREDICTIONS;
TRANSFERS.

Mike GATTING *See* FOOD; LEG SPIN BOWLING; SEX.

German football

We just went out and played the same stale cheese.

Franz Beckenbauer (1945–), German footballer, responding to the
latest in a series of disappointing West German performances in 1988.

We enjoy the expectations people have of us. The higher they are, the more
pressure, the better we like it.

Jürgen Klinsmann (1964–), German footballer, speaking as captain
of Germany at the 1998 World Cup finals.

We are so good at penalties because we have had to rebuild our country
twice.

Jürgen Klinsmann (1964–), German footballer. *On the Spot: The
12–yard Club*, BBC TV documentary, 1999.

If we draw them again, do we get to keep them?

Kevin Keegan (1951–), English footballer and football manager.
Speaking as England coach after England were drawn against
Germany for both the Euro 2000 finals and the qualifying round for
the 2002 World Cup. Quoted in *The Times*, 31 December 1999.

See also EUROPEAN FOOTBALL; FOREIGN SIGNINGS.

Ryan GIGGS

**Welsh footballer (1973–), and a key member of the
successful Manchester United sides of the 1990s.**

I remember the first time I saw him. He was 13 and he just floated over the
ground like a cocker spaniel chasing a piece of silver paper in the wind.

Sir Alex Ferguson (1941–), Scottish footballer manager, 1997.

When he goes at them the way he does, you don't want to be a defender. He
gives them twisted blood.

Gary Pallister (1965–), English footballer, speaking as Giggs's team-
mate at Manchester United in 1997.

David GINOLA

**French footballer (1967–) playing in England from
the mid-1990s, noted both for his flair on the field
and for his Gallic good looks.**

He's a bit tricky. And that's the understatement of the century.

Sol Campbell (1974–), English footballer, referring to his team-
mate at Tottenham Hotspur in 1999.

I rugby tackled him once because it was the only way to stop him. He then
gave me three dummies on the trot. I was out of the game so long I had
time to eat two hot-dogs. And, to make matters worse, he was polite to me
after the game.

Darren Bazeley (1972–), English footballer. Quoted after his team,
Watford, lost 5–2 to Tottenham in 1999.

See also FOOTBALL MANAGERS.

Goalkeepers

The goal stands up, the keeper
Stands up to keep the goal.

A.E. Housman (1859–1936), British poet. 'Bredon Hill' in
A Shropshire Lad (1896).

Good goalkeepers never make great saves.

Warney Cresswell (b. 1897), English goalkeeper.

Maybe Napoleon was wrong when he said we were a nation of shopkeepers
... Today England looked like a nation of goalkeepers.

Tom Stoppard (Tom Straussler; 1937–), Czech-born British
playwright. *Professional Foul* (1977).

Somewhere in there, the grace of a ballet dancer joins with the strength of
an SAS squaddie, the dignity of an ancient king, the nerve of a bomb
disposal officer.

Eamonn Dunphy (1945–), Irish footballer and sportswriter, referring
to the Northern Ireland goalkeeper Pat Jennings.

I've seen forwards get past me with all the confidence of a Pelé or a
Johan Cruyff and then, faced by 'Shilts', suddenly lose their nerve. I
mean, it's happened to me when I've tried to beat him in training. All
he has to do is crouch a little bit, and he sort of spreads and fills the
bloody goal up.

Larry Lloyd (1948–), English footballer. Referring to the English
goalkeeper Peter Shilton (1949–). Quoted in Jason Tomas, *The
Magnificent Obsession* (1982).

The goalkeeper is the jewel in the crown and getting at him should be
almost impossible. It's the biggest sin in football to make him do any
work.

George Graham (1944–), Scottish football manager, speaking as
manager of Leeds United in 1997.

A goalkeeper is a goalkeeper because he can't play football.

Ruud Gullit (1962–), Dutch footballer and manager, 1997.

Golf

Golf is life. If you can't take golf, you can't take life.

Anonymous.

A game in which you claim the privileges of age, and retain the playthings of childhood.

Samuel Johnson (1709–84), British lexicographer.

The game of golf fulfils the axioms laid down for a perfect exercise – a walk with an object.

James Cantlie (1851–1926), Scottish physician and writer.
Physical Efficiency (1906).

Oh! The dirty little pill
Went rolling down the hill
And rolled right into a bunker.
From there to the green,
I took thirteen,
And then, by God, I sunk her!

Popular early-20th-century song.

Golf is in the interest of good health and good manners. It promotes self-restraint and affords a chance to play the man and act the gentleman.

William Howard Taft (1857–1930), US president.

Golf is the only game where the worst player gets the best of it. He obtains more out of it as regards both exercise and enjoyment, for the good player gets worried over the slightest mistake, whereas the poor player makes too many mistakes to worry over them.

David Lloyd George (1863–1945), British Liberal prime minister. Attributed.

You get to know more of the character of a man in a round of golf than in six months of political experience.

David Lloyd George (1863–1945), British Liberal prime minister. Attributed.

I guess there is nothing that will get your mind off everything like golf. I have never been depressed enough to take up the game but they say you get so sore at yourself you forget to hate your enemies.

Will Rogers (1879–1935), US humorist.

It is almost impossible to remember how tragic a place this world is when one is playing golf.

Robert Lynd (1879–1949), Anglo-Irish essayist and critic.

Golf is so popular simply because it is the best game in the world at which to be bad.

A.A. Milne (1882–1956), British writer.

Golf, like the measles, should be caught young, for, if postponed to riper years, the results may be serious.

P.G. Wodehouse (1881–1975), British comic novelist. *A Mixed Threesome* (1922).

Golf ... is the infallible test. The man who can go into a patch of rough alone, with the knowledge that only God is watching him, and play his ball where it lies, is the man who will serve you faithfully and well.

P.G. Wodehouse (1881–1975), British comic novelist. *The Clicking of Cuthbert* (1922).

The least thing upset him on the links. He missed short putts because of the uproar of the butterflies in the adjoining meadows.

P.G. Wodehouse (1881–1975), British comic novelist. His description of a sensitive golfer in *The Clicking of Cuthbert* (1922).

Golf is the Great Mystery.

P.G. Wodehouse (1881–1975), British comic novelist. *The Heart of Gold* (1926).

Golf is a game that is played on a five inch course – the distance between your ears.

Bobby Jones (1902–71), US golfer.

Golf is a game to be played between cricket and death.

Colin Ingleby-McKenzie (1933–), English cricketer.

Golf is like a love affair. If you don't take it seriously, it's no fun; if you do take it seriously, it breaks your heart.

Arthur Daley (1904–74), US sportswriter.

If you watch a game, it's fun. If you play it, it's recreation. If you work at it, it's golf.

Bob Hope (1903–), US comedian. Quoted in *Reader's Digest*, October 1958.

Golf is a fascinating game. It has taken me nearly forty years to discover that I can't play it.

Ted Ray (Charles Olden; 1905–77), British comedian. *Golf – My Slice of Life* (1972).

Golf is a game where a man places a small sphere on top of a larger sphere and attempts to dislodge the small sphere from the larger sphere.

Anonymous. Quoted in Ted Ray, *Golf – My Slice of Life* (1972).

Golf is deceptively simple, endlessly complicated. A child can play it well and a grown man can never master it. It is almost a science, yet it is a puzzle with no answer.

Arnold Palmer (1929–), US golfer.

The number of shots taken by an opponent who is out of sight is equal to the square root of the sum of the number of curses heard plus the number of swishes.

Michael Green (1927–), British humorist. *The Art of Coarse Golf* (1975).

If there is any larceny in a man, golf will bring it out.

Paul Gallico (1897–1976), US journalist, novelist and short-story writer. Quoted in the *New York Times*, 6 March 1977.

Be funny on a golf course? Do I kid my best friend's mother about her heart condition?

Phil Silvers (1912–85), US film and television comedian.

Golf is like an 18-year-old girl with the big boobs. You know it's wrong but you can't keep away from her.

Val Doonican (1928–), Irish singer and entertainer.

Work is the thing that interferes with golf.

Frank Dane, US comedian.

Golf is not and never has been a fair game.

Jack Nicklaus (1940–), US golfer.

Golf and sex are the only things you can enjoy without being good at them.
Jimmy Demaret (1910–), US golfer. Attributed.

If God had intended a round of golf to take more than three hours, He would not have invented Sunday lunch.
Jimmy Hill (1928–), British sports commentator.

See also BALLS; CADDIES; GOLF-BASHERS; GOLF COURSES; GOLFERS; HANDICAPS; TECHNIQUE.

Golf-bashers

Golf is a lot of walking, broken up by disappointment and bad arithmetic.
Anonymous.

Golf is a day spent in a round of strenuous idleness.
William Wordsworth (1770–1850), British poet.

Golf is a good walk spoiled.
Mark Twain (1835–1910), US writer.

Golf is typical capitalist lunacy.
George Bernard Shaw (1856–1950), Irish playwright and critic.

Golf always makes me so damned angry.
George V (1865–1936), king of Great Britain (1910–36).

It's not in support of cricket but as an earnest protest against golf.
Sir Max Beerbohm (1872–1956), British writer, on donating one shilling towards the cricketer W.G. Grace's testimonial. Attributed in *Carr's Dictionary of Extraordinary English Cricketers*.

I regard golf as an expensive way of playing marbles.
G.K. Chesterton (1874–1936), British novelist and poet.

Golf is a game whose aim is to hit a very small ball into an even smaller hole, with weapons singularly ill-designed for the purpose.
Sir Winston Churchill (1874–1965), British Conservative prime minister.

Men who would face torture without a word become blasphemous at the short fourteenth. It is clear that the game of golf may well be included in that category of intolerable provocations which may legally excuse or mitigate behaviour not otherwise excusable.

A.P. Herbert (1890–1971), British humorist. *Misleading Cases* (1935).

If I had my way, any man guilty of golf would be ineligible for any office of trust in the United States.

Henry L. Mencken (1880–1956), US journalist and critic.

All I've got against it is that it takes you so far from the clubhouse.

Eric Linklater (1889–1974), Scottish novelist. *Poet's Pub* (1929).

A golf course outside a big town serves an excellent purpose in that it segregates, as though a concentration camp, all the idle and idiot well-to-do.

Sir Osbert Sitwell (1892–1969), British poet.

Please accept my resignation. I don't want to belong to any club that will accept me as a member.

Groucho Marx (Julius Henry Marx; 1895–1977), US film comedian, declining membership of the Friar's Club in Hollywood. Attributed.

If you want to take long walks, take long walks. If you want to hit things with sticks, hit things with sticks. But there's no excuse for combining the two and putting the results on TV. Golf is not so much a sport as an insult to lawns.

National Lampoon, 1979.

Golf is hockey at the halt.

Arthur Marshall (1910–89), British journalist and writer, 1985.

Golf is a game where white men can dress up as black pimps and get away with it.

Robin Williams (1952–), US comedian, 1986.

It is the unthinkable in pursuit of the unsinkable.

Douglas Watkinson, playwright, *Dragon's Tail* (1986).

All games are silly, but golf, if you look at it dispassionately, goes to extremes.

Peter Alliss (1931–), British television golf commentator.

There is one thing in this world that is dumber than playing golf. That is watching someone else playing golf. What do you actually get to see? Thirty-seven guys in polyester slacks squinting at the sun. Doesn't that set your blood racing?

Peter Andrews, sportswriter.

Golf courses

The greens are harder than a whore's heart.

Sam Snead (1912–), US golfer, referring to the Winged Foot Golf Club in New York.

At Jinja there is both hotel and golf course. The latter is, I believe, the only course in the world which posts a special rule that the player may remove his ball from hippopotamus footprints.

Evelyn Waugh (1903–66), British novelist.

Alaska would be an ideal place for a golf course – mighty few trees and damn few ladies' foursomes.

Rex Lardner (1918–98), US writer. *Out of the Bunker* (1960).

Augusta is the closest thing to heaven for a golfer – and it's just about as hard to get into.

Joe Geshwiler, US journalist, referring to the famous golf course at Augusta, Georgia, in the *San Francisco Examiner*, 1983.

Muirfield without a wind is like a lady undressed. No challenge.

Tom Watson (1949–), US golfer, referring to the Muirfield course in East Lothian, Scotland, in 1987.

See also ST ANDREW'S.

Golfers

The true definition of a golfer is one who shouts 'Fore', takes five, and puts down a three.

Anonymous.

The uglier a man's legs are, the better he plays golf. It's almost a law.

H.G. Wells (1866–1946), British novelist. *Bealby* (1915).

And the wind shall say 'Here were decent godless people;
Their only monument the asphalt road
And a thousand lost golf balls.'

T.S. Eliot (1888–1965), Anglo-American poet, critic and playwright.

Statisticians estimate that crime among good golfers is lower than in any class of the community except possibly bishops.

P.G. Wodehouse (1881–1975), British comic novelist.

Give me a man with big hands and big feet and no brains and I'll make a golfer out of him.

Walter Hagen (1892–1969), US golfer.

The wretched golfer, divot-bound.
Persists in dreams of the perfect round.
And that is why I wander alone,
From tee to green to tee.
For every golfer I've ever known,
Is too good or too bad for me.

Ogden Nash (1902–71), US poet and humorist.

Golf has drawbacks. It is possible, by too much of it, to destroy the mind ... Excessive golfing dwarfs the intellect. Nor is this to be wondered at when we consider the more fatuously vacant the mind is, the better for play. It has been observed that absolute idiots play the steadiest.

Sir Walter Simpson (1843–1898), British writer. *The Art of Golf* (1887).

One who has to shout 'Fore' when he putts.

Michael Green (1927–), British humorist, defining the Coarse
Golfer in *The Art of Coarse Golf* (1967).

Golfers don't fist fight. They cuss a bit. But they wouldn't punch anything or anybody. They might hurt their hands and have to change their grip.

Dan Jenkins, US sportswriter. *Dead Solid Perfect* (1974).

If I had my way the social status of professional golfers would be one notch below that of Nazi war criminals.

Andy Lyons (1963–), British sportswriter in *Melody Maker*, 1988.

See also Seve BALLESTEROS; HEALTH; Jack NICKLAUS; Arnold PALMER;
Sam SNEAD; Lee TREVINO; Tiger WOODS.

David GOWER

**Blonde-haired English cricketer (1957–), possessed of
particularly sweet timing, who scored over 7000 runs in
Test cricket and captained England in the 1980s.**

Quotes about David Gower

He looked so frail and wispish, like a pedigree two-year-old filly, as he
walked disconsolately back to his team-mates in the dressing-room.

Frances Edmonds, writer, novelist and wife of England cricketer Phil
Edmonds, describes Gower's appearance after getting out on the
England tour of the West Indies, 1986. *Another Bloody Tour* (1986).

David Gower makes batting look as easy as drinking tea.

Sir Len Hutton (1916–90), English cricketer.

It's difficult to be more laid back than David Gower without being actually
comatose.

Frances Edmonds, writer, novelist and wife of England cricketer Phil Edmonds.

Quotes by David Gower

What do they expect me to do? Walk around in a T-shirt with 'I'm in charge'
on it?

Responding to allegations of weak captaincy in 1986.

Captaincy means more than vigorous arm-waving.

Quoted in 1986.

W.G. GRACE

**Prodigiously bearded English cricketer (1848–1915),
generally regarded as the 'father of modern cricket'.**

Quotes about W.G. Grace

They have paid to see Dr Grace bat, not to see you bowl.

Anonymous umpire, refusing a bowler's appeal to give the great English cricketer
W.G. Grace out when bowled first ball. Occasionally attributed to Grace himself,
sometimes in the form 'They haven't come to see you umpiring, they have come
to see me bat'. Quoted in Harry Furniss, *A Century of Grace* (1985).

Had Grace been born in ancient Greece, the *Iliad* would have been a different book.

The bishop of Hereford.

He revolutionized cricket. He turned it from an accomplishment into a science, he turned a one-stringed instrument into a many-chorded lyre ... W.G. discovered batting; he turned its many narrow straight channels into one great winding river.

Prince Ranjitsinhji (1872–1933), Indian cricketer. *The Jubilee Book of Cricket* (1897).

He has one of the dirtiest necks I have kept wicket behind.

Viscount Cobham (1909–), English aristocrat and cricketer.

He orchestrated the folk music of cricket.

Sir Neville Cardus (1889–1975), British journalist and writer.

Like Dr Johnson, he endures not by reason of his works but by reason of his circumferential humanity.

Sir Neville Cardus (1889–1975), British journalist and writer, from
'William Gilbert Grace', in *Great Victorians* (1932).

W.G. Grace was by no conceivable standard a good man. He was a cheat on and off the cricket field.

C.P. Snow (1905–80), British novelist and physicist.

His personality was such that it is remembered by those who played with him to the exclusion of his actual performance.

John Arlott (1914–91), English cricket writer and commentator.

Quotes by W.G. Grace

I cannot remember when I began to play cricket. Respect for the truth prevents me from saying I played the first year of my existence, but I have little hesitation in declaring that I handled a bat and ball before the end of my second.

Attributed.

I don't like defensive shots, you can only get threes.

Attributed.

See also BEARDS AND MOUSTACHES; CRICKET; CRICKETERS; EXCUSES; LITERATURE AND SPORT; SMOKING; TACTICS.

Jimmy GREAVES

English footballer, and later a commentator (1940–),
considered one of the most gifted strikers of his generation.

He was the Fagin of the penalty area, the arch-pickpocket of goals.

Geoffrey Green (1911–), British sportswriter.

Jimmy Greaves used to hang around like a substitute best man at a
wedding for 85 minutes and still win more matches than any other player.

Ian Wooldridge (1932–), British sportswriter. *Football Monthly*, 1973.

A walrus in a woolly jumper ... as illuminating as the average taxi driver,
without the saving grace of getting you anywhere.

Victor Lewis-Smith (1961–), British journalist. *Evening Standard*,
1992.

See also George BEST; Sir Bobby CHARLTON; CLASSIC COMMENTARIES;
Tom FINNEY; Sir Geoff HURST.

Greyhound racing

He must be heeded lyke a snake,
And neckyd lyke a drake,
Backed lyke a bream,
Footed lyke a catte,
Taylled lyke a ratte.

Dame Juliana Berners (*fl.*1450s), English prioress. Her
recommendation for the perfect greyhound. Quoted in John Arlott,
The Oxford Companion to Sports and Games (1975).

Remember'st thou my greyhounds true?
O'er holt or hill there never flew.
From slip or leash there never sprang,
More fleet of foot, more sure of fang.

Sir Walter Scott (1771–1832), Scottish novelist and poet.

Don't let's go to the dogs tonight,
For mother will be there.

A.P. Herbert (1890–1971), British humorist. 'Don't Let's Go to the
Dogs Tonight' (1926).

No dog can go as fast as the money you bet on him.

Bud Flanagan (1896–1968), British comedian.

Gymnastics

O, he flies through the air with the greatest of ease,
This daring young man on the flying trapeze.

George Leybourne (1842–84), British singer and songwriter. 'The
Daring Young Man on the Flying Trapeze' (1868).

If there had not been such a thing as gymnastics, I would have had to
invent it because I feel at one with the sport.

Olga Korbut (1956–), Russian gymnast, 1972.

In Russia, show the least athletic aptitude and they've got you dangling off
the parallel bars with a leotard full of hormones.

Victoria Wood (1953–), British comedienne. *Up to you Porky* (1985).

Her legs are kept tightly together: she's giving nothing away.

Extract of gymnastics commentary, BBC TV.

Sir Richard HADLEE

New Zealand cricketer (1951–). Not only New Zealand's greatest ever all-rounder, but also one of the greatest of all fast bowlers.

Quotes about Sir Richard Hadlee

Richard Hadlee has the appearance of a rickety church steeple and a severe manner which suggests that women are not likely to be ordained yet.

Peter Roebuck (1956–), English cricketer. The *Cricketer*.

Quotes by Sir Richard Hadlee

I regard an over as having six bullets in a gun. I use those bullets strategically, to manipulate the batsman into a certain position or state of mind, so that I can eliminate him.

Defining his tactics as a bowler.

It's a bit like the four-minute mile or climbing Mount Everest. Someone is going to do it eventually, but no one forgets the person who did it first.

Reflecting on becoming the first man to take 400 Test wickets, 1990.

Hammer

Mention that you are a hammer thrower to someone who is not an athletics enthusiast and you will be met with any reaction from a puzzled frown to raucous laughter. If you have the misfortune to say it to a groundsman you may face physical violence.

Howard Payne (1931–92), British hammer thrower. *Hammer Throwing* (1969).

Walter ('Wally') HAMMOND

English cricketer (1903–65), an imperious batsman whose feats included scoring over 50,000 runs for Gloucestershire and taking a record 10 catches in a single match.

Whenever I saw Wally Hammond batting, I felt sorry for the ball.

Sir Len Hutton (1916–90), English cricketer.

The greatest player we shall ever see – but a funny bugger.

Unidentified Gloucestershire team-mate.

Handicaps

Drink and debauchery.

Valentine Browne, Viscount Castlerosse (1891–1943), Irish journalist. His response when asked by Nancy Cunard what his golf handicap was. Quoted in Philip Ziegler, *Diana Cooper* (1981).

A handicapper being a character who can dope out from the form what horses ought to win the races, and as long as his figures turn out all right, a handicapper is spoken of most respectfully by one and all, although of course when he begins missing out for any length of time as handicappers are bound to do, he is no longer spoken of respectfully, or even as a handicapper. He is spoken of as a bum.

Damon Runyon (1884–1946), US author and journalist. From 'All Horse Players Die Broke', *Take it Easy* (1938).

I'm a coloured, one-eyed Jew – do I need anything else?

Sammy Davis Jr (1925–90), US entertainer. His reply when asked what his golf handicap was. *Yes I Can* (1966).

It is as easy to lower your handicap as it is to reduce your hat size.

Henry Beard, US humorist, referring to golfing handicaps in *Mulligan's Law* (1994).

Hang-gliding

If at first you don't succeed, so much for hang-gliding.

Anonymous.

Hang-gliding will be commonplace by the year 2000. They will be the bicycles of the air.

Martin Hunt, British hang-gliding administrator. A rather over-optimistic view of the future of hang-gliding, 1977.

Hard men

If you shout hooray for the Pennsylvania Dutchmen
Every team that they play will be carried away with a crutch when
They're out on the field if they're wearing the shield of the Dutchmen.

Hugh Martin (1914–) and **Ralph Blane** (1914–95), US songwriters.
'Buckle Down Winsocki' (1941).

There was plenty of fellers who would kick your bollocks off. The difference was that at the end they'd shake your hand and help you look for them.

Nat Lofthouse (1925–), English footballer, recalling English football in the 1950s.

Nobby Stiles a dirty player? No, he's never hurt anyone. Mind you, he's frightened a few!

Sir Matt Busby (1909–94), Scottish football manager. He was speaking as manager of Manchester United in the 1960s about the formidable Nobby Stiles (1942–), variously known as the 'Toothless Tiger' and (during the 1966 World Cup campaign) 'El Bandito', on account of his ruthless tackling.

I have a little black book with two players in it, and if I get a chance to do them I will. I will make them suffer before I pack this game in. If I can kick them four years over the touch-line, I will.

Jack Charlton (1935–), English footballer and manager. Said to journalists in 1970, this threat landed him trouble with the football establishment.

Norman Hunter doesn't tackle opponents so much as break them down for resale as scrap.

Julie Welch (1948–), British journalist. Referring to English footballer Norman Hunter (1943–), nicknamed 'Bites Yer Legs' on account of the fierceness of his tackles.

I enjoy hitting a batsman more than getting him out. I like to see blood on the pitch. And I've been training on whisky.

Jeff Thomson (1950–), Australian cricketer, 1974.

See also BITING; Vinny JONES; VIOLENCE.

Headlines

£8000 Facelift for Westerham Sportswomen.

Sevenoaks News, 1979.

New York Ban On Boxing After Death.

The Times, introducing a report on the death of a boxer in the ring.

Para Girl to repeat Fatal Jump.

World in Runcorn.

Norse Manure.

Headline in the *Sun* following England's defeat by Norway in 1993.

Out On His Arsenal.

The *Daily Star* greets the news of manager George Graham's sacking as Arsenal manager in 1995.

Moses finds the Promised Land.

The *Observer*. Referring to the Kenyan runner Moses Kiptanui after he became the first athlete to run the 3000 metres steeplechase in under eight minutes, 1995

Football Violence: Judge Hits Out.

Nottingham Evening Post.

See also BALL-TAMPERING; David BECKHAM; Eric CANTONA.

Health

Sport is a preserver of health.
Hippocrates (460–377 BC), Greek physician.

Orandum est ut sit mens sana in corpore sano.
Your prayer must be for a sound mind in a sound body.
Juvenal (*c.*55–*c.*140 AD), Roman satirist. *Satirae*, X.

I was shown one particular set of golfers, the youngest of whom was
turned of four-score. They were all gentlemen of independent fortunes
who had amused themselves with this pastime for the best part of a
century without ever having felt the least alarm from sickness or disgust;
and they never went to bed without having each the best part of a gallon
of claret in his belly. Such uninterrupted exercise, co-operating with the
keen air from the sea, must, without all doubt, keep the appetite always
on edge, and steel the constitution against all the common attacks of
distemper.
Tobias Smollett (1721–71), Scottish novelist. *The Expedition of
Humphrey Clinker* (1771).

Sport is the bloom and glow of perfect health.
Ralph Waldo Emerson (1803–82), US writer and philosopher.

Health is something a runner goes through on his way to fitness.
Dr George Sheehan (1918–93), US cardiologist, 1975.

See also EXERCISE; JOGGING.

Henley
**Annual rowing regatta held in July at Henley on the
River Thames in Oxfordshire, and a highlight of the British
social calendar.**

You talk about the Rose Bowl, you can have your World Series or
Heavyweight Championship, but when a US oarsman, any oarsman, hears
the crowd cheer at Henley he's heard everything.
Randy Jablonic, US rower, 1970.

Henley is full of haughty happiness, hats, haves and very few have-nots.

Frank Keating (1937–), British sportswriter, in the *Guardian*, 1 July 1983.

See also OFFICIALS; ROWING.

Sir Jack HOBBS

English cricketer (1882–1963) whose achievements as a batsman included 197 first-class centuries, half of them scored after he had reached the age of 40.

A professional who bats exactly like an amateur.

Sir Pelham Warner (1873–1963), Trinidadian-born English cricketer. The remark was intended as a compliment on the classical style of Hobbs's batting.

It were impossible to fault him. He got 'em on good 'uns, he got 'em on bad 'uns, he got 'em on sticky 'uns, he got 'em on t'mat, against South African googlers, and he got 'em all over t'world.

Wilfred Rhodes (1877–1973), English cricketer.

Jack Hobbs could have scored thousands more runs, but he often was content to throw his wicket away when he had reached his hundred and give someone else a chance.

Wilfred Rhodes (1877–1973), English cricketer.

A snick by Jack Hobbs is a sort of disturbance of a cosmic orderliness.

Sir Neville Cardus (1889–1975), British journalist.

It's like trying to bowl to God on concrete.

R.C. Robertson-Glasgow (1901–65), English cricketer, describing the experience of bowling to Hobbs and his Surrey colleague Andrew Sandham. Quoted in Ben Travers, *94 Declared*.

The Master: records prove the title good:
Yet figures fail you, for they cannot say
How many men whose names you never knew
Are proud to tell their sons they saw you play.

John Arlott (1914–91), English cricket writer. 'To John Berry Hobbs on his Seventieth Birthday' (16 December 1952).

Others scored faster; hit the ball harder; more obviously murdered bowling. No one else, though, ever batted with more consummate skill.

John Arlott (1914–91), English cricket writer and commentator.
Jack Hobbs: Profile of The Master (1981).

See also Sir Donald BRADMAN.

Hockey

The most odious of all games for a woman.
Badminton magazine, 1900.

Street hockey is great for kids. It's energetic, competitive, and skilful. And best of all it keeps them off the street.
Newsbeat BBC Radio 1.

It was worth getting your knickers wet for.
Jenny Cardwell, British hockey player, following England's victory, in wet conditions, against reigning Olympic champions Spain in 1992.

See also ICE HOCKEY.

Glenn HODDLE
Highly skilled English footballer (1957–). He attracted notoriety as England manager when he called in a faith-healer to help the team during their 1998 World Cup campaign.

Quotes about Glenn Hoddle
If Glenn Hoddle is right then I must have been a failed football manager in a previous existence.
David Blunkett (1947–), British Labour politician, in 1998. He was referring to his own blindness, in the context of Hoddle's comments on disabled people paying the price of their sins in a past life.

If his theory is correct, he is in for real problems in the next life. He will probably be doomed to come back as Glenn Hoddle.
Tony Banks (1943–), British Labour politician and sports minister, responding to Hoddle's ill-advised comments on reincarnation.
Quoted in *The Times*, 31 December 1999.

Quotes by Glenn Hoddle

Jesus was a normal, run-of-the-mill sort of guy who had a genuine gift, just as Eileen has.

Referring to the faith healer Eileen Drewery, whose influence over
Hoddle as manager of the England team during the 1998 World Cup
campaign provoked derision in the press. 'Quotes of the Year 1998',
the *Daily Telegraph*, 28 December 1998.

With hindsight, the biggest mistake I think I made was in not getting Eileen Drewery out to join us in France from the start.

Looking back on England's 1998 World Cup campaign.

You and I have been physically given two hands and two legs and half-decent brains. Some people have not been born like that for a reason. The karma is working from another lifetime. It is not only people with disabilities. What you sow you have to reap.

Quoted in *The Times*, 31 December 1999.

At this moment in time I did not say them things.

Quoted in 1999.

See also AGE; David BECKHAM; FOOTBALL (ASSOCIATION); Diego MARADONA; SPORTING ROYALS.

Hooliganism

That Association Football is becoming notorious for scenes and disgraceful exhibitions of ruffianism. The rabble will soon make it impossible for law-abiding citizens to attend matches.

Scottish Athletic Journal, 1887.

A limit to youthful enthusiasm is reached when these delightful young rascals career over the playing area after scalps.

The *Cricketer*, reporting on the enthusiasm of autograph hunters at Lord's in 1921.

Football hooligans? Well, there are 92 club chairmen for a start.

Brian Clough (1935–), English footballer and manager, 1980.

There are more hooligans in the House of Commons than at a football match.

Brian Clough (1935–), English footballer and manager, 1980.

If we can stop hooliganism, we can go a long way towards stemming this great tide of people not going to football matches.

Brian Clough (1935–), English footballer and manager.

We do not believe there will be trouble. Because of the cost of getting here, we expect an upper middle-class sort of person, the type who represents the British tradition of education ... like gentlemen, like an officer trained at Sandhurst. Someone like David Niven.

Guillermo Urquigo, Monterrey police spokesman, speaking prior to
the arrival of England football fans in Monterrey, Mexico, in 1986.

If we were doing this in the Falklands they would love it. It's part of our heritage. The British have always been fighting wars.

Anonymous English football hooligan, answering charges in court.
Quoted in the *Independent*, 23 December 1988.

They deserve to be flogged and made to break rocks for five years – with their heads.

Daily Star, condemning English football hooligans in 1993.

Now that we don't have a war, what's wrong with a good punch-up? We are a nation of yobs. Without that characteristic, how did we colonise the world? I don't agree with broken glass and knives. But what an English guy does is fight with his fists; a good clean fight. with so many milksops, left-wing liberals and wetties around, I just rejoice that there are people who keep up our historic spirit.

Dowager Marchioness of Reading (1919–), English aristocrat,
responding, in 1998, to the latest outbreak of violence involving
England supporters.

See also FANS; TRAGEDIES; VIOLENCE;

Horse racing

The sport of kings.

Anonymous.

Riding is the art of keeping a horse between yourself and the ground.

Anonymous.

In case my godson Philip Stanhope shall at anytime keep or be concerned in keeping any racehorse or pack of hounds, or reside one night at Newmarket, that infamous seminary of iniquity and ill-manners, during the course of the races there, or shall resort to the said races or shall lose in one day at any game or bet whatsoever the sum of £500 then in any of the cases aforesaid it is my express will that he, my said godson, shall forfeit and pay out of my estate the sum of £50,000 to and for the use of the Dean and Chapter of Westminster.

Earl of Chesterfield (1694–1773), English aristocrat. Clause of his will prohibiting his godson from having anything to do with horse-racing – conditions that the latter managed to observe, although the family later established close links with the sport. Quoted in David Randall, *Great Sporting Eccentrics* (1985).

The world should be postponed for a whore and a horse race.

Horace Walpole (1717–97), British novelist and Whig politician.

It will be Eclipse first, the rest nowhere.

Dennis O'Kelly (1720–87), Irish-born racehorse owner and gambler. Predicting the result of a race at Epsom, 3 May 1769, in which his horse, Eclipse, was running.

The swindling, dangerous and absurd practice of steeple-chasing, things merely got up by publicans and horse-dealers to pillage the unwary and enrich themselves.

The Times, 1838.

There is no secret so close as that between a rider and his horse.

Robert S. Surtees (1803–64), British journalist and novelist. *Mr Sponge's Sporting Tour* (1853).

Oh! doodah day!
Gwine to run all night!
Gwine to run all day!
I bet my money on de bobtail nag.
Somebody bet on de bay.

Stephen Foster (1826–64), US songwriter. 'Camptown Races' (1850).

It is difference of opinion that makes horse races.

Mark Twain (1835–1910), US writer. *Pudd'nhead Wilson* (1893).

There are no handles to a horse, but the 1910 model has a string to each side of its face for turning its head when there is anything you want it to see.

Stephen Leacock (1869–1944), Canadian humorist. 'Reflections on Riding', *Literary Lapses* (1910).

I have seen flowers come out in stony places,
And kind things done by men with ugly faces,
And the Gold Cup won by the worst horse at the races.

John Masefield (1879–1967), British poet.

How amusing racing would be if it were not for the horses. They take people's minds off conversation.

Valentine Browne, Viscount Castlerosse (1891–1943), Irish journalist. Quoted in the *Sunday Express*.

My horse was in the lead, coming down the home stretch, but the caddie fell off.

Samuel Goldwyn (1882–1974), US film producer.

Leathery breeches, spreading stables,
Shining saddles left behind,
To the down the spring of horses,
Moving out of sight and mind.

John Betjeman (1906–84), British poet.

I have no intention of watching undersized Englishmen perched on horses with matchstick legs race along courses planned to amuse Nell Gwynn.

Gilbert Harding (1907–60), British broadcaster.

A real racehorse should have a head like a lady and a behind like a cook.

Jack Leach, British jockey.

There are, they say, fools, bloody fools, and men who remount in a steeplechase.

John Oaksey (1929–), British sports commentator and jockey.

In racing to insult a man's horse is worse than insulting his wife.

John Oaksey (1929–), British sports commentator and jockey.

She's about as cuddly as a dead hedgehog. The alsatians in her yard would go around in pairs for protection.

John Francome (1952–), British jockey, referring to British racehorse trainer Jenny Pitman. *The Times*, 31 December 1999.

See also ASCOT; The DERBY; GAMBLING; JOCKEYS AND RIDERS; RED RUM.

Hunting

If some animals are good at hunting and others are suitable for hunting, then the Gods must clearly smile on hunting.

Aristotle (384–322 BC), Greek philosopher.

The chase, the sport of kings;
Image of war, without its guilt.

William Somerville (1675–1742), British poet. *The Chase* (1735).

The hounds all join in glorious cry,
The huntsman winds his horn:
And a-hunting we will go.

Henry Fielding (1707–54), British novelist. 'A-Hunting
We Will Go'.

D'ye ken John Peel with his coat so gay?
D'ye ken John Peel at the break of the day?
D'ye ken John Peel when he's far far away
With his hounds and his horn in the morning?

'Twas the sound of his horn called me from my bed,
And the cry of his hounds has me oft-times led;
For Peel's view-hollo would waken the dead,
Or a fox from his lair in the morning.

John Woodcock Graves (1795–1886), British poet, huntsman and songwriter. 'John Peel'.

J'aime le son du cor, le soir, au fond des bois.
I love the sound of the horn, at evening, from the depths of the woods.

Alfred de Vigny (1797–1863), French poet. 'Le Cor'.

'Unting is all that's worth living for – all time is lost wot is not spent in 'unting – it is like the hair we breathe – if we have it not we die – it's the sport of kings, the image of war without its guilt, and only five-and-twenty per cent of its danger.

Robert S. Surtees (1805–64), British journalist and novelist. *Handley Cross* (1843).

It ar'n't that I loves the fox less, but that I loves the 'ound more.

Robert S. Surtees (1805–64), British journalist and novelist. *Handley Cross* (1843).

The horse loves the hound, and I loves both.

Robert S. Surtees (1805–64), British journalist and novelist. *Handley Cross* (1843).

There is a passion for hunting something deeply implanted in the human breast.

Charles Dickens (1812–70), British novelist. *Oliver Twist* (1837–39).

There are three kinds of man you must never trust: a man who hunts south of the Thames, a man who has soup for lunch; and a man who waxes his moustache.

Sir James Richards (1907–92), British historian and critic. Recalling advice given to him by his father.

It isn't mere convention. Everyone can see that the people who hunt are the right people and the people who don't are the wrong ones.

George Bernard Shaw (1856–1950), Irish playwright and critic. *Heartbreak House* (1919).

Three jolly gentlemen,
In coats of red,
Rode their horses
Up to bed.

Walter de la Mare (1873–1956), British poet and novelist. 'The Huntsmen'.

It was a confusion of ideas between him and one of the lions he was hunting in Kenya that had caused A.B. Spottsworth to make the obituary column. He thought the lion was dead, and the lion thought it wasn't.

P.G. Wodehouse (1881–1975), British comic novelist. *Ring for Jeeves*.

For when I'm not shootin' or ridin',
I'm huntin' or fishin' or shootin'.
Well, a chap must do something I always tell the chaps,
For if a chap doesn't a chap will collapse.

A.P. Herbert (1890–1971), British humorist, 1930.

Conservatives do not believe that the political struggle is the most important thing in life ... The simplest of them prefer fox-hunting, the wisest religion.

Quintin Hogg, Baron Hailsham of St Marylebone (1907–), British
Conservative politician. *The Case for Conservatism* (1947).

I don't think a prostitute is more moral than a wife, but they are doing the same thing.

Prince Philip, Duke of Edinburgh (1921–), Greek-born consort of
Queen Elizabeth II, illustrating his thoughts on the morality of blood
sports during a speech on 6 December, 1988. *Daily Mail*, 7
December 1988.

See also ANGLING; ANTI-BLOOD SPORTS; SHOOTING.

Sir Geoff HURST

**English footballer (1941–) whose hat-trick in the 1966
World Cup Final against West Germany secured victory
for England.**

Quotes about Sir Geoff Hurst

Geoff Hurst had a hammer in his left boot and good left feet are like bricks of gold.

Jimmy Greaves (1940–), English footballer.

Quotes by Sir Geoff Hurst

As I was heading towards goal, Alan Ball was shouting: 'Hursty, Hursty, give me the ball!' I said to myself: 'Sod you, Bally, I'm on a hat-trick.'

Referring to his memorable third goal in the 1966 World Cup Final
against West Germany. *Match of the Day*, BBC TV, 1999.

See also CLASSIC COMMENTARIES.

Sir Len HUTTON

English cricketer (1916–90) whose feats as a batsman
included the then record score of 364 in a Test match
against Australia in 1938.

Quotes about Sir Len Hutton

There's nothing we can teach this lad.

George Hirst (1871–1954), English cricketer, speaking as Yorkshire
coach in 1930, when Hutton first joined.

I'm only setting up these records for Hutton to break them.

Herbert Sutcliffe (1894–1978), English cricketer, referring to the
inevitability of the young-and-upcoming Hutton surpassing his own
batting records.

I saw Len Hutton in his prime.
Another time, another time.

Harold Pinter (1930–), British playwright. 'Poem' (1986).

Quotes by Sir Len Hutton

If my mother hadn't thrown my football boots on the fire, I might have
become as famous as Denis Compton.

Referring to his youthful passion for football and to Denis
Compton's fame as a player at the top level in both sports.

See also Ian BOTHAM; CRICKET BATS; CRICKET PITCHES; David GOWER; Walter
('Wally') HAMMOND; SEXISM IN SPORT; YORKSHIRE COUNTY CRICKET CLUB.

Ice hockey

Hockey captures the essence of Canadian experience in the New World. In a land so inescapably and inhospitably cold, hockey is the chance of life, and an affirmation that despite the deathly chill of winter we are alive.

Stephen Leacock (1869–1944), Canadian humorist.

I went to a fight the other night and a hockey game broke out.

Rodney Dangerfield (1921–), US comedian. 'Scorecard', *Sports Illustrated*, 4 September 1978.

A puck is a hard rubber disc that hockey players strike when they can't hit one another.

Jimmy Cannon (1910–73), US sportswriter.

Ice hockey is a form of disorderly conduct in which the score is kept.

Doug Larson, US writer.

This game is 50% mental and 50% being mental.

Jim McKenny (1946–), US ice hockey player and broadcaster.

If you take the game seriously, you go crazy anyway, so it helps if you're a bit nuts to start with because you don't waste time getting that way.

Bob Plager (1943–), US ice hockey player.

How would you like a job where, every time you make a mistake, a big red light goes on and 18,000 people boo?

Jacques Plante (1929–86), Canadian ice hockey player.

Ice skating

... then over the parke (where I first in my life, it being a great frost, did see people sliding with their sckeates, which is a very pretty art) ...
Samuel Pepys (1633–1703), British diarist. *Diary*,
1 December 1662.

Skating is a chilly pleasure, and therefore, no sin.
Heinrich Heine (1797–1856), German poet.

In skating over thin ice, our safety is in our speed.
Ralph Waldo Emerson (1803–82), US philosopher and poet.

The thinner the ice, the more anxious everybody is to see if it will bear.
Josh Billings (1818–85), US humorist.

No boy may go ice-skating on any water not passed by the headmaster.
Eton School notice.

You've got so much ice on your hands I could skate on them.
John Curry (1949–94), British ice skating champion, on observing the diamond rings adorning the fingers of the US pianist and entertainer Liberace. Quoted in Ned Sherrin, *Cutting Edge* (1984).

It has always seemed to me hard luck on the very best ice-dancing skaters that they have to spend so much of their time whizzing along backwards, with their bottoms sticking rather undecoratively out.
Arthur Marshall (1910–89), British journalist and writer. *Sunday Telegraph*, 1986.

Ice-skating – with its meticulously preordinated choreography, fanciful dress and movements that consist of wandering around in apparently pointless, ever-decreasing circles – is closer to Trooping the Colour than to a sport.
Julie Burchill (1960–), British journalist. 'Only a Game'.

Olympic figure skating – a sport where competitors are dressed as dinner mints.
Jere Longman, US sportswriter. *Philadelphia Inquirer*.

This is a sport where you talk about sequins, earrings and plunging necklines – and you are talking about the men.

Christine Brennan, US journalist, *Washington Post*.

Paul INCE

English footballer (1967–) who emerged as a star with West Ham United and Manchester United in the 1990s.

He looked like a pint of Guinness running round in the second half.

Paul Gascoigne (1967–), English footballer, remarking upon Ince's appearance after his head was bandaged following an injury during a match in Rome in 1997.

I used to have a saying that when a player is at his peak, he feels as though he can climb Mount Everest in his slippers. That's what he was like.

Sir Alex Ferguson (1941–), Scottish football manager, referring to Ince in 1997.

Incompetence

When I take a gun in hand, the safest place for a pheasant is just opposite the muzzle.

Rev. Sydney Smith (1771–1845), British clergyman and essayist.

What's the good of me goin' in? If I miss 'em I'm out and if I hit 'em I'm out. Let's start the next innings.

Billy Buttress (*fl.* mid-19th century), English cricketer. Although much admired as a bowler, Buttress was repeatedly humiliated as a batsman. This plea, uttered by Buttress after he was found hiding up a tree in order to avoid having to go in to bat at the end of the order, was reluctantly accepted.

I once delivered a simple ball, which I was told, had it gone far enough, would have been considered a wide.

Lewis Carroll (C.L. Dodgson; 1823–98), British writer, recollecting his limited experience of cricket.

I bowl so slow that if after I have delivered the ball and don't like the look of it, I can run after it and bring it back.

J.M. Barrie (1860–1937), Scottish novelist and playwright, 1926.
quoted in Neville Cardus, *Autobiography* (1947).

Randolph Turpin does everything wrong – right.

Sugar Ray Robinson (1920–89), US welterweight and middleweight
boxer, referring to middleweight boxer Randolph Turpin.

Although he is a bad fielder he is also a bad hitter.

Ring Lardner (1885–1933), US humorist and writer, referring to an
unidentified baseball player. Quoted in R.E. Drennan, *Wit's End* (1973).

A stiff is a guy without much talent, but who helps you win games. A guy without much talent who doesn't is a dog. A no-hoper is a guy who's not quite good enough to be a stiff yet.

Doug Moe (1938–), US basketball coach, speaking as coach of the
Philadelphia 76ers.

It is more satisfying to be a bad player at golf. The worse you play, the better you remember the occasional good shot.

Nubar Gulbenkian (1896–1972), British philanthropist, 1972.

The only time our girls looked good in Munich was in the discotheque, between 9 and 11 every night.

Anonymous US athletics coach at the 1972 Olympics.

I am to cricket what Dame Sybil Thorndike is to non-ferrous welding.

Frank Muir (1920–98), British humorist, 1972.

My back swing off the first tee had put him in mind of an elderly woman of dubious morals trying to struggle out of a dress too tight around the shoulders.

Patrick Campbell (1913–80), British writer.

He can't run, he can't tackle and he can't head the ball. The only time he goes forward is to toss the coin.

Tommy Docherty (1928–), Scottish football manager, referring to
Manchester United footballer Ray Wilkins. These drawbacks did not
prevent Wilkins going on to collect 84 England caps.

I was called 'Rembrandt' Hope in my boxing days, because I spent so much time on the canvas.

Bob Hope (1903–), US comedian.

I would like to deny all allegations by Bob Hope that during my last game of golf, I hit an eagle, a birdie, an elk and a moose.

Gerald Ford (1913–), US president.

Whenever I play with him, I usually try to make it a foursome – Ford, me, a paramedic, and a faith healer.

Bob Hope (1903–), US comedian, referring to US president and amateur golfer Gerald Ford.

Sammy Davis Jr hits the ball 130 yards and his jewellery goes 150.

Bob Hope (1903–), US comedian.

It took me 17 years to get 3000 hits in baseball. I did it in one afternoon on the golf course.

Henry 'Hank' Aaron (1934–), US baseball player.

Every day you guys look worse and worse. And today you played like tomorrow.

John Mariucci (1916–), US ice hockey coach, addressing his lacklustre US Olympic squad after another disappointing performance.

I wanted to be an Olympic swimmer, but I had some problems with buoyancy.

Woody Allen (1935–), US comedian.

My golf game's gone off so much that when I went fishing a couple of weeks ago my first cast missed the lake.

Ben Crenshaw (1952–), US golfer, 1977.

I'm not saying my golf game went bad, but if I grew tomatoes they'd come up sliced.

Lee Trevino (1939–), US golfer. Quoted in 'Coaches' Corner', *Scholastic Coach*, December 1982.

Duffers who consistently shank their balls are urged to buy and study *Shanks – No Thanks* by R.K. Hoffman, or in extreme cases, M.S. Howard's excellent *Tennis for Beginners*.

Henry Beard, US humorist. *Golfing* (1985).

England have only three major problems – they can't bat, they can't bowl and they can't field.

Martin Johnson (1949–), British sportswriter, referring to the England cricket team at the beginning of the 1986–87 tour of Australia in the *Independent*, 1986. When England unexpectedly won the Ashes, he was moved to remark of his prediction: 'Right quote; wrong team.'

Francesco Damiani punches with all the violence and bad intentions of Mahatma Gandhi.

Jerry Izenberg (1930–), US sportswriter, in the *Newark Star-Ledger*.

I know it's said I can't punch, but you should see me putting the cat out at night.

Chris Finnegan (1944–), British middleweight boxer.

I was swinging like a toilet door on a prawn trawler.

David Feherty (1958–), Northern Ireland-born golfer, 1993.

I can't bat, can't bowl and can't field these days. I've every chance of being picked for England.

Ray East (1947–), English cricketer, 1993.

We couldn't even score against a team of journalists.

Arrigo Sacchi (1946–), Italian football coach. Quoted after a humiliating series of disappointing results by his team Atletico Madrid in 1998. 'Sporting Quotes of the Year 1998', the *Daily Telegraph*, 28 December 1998.

Pathetic, abysmal, gutless and disgraceful. If my footballers were bricklayers the house they built would fall down.

Alan Ball (1947–), English footballer and manager, speaking as manager of Portsmouth after a disappointing performance against Ipswich, 1999.

Injuries

Without danger the game grows cold.

George Chapman (1559–1634), English playwright.

I've watched the seconds pat and nurse
Their man; and seen him put to bed;

With twenty guineas in his purse,
And not an eye within his head.

John H. Reynolds (1794–1852), British poet, referring to boxing.

He was once known along Broadway as a heavyweight fighter and he was by no means a bad fighter in his day, and he now has a pair of scrambled ears to prove it. Furthermore he is bobbing slightly, and seems to have a few marbles in his mouth, but he is greatly pleased to see me.

Damon Runyon (1884–1946), US author and journalist. *Take It Easy* (1938).

Nobody gets hurt, but the customer.

Joe Louis (1914–81), US heavyweight boxer, referring to injuries
sustained in boxing.

He hit me, man, and knocked me face down on the canvas. I was in the land of make-believe. I heard saxophones, trombones. I saw little blue rats, and they were all smoking cigars and drinking whisky.

James 'Quick' Tillis, US heavyweight boxer, recalling what it felt like
to be knocked down by his opponent Earnie Shavers.

There's a whole lot of difference between pain and damage. The bruises from punches are like icebergs. You see only a small part of the damage on the surface.

Abe Simon, US heavyweight boxer.

In St Moritz everyone who is anything goes around in plaster, which may be fashionable, but is damned uncomfortable. I value my legs as much as Marlene Dietrich values hers.

Noël Coward (1899–1973), British playwright, actor and composer.

I'll stay in football. I don't mind if they stand me up and use me as a corner flag.

Derek Dooley (1929–), English footballer. Quoted in 1953, after
having had his leg amputated.

Oh wasn't it naughty of Smudges?
Oh, Mummy, I'm sick with disgust.
She threw me in front of the Judges
And my silly old collarbone's bust.

John Betjeman (1906–84), British poet. 'Hunter Trials', in
A Few Late Chrysanthemums (1954).

He played too much football without a helmet.

Lyndon B. Johnson (1908–73), US president, referring to Gerald
Ford, who as a young man had some success as a gridiron footballer.
Quoted in Denys Cook, *Presidents of the USA* (1981).

You don't feel a thing. Honest. No pain at all. Sometimes I've gone down
and it feels sweet as hell, like it must be the other guy falling, not you
yourself. In a way it's a very lovable feeling.

Floyd Patterson (1935–), US heavyweight boxer, describing in
1970 what it feels like to be knocked down during a boxing bout.

I'll beat Floyd Patterson so bad, he'll need a shoehorn to put his hat on.

Muhammad Ali (Cassius Clay; 1942–), US heavyweight boxer. Ali
won the bout.

In my time I've had my knee put out, broken my collar-bone, had my nose
smashed, a rib broken, lost a few teeth, and ricked my ankle, but as soon as
I get a bit of bad luck I'm going to quit the game.

J.W. Robinson, rugby player.

It's like a woman concentrating on intricate sewing. If she pricked her
finger she'd hardly notice it and just carry on.

Joe Bugner (1950–), Hungarian-born heavyweight boxer,
describing how a good boxer absorbs blows from his opponent.

I've had about ten operations. I'm a bit like a battered old Escort. You might
find one panel left that's original.

Ian Botham (1955–), English cricketer, 1993.

For many sportsmen, coming face to face with irrefutable evidence of their
mortality is the moment they dread above all others.

Ian Botham (1955–), English cricketer, discussing the impact of
injuries upon sportsmen in *Botham: My Autobiography* (1994).

For me injuries don't come in threes, they come in 33s.

Paul Gascoigne (1967–), English footballer, 1994.

This is one of the freakiest injuries I've seen. And a bit annoying, because I
had to look up a number later.

John Adam, US baseball coach. Said after one of his team, the
Milwaukee Brewers, dislocated a shoulder while attempting to tear a
telephone directory in half.

If this keeps up, our team picture this year will be an X-ray.

John Cooper, American football coach. Commenting upon a recent
run of injuries sustained by members of the Arizona state side.

It could be bad news for Andy Sinton. His knee is locked up in the
dressing room.

George Gavin, British television presenter. Referring to an injury
sustained by English footballer Andy Sinton. Sky Sport, 1997.

Whenever I break down with injury, it's always 'Sicknote'. People read it
and think it's funny. I've been out on the street, just walking along and they
shout: 'Sicknote!' It's not nice.

Darren Anderton (1972–), English footballer, lamenting, in 1998,
his nickname, inspired by his reputation for missing numerous games
through injury.

See also MEDICAL TREATMENT; VIOLENCE.

Intelligence

In my experience officers with high athletic qualifications are not usually
successful in the higher ranks.

Winston Churchill (1874–1965), British Conservative prime
minister, 1941.

With one or two exceptions, colleges expect their players of games to be
reasonably literate.

Sir Maurice Bowra (1898–1971), British scholar.

The word 'genius' isn't applicable in football. A genius is a guy like
Norman Einstein.

Joe Theisman (1949–), American football player and commentator.

I prefer players not to be too good or clever at other things. It means they
concentrate on football.

Bill Nicholson (1919–), English footballer and manager, 1973.

I don't seem to use my intelligence intelligently.

Virginia Wade (1945–), British tennis player, 1977.

Show me a talented player who is thick and I'll show you a player who has problems.

Brian Clough (1935–), English football manager.

If my IQ had been two points lower, I'd have been a plant somewhere.

Lee Trevino (1939–), US golfer.

I was twenty before I realised that Manual Labour wasn't a Mexican.

Lee Trevino (1939–), US golfer.

I know a lot of people think I'm dumb. Well, at least, I ain't no educated fool.

Leon Spinks (1953–), US heavyweight boxer.

When I went to Catholic High School in Philadelphia, we just had one coach for football and basketball. He took all of us who turned out and had us run through a forest. The ones who ran into the trees went on the football team.

George Raveling (1937–), US basketball coach.

I asked the doctor before he closed the wound if he could put some brains in there.

Rex Hudler (1963–), US baseball player, after receiving treatment
for a head injury.

Sometimes, God gives you physical talent and takes away the brain.

Mike Ditka (1939–), American football coach.

He's one of those footballers whose brains are in his head.

Derek Johnstone, Scottish football player and commentator. Extract
of football match commentary, BBC TV Scotland, 1994.

He's got all the ability in the world but there's something missing. He must be a brain donor. Brian wanted a Colly but all he got was a cabbage.

Tommy Docherty (1928–), Scottish football manager, referring in
1998 to English footballer Stan Collymore (1971–) and his
disappointing performances for Aston Villa after being signed for the
team by Brian Little.

See also AMERICAN FOOTBALL; EDUCATION.

Italian football

Italian players have a very closed life. Football is all their life is. The game is so serious, there is no fun. Other things are important to me too, and that is why I like the English way. Here, after the game, the two teams meet up for half an hour in the bar and the bad tackle is forgotten, which is good.

Gianfranco Zola (1966–), Italian footballer, 1997.

We played the Italians at their own game. They are very good at diving, cheating, trying to waste time.

Paul Gascoigne (1967–), English footballer, following a draw
against Italy in 1997.

When Italians tell me it's pasta I check under the sauce to make sure it is. They're masters of the smokescreen. They come out with the 'English are so strong, we're terrible in the air, we can't do this, we can't do that'. Then they beat you 3–0.

Sir Alex Ferguson (1941–), Scottish football manager, speaking as
manager of Manchester United just before a match with Inter Milan
in 1999.

See also Gianfranco ZOLA;

• J •

Jockeys and riders

It takes a good deal of physical courage to ride a horse. This, however, I have. I get it at about forty cents a flask, and take it as required.

Stephen Leacock (1869–1944), Canadian humorist. 'Reflections on
Riding', *Literary Lapses* (1910).

Mother always told me my day was coming, but I never realised I'd end up being the shortest knight of the year.

Sir Gordon Richards (1904–86), British jockey, his reaction on receiving news
of his knighthood, in recognition of his success as a jockey, in 1953.

A jump jockey has to throw his heart over the fence – and then go over and catch it.

Dick Francis (1920–), British jockey and novelist.

When I appear in public people expect me to neigh, grind my teeth, paw the ground and swish my tail – none of which is easy.

Princess Anne (1950–), British Princess Royal. 'Sayings of the Week',
the *Observer*, 22 May 1977.

See also Steve CAUTHEN; Lester PIGGOTT; Bill SHOEMAKER.

Jogging

Jogging is very beneficial. It's good for your legs and your feet. It's also very good for the ground. It makes it feel needed.

Charles Schulz (1922–2000), US cartoonist. *Peanuts.*

The only reason I would take up jogging is so that I could hear heavy breathing again.

Emma Brombeck (1927–), US writer and humorist.

I don't jog. If I die I want to be sick.

Abe Lemmons, US basketball coach.

My doctor told me my jogging could add years to my life. I told him 'Yeah, since I began, I already feel ten years older!'

Lee Trevino (1939–), US golfer.

It's unnatural for people to run around the city streets unless they are thieves or victims. It makes people nervous to see someone running. I know that when I see someone running on my street, my instincts tell me to let the dog go after him.

Mike Royko (1932–97), US journalist.

Jogging is for people who aren't intelligent enough to watch Breakfast TV.

Victoria Wood (1953–), British comedienne. *Mens Sana in Thingummy Doodah* (1991).

See also EXERCISE; HEALTH.

Ben JOHNSON

Jamaican-born Canadian sprinter (1961–) whose career came to grief when he was found to have used performance-enhancing drugs at the 1988 Seoul Olympics.

Quotes about Ben Johnson

It should not have surprised anyone that Ben Johnson was using steroids. You don't go from 10.17 to 9.83 on unleaded gas.

Jamie Astaphan, Johnson's doctor, 1989.

Ben Johnson must still be the fastest human in the world. He served a lifetime sentence in just two years.

Mike Littwin, US journalist, referring in the *Baltimore Sun* in 1990 to the recent reduction in Johnson's ban for the use of illegal drugs.

Quotes by Ben Johnson

I have never, ever knowingly taken illegal drugs, and I would never embarrass my family, my friends, my country, and the kids who love me.

Claim made by Johnson at a press conference in Toronto on 4
October 1988, after he was deprived of his Olympic gold medal
following tests revealing he had taken banned drugs. He later
confessed to having taken anabolic steroids.

Earvin ('Magic') JOHNSON

US basketball player (1959–) who emerged as a top
basketball star in the 1980s.

Quotes about Magic Johnson

Giving 'Magic' the basketball is like giving Hitler an army, Jesse James a
gang, or Genghis Khan a horse. Devastation. Havoc.

Jim Murray, US journalist, in the *Los Angeles Times*.

Quotes by Magic Johnson

I only know how to play two ways: reckless and abandon.

Attributed.

See also TEAM SPIRIT.

Brian JOHNSTON

British cricket commentator (1913–94), nicknamed
'Johnners', who was hugely loved for his rumbustious
style and irrepressible good humour.

Quotes about Brian Johnston

A man with a music-hall imagination.

John Arlott (1914–91), British journalist and cricket commentator.

In Arlott's day the radio team had a centre of gravity; in the age of Johnston
a centre of levity.

Russell Davies (1946–), British writer and broadcaster, marking
Johnston's death in the *Sunday Telegraph* in 1994.

He was a man whose personal church clock stood perpetually at ten to
three, and for whom there was always honey for tea. Not just honey either:
cream cake and sponge cake and cherry cake and Dundee cake and walnut

cake ... Johnston's enduring contribution to Western civilization is the cake-by-cake commentary.

The Times, obituary for Brian Johnston, 1994. The allusion is to the poem 'The Old Vicarage, Grantchester', by Rupert Brooke (1887–1915), in which appear the lines 'Stands the Church clock at ten to three? / And is there honey still for tea?'.

He had, over half a century, perfected and personified that hardly definable English sound, the burble.

Godfrey Smith (1926–), British writer, marking Johnston's death in the *Sunday Times* in 1994.

Quotes by Brian Johnston

Fred Titmus has two short legs, one of them square.

Extract of commentary, commenting specifically on the placing of two fielders at the short leg position by English spin bowler Fred Titmus (1932–).

The bowler's Holding, the batsman's Willey.

Said while commentating on a Test match between England and the West Indies, 1976, when England batsman Peter Willey was facing West Indies fast bowler Michael Holding.

Turner looks a bit shaky and unsteady, but I think he's going to bat on – one ball left.

Extract of commentary on a Test match during which the New Zealand batsman Glenn Turner was struck in the box area, with one ball of the over remaining.

You've come over at a very appropriate time; Ray Illingworth has just relieved himself at the pavilion end.

Extract of commentary broadcast from a match at Grace Road, Leicester.

Neil Harvey's at slip, with his legs wide apart, waiting for a tickle.

Extract of commentary broadcast from a match between England and Australia.

Vinny JONES

Welsh footballer (1965–) who made a reputation as one of English football's 'hard men' in the 1980s and 1990s.

Quotes about Vinny Jones

Vinny Jones is as discreet as a scream in a cathedral.

Frank McGhee, British journalist. The *Observer*, 1988.

Vinny Jones is a player who regards it as a matter of personal honour to intimidate the nation's finest, to castrate them with a shattering, late tackle early in the game, to rip their ears off and spit in the hole.

Jasper Rees, British journalist. The *Independent on Sunday*, 1992.

Quotes by Vinny Jones

I'd like to get ten goals this season, but the authorities don't normally let me play for a whole season.

Referring in 1991 to the many suspensions imposed upon him throughout his career.

The FA have given me a pat on the back. I've taken violence off the terracing and onto the pitch.

Speech, Oxford Union, 1995.

I can't run, can't pass, can't tackle, can't shoot, but I'm still here.

Quoted in 1997.

See also FAMOUS LAST WORDS; TACTICS; VICTORY.

Kevin KEEGAN

**Irrepressible English footballer and manager
(1951–) who was European Footballer of the
Year in 1978 and 1979 and subsequently enjoyed
success as manager of Newcastle United and Fulham
before accepting the post of England coach in 1999.**

To call Keegan a superstar is stretching a point. He's been very, very lucky,
an average player who came into the game when it was short of
personalities. He's not fit to lace my boots as a player.

George Best (1946–), Northern Ireland footballer. Sportswriter John
Roberts was moved to observe that in his opinion Keegan was not
fit even to lace Best's drinks.

The Julie Andrews of football.

Duncan McKenzie, English football player and commentator, 1981.

If Kevin Keegan fell into the Tyne, he'd come up with a salmon in his
mouth.

Jack Charlton (1935–), English footballer and manager, 1995.

See also CLASSIC COMMENTARIES; FAMOUS LAST WORDS; FOOTBALL
(ASSOCIATION); FOOTBALL MANAGERS; FOOTBALL REFEREES; GERMAN
FOOTBALL.

Keep-fit *See* EXERCISE.

Billie Jean KING

**US tennis player (1943–) who won a record 20
Wimbledon titles in the 1960s and 1970s, including the
womens' singles title on six occasions.**

Quotes about Billie Jean King

You'll be good, because you're ugly, Billie Jean.

Frank Brennan, sportswriter.

She's a great player, for a gal. But no woman can beat a male player who
knows what he's doing. I'll put Billie Jean and all the other Women's
Libbers back where they belong – in the kitchen and the bedroom.

Bobby Riggs (1918–95), US tennis player. Quoted in 1973, shortly
before losing in straight sets to Billie Jean King in the notorious
'Battle of the Sexes' match, the result of which ironically did much to
promote women's tennis.

Quotes by Billie Jean King

My ego operates this way – every time you tell me I can't do something, that
ego tells me I not only can, but must.

Attributed.

Ask Nureyev to stop dancing, ask Sinatra to stop singing, then you can ask
me to stop playing.

Attributed.

Don KING

**US boxing promoter (1932–) renowned for his outrageous
public persona.**

Quotes about Don King

Don King is a man who wants to swallow mountains, walk on water and
sleep on clouds.

Mark Kram, US sportswriter.

Don King doesn't care about black or white. He just cares about green.

Larry Holmes (1949–), US heavyweight boxer, referring to the
green colour of the US dollar bill.

Don King dresses like a pimp and speechifies like a store-front preacher.

John Schulian (1945–), US writer.

Don King is one of the great humanitarians of our time. He has risen above that great term, prejudice. He has screwed everybody he has ever been around. Hog, dog or frog, it don't matter to Don. If you got a quarter, he wants the first 26 cents.

Randall 'Tex' Cobb (1950–), US heavyweight boxer and actor.

One day Don King will asphyxiate by the force of his own exhaust.

Carmen Graziano, US boxing trainer, 1989.

Quotes by Don King

Only in America could a Don King happen.

Hence the sobriquet Don 'Only in America' King.

People don't like me for the same reason they didn't like Muhammad Ali. We're the wrong kind of nigger. We're not quiet. We stand up to be counted.

Attributed.

I'm one of the world's great survivors. I'll always survive because I've got the right combination of wit, grit and bullshit.

Quoted in the *Sunday Times*, 18 December 1994.

I am the living attestation of the American dream. I am the extolment of this great nation.

Quoted in the *Independent on Sunday*, 10 March 1996.

I am the promoter. First, there was the prophet Isaiah. Then, Nostradamus. Then P.T. Barnum and Buffalo Bill – and then me!

Attributed.

I dare to be great. The man without imagination stands unhurt and hath no wings. This is my credo, this is my forte.

Independent on Sunday, 10 March 1996.

See also CORRUPTION; RACE; Mike TYSON.

Kit

It is a good plan, if it can previously be so arranged, to have one side with striped jerseys of one colour, say red; and the other with another, say blue. This prevents confusion and wild attempts to run after and wrest the ball from your neighbour. I have often seen this done, and the invariable apology – 'I beg your pardon, I thought you were on the opposite side.'

Routledge's *Handbook of Football* (1867).

Stretch pants – the garment that made skiing a spectator sport.

Time Magazine, 23 February 1961.

Dressing a pool player in a tuxedo is like putting whipped cream on a hot dog.

Minnesota Fats (1913–96), US pool player. Quoted in 'Scorecard',
Sports Illustrated, 4 April 1966.

I'd give up golf if I didn't have so many sweaters.

Bob Hope (1903–), US comedian.

Massive bats, helmets, big gloves ... it's rather like sending Nureyev onto the stage at Covent Garden to dance the *Nutcracker Suite* in sea-fisherman's waders.

Denis Compton (1918–97), English cricketer, commenting on the
garb worn by the modern cricketer. *Cricket and All That* (1978).

Sporting Lisbon in their green and white hoops, looking like a team of zebras.

Peter Jones (1930–1990), British football commentator. Extract of
BBC radio match commentary.

Doug Sanders' outfit has been described as looking like the aftermath of a direct hit on a pizza factory.

Dave Marr (1933–97), US golfer and commentator, referring to the
colourful garb favoured by the golfer Doug Sanders in 1983.

I would rather see the whole village dead at my feet than a man bowling in braces.

Adrian Allington, British writer, 1984.

The traditional dress of the Australian cricketer is the baggy green cap on the head and the chip on the shoulder. Both are ritualistically assumed.

Simon Barnes (1951–), British sportswriter. *The Times*, 9 May 1985.

Next to hooligans the people I'd most like to lose interest in football are kit manufacturers.

Patrick Barclay (1947–), British sportswriter. The *Guardian*, 1985.

'Play it as it lies' is one of the fundamental dictates of golf. The other is 'Wear it if it Clashes'.

Henry Beard, US humorist. *Golfing* (1985).

Come on you blue two-tone hoops with red and white trim and a little emblem on the sleeve and the manufacturer's logo and the sponsor's name across the chest and ...

Mike Ticher, British sportswriter. *When Saturday Comes* (1986).

The idea is to look like a cross between subway graffiti and Papua New Guinea. The skier, even at a dead stop, will snap, sizzle and smoke.

Maria Sterling, US fashion critic, discussing ski fashion in 1987.

I only wish some of the players' trousers fitted better.

Prince Philip, Duke of Edinburgh (1921–), Greek-born consort of Queen Elizabeth II: his reply when asked for his view of modern cricket in 1987.

I cannot for the life of me see why the umpires, the only two people on a cricket field who are not going to get grass stains on their knees, are the only two people allowed to wear dark trousers.

Katharine Whitehorn (1926–), British journalist.

Nearly all the Brazilian supporters are wearing yellow shirts. It's a fabulous kaleidoscope of colour.

John Motson (1945–), British television sports commentator. *Colemanballs 4* (1988).

Azinger is wearing an all black outfit: black jumper, blue trousers, white shoes and a pink 'tea cosy' hat.

Renton Laidlaw (1939–), Scottish sportswriter and commentator, describing the appearance of US golfer Paul Azinger.

I feel calm in calm colours. I don't want people to watch the way I dress. I want people to watch the way I play.

Seve Ballesteros (1957–), Spanish golfer.

The Dutch look like a huge jar of marmalade.

Barry Davies (1939–), British television sports commentator. Extract of match commentary, referring to the orange shirts of massed Dutch fans.

Trousers are now allowed to be worn by ladies on the course. But they must be removed before entering the clubhouse.

Notice at Irish golf club.

Contour-hugging cycle shorts can cruelly expose anyone whose performance falls an inch or two short of an all-comers' record. You need a full kitbag to get away with this particular garb. That might explain why so many men wear their cycle shorts under their regular strip.

Richard Littlejohn, British journalist, in *Punch*, 1992.

It looks like something you'd reject for the kitchen curtains.

Brian Moore (1932–), British television sports commentator, referring to Arsenal's away strip. ITV television sports commentary, 1993.

Modern football shirts look like the work of a chimpanzee on drugs let loose at Brentford Nylons.

Andrew Shields, British writer. *Time Out*, 1994.

This spring, Arsenal's goalkeeper David Seaman is wearing a banana-yellow abattoir worker's smock with a fetching inlaid testcard motif, which is attractively repeated in a pair of radioactive side panels on his lycra-style shorts, for that fire-damaged tarpaulin look.

Giles Smith, British journalist. *Independent on Sunday*, 1994.

When I was a lad, when we played Wednesday, they'd wear blue and white stripes and we'd wear red and white stripes. Now they wear all sorts of stuff, like a fashion parade. Where have our stripes gone this season? Blades' strip looks as if it was designed by Julian Clary when he had a migraine.

Sean Bean (1959–), British actor, speaking as a Sheffield United ('Blades') fan in 1996.

The worst thing about playing for Great Britain is the sleeveless shirts. It means you have to shave your armpits before every game.

Karen Brown (1963–), British hockey player.

On the correctly formed pubescent girl, a Speedo looked wonderful. When it was wet, it was an incitement to riot.

Clive James (1939–), Australian writer and broadcaster, referring to fashionable swimwear.

When I see all my legs out, I have confidence. I look at my muscles and they look big and I feel strong. With big shorts, I can't see my muscles at all.

Paolo di Canio (1968–), Italian footballer, explaining in the late 1990s why he chose to wear unfashionably short shorts.

See also BALLS; CRICKET BATS; BOXING GLOVES.

Lacrosse

I thought lacrosse was what you find in la church.

Robin Williams (1952–), US comedian. Interview in *Playboy*, 1982.

Jake LaMOTTA

**US middleweight boxer (1922–), the subject of Martin
Scorsese's film *Raging Bull* (1980).**

Me and Jake LaMotta grew up in the same neighbourhood. You wanna
know how popular Jake was? When we played hide and seek, nobody
ever looked for LaMotta.

Rocky Graziano (1922–90), US middleweight and welterweight
boxer.

LaMotta couldn't punch at all but he was tough, kept coming. He wore you
out. You couldn't miss him. You'd throw a punch backwards, you'd hit him.
You'd throw it under his legs, you'd hit him. He was tough.

Fritzie Zivic (1913–84), US welterweight boxer.

See also Sugar Ray ROBINSON; VIOLENCE.

Brian LARA

**Temperamental West Indian cricketer (1969–) who
captured the headlines in 1994 by breaking batting records
in both Test and English county cricket.**

Quotes about Brian Lara

I couldn't bat for the length of time required to score 500. I'd get bored
and fall over.

Denis Compton (1918–97), English cricketer, acknowledging Lara's feat
of becoming the first man to score 500 runs in a first-class cricket match,
in 1994. Quoted in the *Daily Telegraph*, 27 June 1994.

Quotes by Brian Lara

I still don't think this 500 makes me a great cricketer. I've still much
to learn.

Reflecting upon his score of 501 for Warwickshire in June 1994, the
highest score ever made in first-class cricket.

I woke up at 4 a.m. with my hands sweating and couldn't get back to
sleep. I've been batting the innings since then, and now it's finished I'm
very happy.

Recollecting his feelings after breaking Sir Gary Sobers' record Test
score of 365 by making 375 runs against England at Antigua in
1994.

Last words

Bury me twenty-two yards from Arthur, so I can send him down a ball,
now and then.

Alfred Shaw (1842–1907), English cricketer: his request in 1907 that
he be buried close to his fellow cricketer and good friend Arthur
Shrewsbury. Their graves are twenty-seven yards distant, allowing
for Shaw's customary five-yard run-up.

Some time, Rock, when the team's up against it, when things are wrong
and the breaks are beating the boys – tell them to go in there with all
they've got and win just one for the Gipper.

George Gipp (1895–1920), American football player: his last request,
addressed to coach Knute Rockne. Rockne found occasion to pass on
Gipp's message during a game in 1928. Since then many flagging teams

have been spurred to new efforts with the exhortation 'Win one for the Gipper'. President Ronald Reagan, who played Gipp in the film *Knute Rockne – All-American Hero* (1940), gave the quotation a new lease of life when he quoted it, more than once, while in office.

No, get me a people doctor.

Max Baer (1909–59), US heavyweight boxer. Final utterance when taken ill at a hotel and asked if he would like to see the house doctor.

Put me back on my bike.

Tommy Simpson (1938–67), British cyclist. Said moments before his death from heart failure during the ascent of Mt Ventoux in the 1967 Tour de France.

That was a great game of golf.

Bing Crosby (1904–77), US film actor and singer. Spoken just before he died from a heart attack at the 18th hole.

Lawyers

The niblick, with its heavy head of iron, is a capital club for knocking down solicitors.

Anonymous paean of praise for the niblick golfing club.

My definition of utter waste is a coachload of lawyers going over a cliff, with three empty seats.

Lamar Hunt (1932–), owner of the Kansas City Chiefs football club.

The way things are going the faces on next year's bubble gum cards will be lawyers.

Reggie Jackson (1946–), US baseball player, lamenting the growth in lawsuits and other legal dealings associated with baseball.

Leeds United

When I was just a little boy,
I asked my mother 'What should I be?
Should I be Chelsea?
Should I be Leeds?'
Here's what she said to me...

'Wash your mouth out son,
And go get your father's gun,
And shoot all the Chelsea scum,
Leeds are number one.'

Leeds United supporters' song, to the tune of 'Que sera, sera'.

We're all Leeds admirers now. Who'd have thought it, eh? Leeds, that team of bawling, bullying bruisers being transformed into the best thing since sliced bread – white sliced bread with a yellow-and-blue trim, that is.

Programme for Charlton Athletic–Leeds United fixture, 1999.

Leg spin bowling

Googly. In cricket, a deceptive delivery depending on hand action by the bowler in which an off-break is bowled to a right-handed batsman with what appears to be a leg-break action. It was invented and developed by B.J.T. Bosanquet from 1890, and he used it against the Australians in 1903. In Australia it is called a 'Bosey'. The origin of the term is uncertain. It may have evolved from 'goggle', since the bowl that you see is not the ball that you get.

The definition of a 'googly' in *Brewer's Dictionary of Phrase and Fable, Millennium Edition* (1999).

Chinaman. A cricketing term (not to be confused with GOOGLY) denoting an offbreak bowled by a left-handed bowler to a right-handed batsman. It is said that the name derives from the bowler Ellis Achong, who, although he played for the West Indies, was actually Chinese and who practised this kind of bowling, although not the first to do so.

The definition of a 'chinaman' in *Brewer's Dictionary of Phrase and Fable, Millennium Edition* (1999).

Shane Warne bowled Mike Gatting with the ball of the decade. It also happened to be Warne's first delivery in an Ashes contest. It fizzed down a foot outside leg on a perfect length, bounced generously and turned virtually at right angles to flick the top of off stump. No wonder Gatting looked so bewildered – he couldn't have played it in his dreams.

Simon Hughes (1959–), Middlesex cricketer and cricket writer, describing Shane Warne's famous dismissal of Mike Gatting in the Old Trafford Test match of June 1993. *A Lot of Hard Yakka* (1997).

Carl LEWIS

US track and field athlete (1961–) remembered for winning gold medals in the 100 and 200 metres, 400-metre relay and long jump at the 1984 Los Angeles Olympics.

There's going to be some serious celebrating when Carl gets beaten.

Larry Myricks (1956–), US long jumper, 1984.

Is the world's second-best athlete gay?

Daley Thompson (1958–), British decathlete. Slogan on a T-shirt he wore at the 1984 Olympics, reflecting speculation about Lewis's sexuality. The immodest implication was that 'the world's best athlete' was Thompson himself.

I wouldn't be surprised if one day Carl's halo slipped and choked him.

Allan Wells (1952–), Scottish sprinter, referring in 1989 to Lewis's wholesome public image.

Dennis LILLEE

Australian cricketer (1949–) who established a reputation as the most formidable fast bowler of his time and formed a terrifying new-ball partnership with Jeff Thomson in the 1970s.

Quotes about Dennis Lillee

Leaving out Dennis Lillee against England would be as unthinkable as the Huns dropping Attila.

Australian television commentator, 1982.

Quotes by Dennis Lillee

I try to hit a batsman in the ribcage when I bowl a purposeful bouncer, and I want it to hurt so much that the batsman doesn't want to face me any more.

Quoted in David Frith, *The Fast Men* (1975).

I don't want to do the batsman permanent injury, just to cause him concern – to hurt him a bit.

Attributed.

See also BEARDS AND MOUSTACHES; FAST BOWLING; GAFFES.

Gary LINEKER

English footballer (1960–) who after a successful career as
a player and captain of England became a popular media
personality on the strength of his wholesome, easygoing
public image.

The Queen Mother of football.

Arthur Smith and **Chris England**, British writers. *An Evening with
Gary Lineker* (1990).

Alan Hansen and Gary Lineker are Mr and Mrs Mogadon.

'Zit'. Condemning the relaxed and homely television commentary
style of Lineker and fellow presenter Alan Hansen in 1993.

See also CLICHÉS; RACE; SPITTING; WORLD CUP.

Literature and sport

I have a much greater ambition to be the best racket player than the best
prose writer.

William Hazlitt (1778–1830), British essayist and critic.

I plume myself on this achievement more than I could possibly do on any
kind of glory, political, poetical or rhetorical.

Lord Byron (1788–1824), British poet, referring to his successful
attempt to emulate Leander's swim across the dangerous Hellespont
Straits between Europe and Asia, which he achieved on 3 May 1810.

Wake! for the Ruddy Ball has taken flight
That scatters the slow Wicket of the Night;
And the swift Batsman of the Dawn has driven
Against the Star-spiked Rails a fiery smite.

Francis Thompson (1859–1907), British poet, parodying Edward
Fitzgerald's *The Rubaiyat of Omar Khayyám*. 'Wake! for the Ruddy
Ball has Taken Flight'.

Never read print, it spoils one's eye for the ball.

W.G. Grace (1848–1915), English cricketer. Advice to
fellow-players. Quoted in Harry Furniss, *A Century of
Grace* (1985).

I always wanted to be a minor poet. I remember when I did my record long jump saying to myself, when I was in the air half-way, 'This may be pretty good jumping. It's dashed poor minor poetry!'

C.B. Fry (1872–1956), English cricketer, footballer and athlete.

In the years 1910 and 1911 I had 51 innings with 10 not outs and an average of 19. This I consider a creditable record for a poet.

Siegfried Sassoon (1886–1967), British poet.

My writing is nothing, my boxing is everything.

Ernest Hemingway (1898–1961), US novelist.

He still took an interest in the game when he was at Belvedere, and eagerly studied the feats of Ranji and Fry, Trumper and Spofforth.

Stanislaus Joyce on his cricket-loving brother, the Irish novelist
James Joyce. *My Brother's Keeper* (1958).

I was less the keeper of a soccer goal than the keeper of a secret. As with folded arms I leant my back against the left goalpost, I enjoyed the luxury of closing my eyes, and thus I would listen to my heart knocking and feel the blind drizzle on my face and hear, in the distance, the broken sounds of the game, and think of myself as of a fabulous exotic being in an English footballer's disguise, composing verse in a tongue nobody understood about a remote country nobody knew. Small wonder I was not very popular with my team-mates.

Vladimir Nabokov (1899–1977), Russian-born US novelist,
recalling his participation in college football at Cambridge in
Speak, Memory (1966).

All that I know surely about morality and the obligations of man, I owe to football.

Albert Camus (1913–60), French novelist. Although known
primarily as the author of *La Peste* ('The Plague') and
other novels, Camus was also an enthusiastic footballer,
appearing as goalkeeper for the Oran football club
in Algeria.

What other people may find in poetry, I find in the flight of a good drive.

Arnold Palmer (1929–), US golfer.

I enjoyed it, but if I go back again I'll wear a tin hat.

Laurie Lee (1914–97), British poet and novelist, reflecting on his
experience of watching a Test match in 1974, during which he was
knocked unconscious by a beer bottle.

For Ali to compose a few words of real poetry would be equal to an
intellectual throwing a good punch.

Norman Mailer (1923–), US novelist. *The Fight* (1976).

Conventional wisdom notwithstanding, there is no reason either in football
or in poetry why the two should not meet in a man's life if he has the
weight and cares about the words.

Archibald MacLeish (1892–1982), US poet. *Riders on Earth* (1978).

When I asked Harvey Smith to choose a book to take to the desert island, he
laughed and said he had never read a book in his life.

Roy Plomley (1914–1985), British radio presenter, recalling the
appearance of British showjumper Harvey Smith on the BBC
radio programme *Desert Island Discs*.

I approach Chapter One each year with a deeper foreboding than I ever felt
facing Beecher's.

Dick Francis (1920–), British jockey and novelist.

But the real tragedy was that 15 hadn't been coloured yet.

Steve Spurrier (1945–), American football coach, commenting
on a fire in the Florida Auburns' dormitory, in which 20 books
were destroyed.

He has turned defensive boxing into a poetic art. Trouble is, nobody ever
knocked anybody out with a poem.

Eddie Shaw, boxing trainer. Referring to British middleweight boxer
Herol 'Bomber' Graham (1960–).

There isn't much cricket in *Hamlet*...
There isn't much cricket in *Lear*.
I don't think there's any in *Paradise Lost* –
I haven't a copy right here.

Wendy Cope (1945–), British poet. 'The Cricketing Versions' (1992).

Liverpool

Liverpool are the most uncomplicated side in the world. They all drive forward when they've got the ball, and they all get behind it when they haven't.

Joe Mercer (1914–90), English football manager, 1973.

For those of you watching in black and white, Liverpool are the team with the ball.

Liverpool fans' joke. Quoted in Brian Barwick and Gerald Sinstadt, *The Great Derbies, Everton v Liverpool* (1988).

The only way to beat them is to let the ball down.

Alan Ball (1947–), English footballer and manager, speaking   as manager of Portsmouth in 1988.

I always enjoy the summer. You can't lose any matches.

Roy Evans (1948–), English football manager. Reflecting in 1997 upon Liverpool's lack of success under his management.

You have to ask what we are getting for that sort of money. It's not just the level of performance from the players, but the fact that they don't look interested. That's what really hurts; the players don't seem too fussed.

Rex Nash, British academic. Speaking in 1999 as a lecturer of the football research unit at Liverpool University, contrasting the high level of player's salaries with the club's low level of success in the 1990s.

See also BILL SHANKLY; TRAGEDIES.

Clive LLOYD
West Indian cricketer (1944–) who captained the West Indies during their golden era in the late 1970s and early 1980s, when their triumphs included two World Cups.

Clive Lloyd hits him high away over mid-wicket for four, a stroke of a man knocking a thistle top with a walking stick.

John Arlott (1914–91), English cricket writer and commentator, 1975.

Whoever it was that described Clive Lloyd as a 'great, gangling, begoggled super-cat', must (temporarily at least) have been inspired.

Mike Stevenson, British sportswriter.

Lord's cricket ground

Australians will always fight for those 22 yards. Lord's and its traditions belong to Australia just as much as to England.

John Curtin (1885–1945), Australian Labour prime minister, 1945.

Sir – Now I know this country is finished. On Saturday, with Australia playing, I asked a London cabby to take me to Lord's and had to show him the way.

Letter published in *The Times* in the 1970s.

The general atmosphere of Lord's is more like a prayer meeting than a ball game.

Alistair Cooke (1908–), British-born US journalist and broadcaster.

See also MARYLEBONE CRICKET CLUB (MCC).

Losing streaks

The last time the Cubs won a World Series was in 1908. The last time they were in one was 1945. Hey, any team can have a bad century.

Tom Trebelhorn (1948–), US baseball manager, speaking as
manager of the Chicago Cubs.

It's like having heart attacks. You can survive them, but there's always scar tissue.

Sam Rutigliano (1932–), American football player, describing
what it is like to suffer a long run of defeats, in 1978.

I'm going down so often these days you'd think I was making a blue movie.

John Conteh (1951–), British light-heavyweight boxer. Said during
a long run of defeats in 1980.

We can't win at home and we can't win on the road. My problem as general manager is I can't think of another place to play.

Pat Williams, US basketball manager. Said during a lengthy losing streak suffered by his team, Orlando Magic, in 1992.

If we had not won the European Cup, this would have been one of the worst seasons in recent years.

Lorenzo Sanz, Spanish president of Real Madrid, justifying the sacking of coach Jupp Heynckes shortly after the club's European Cup triumph in 1998.

We've won one on the trot.

Alec Stewart (1963–), England cricketer, greeting a rare Test victory, against South Africa, in 1998. 'Quotes of the Year', the *Guardian*, 24 December 1998.

See also DEFEAT; WINNING STREAKS.

Joe LOUIS

US heavyweight boxer (Joseph Louis Barrow; 1914–81), nicknamed the 'Brown Bomber', who won the world heavyweight title in 1937 and held it for a record 12 years.

Quotes about Joe Louis

I looked across the ring and realised I wanted to go home.

Max Baer (1909–59), US heavyweight boxer, describing his feelings on meeting Joe Louis in a bout in 1935.

It's like someone jammed an electric light bulb in your face, and busted it. I thought half my head was blowed off.

James J. Braddock (1905–74), US heavyweight boxer, describing what it felt like being punched by Joe Louis, 1937.

I only have to read Joe Louis' name and my nose starts to bleed again.

Tommy Farr (1914–86), Welsh boxer.

The most beautiful fighting machine I have ever seen.

Ernest Hemingway (1899–1961), US novelist.

A clean fighter in a dirty game.

Wilfrid Diamond (1931–), US sportswriter. *How Great Was Joe Louis?* (1955).

Joe Louis was my inspiration. I idolize him. I just give lip service to being the greatest. He was the greatest.

Muhammad Ali (Cassius Clay; 1942–), US heavyweight boxer, on learning of Louis' death in 1981.

Ali wouldn't have hit Joe Louis on the bum with a handful of rice.

Tommy Farr (1914–86), Welsh boxer, comparing Muhammad Ali with Joe Louis.

Quotes by Joe Louis

He can run, but he can't hide.

Comment made on 19 June 1941 during a bout against Billy Conn, which ended with Conn being knocked unconscious in the 13th round. Quoted in Louis: *My Life Story* (1947).

See also DEFEAT; INJURIES; MONEY; VIOLENCE.

Luck

The mark of a champion is the ability to make the most of good luck and the best of bad.

Anonymous.

If thou dost play with him at any game
Thou art sure to lose, and, of that natural luck,
He beats thee 'gainst the odds.

William Shakespeare (1564–1616), English playwright. *Antony and Cleopatra* (c.1606).

True luck consists not in holding the best of cards at the table; luckiest he who knows just when to rise and go home.

John Hay (1838–1905), US statesman.

I'd rather be lucky than good.

Vernon 'Lefty' Gomez (1908–89), US baseball player.

They throw, I swing. Every once in a while they're throwing where I'm swinging and I get a hit.

Vernon 'Lefty' Gomez (1908–89), US baseball player.

It's funny, but the more I practice, the luckier I become.

Gary Player (1935–), South African golfer.

The harder you work, the luckier you get.

O.J. Simpson (1947–), American football player.

I'm not a believer in luck ... but I do believe you need it.

Alan Ball (1945–), English footballer and manager.

Luck is what happens when preparation meets opportunity.

Darrell Royal (1924–), American football coach.

In the United States, I'm lucky; in Europe, I'm good.

Seve Ballesteros (1957–), Spanish golfer.

Napoleon wanted his generals to be lucky. I don't think he would have worked with me.

Graham Taylor (1944–), English football manager, speaking as manager of England after the national side failed to qualify for the 1994 World Cup.

See also SUPERSTITIONS.

Luge

That's what I call the ultimate laxative.

Otto Jelinek (1940–), Canadian politician and former champion ice skater. His reaction, as Canadian minister of sports, after trying the luge course at the 1988 Calgary Winter Olympics.

·M·

John McENROE

US tennis player (1959–). The on-court tantrums of
'Superbrat', who won three Wimbledon titles in the early
1980s, outraged and delighted fans around the world.

Quotes about John McEnroe

The Benson and Hedges Cup was won by McEnroe ... he was as charming
as always, which means that he was as charming as a dead mouse in a loaf
of bread.

Clive James (1939–), Australian broadcaster and journalist, in the
Observer, 1980.

John McEnroe's so good. Against him, all you can do is shake hands and
take a shower.

Tomas Smid (1956–), Czech tennis player, 1984.

The best doubles pair in the world is John McEnroe and anyone else.

Peter Fleming (1955–), for many years McEnroe's doubles
partner, 1990.

Hooliganism incarnate, a walking, talking, screaming, squawking metaphor
for What's Wrong With Young People Today.

Julie Burchill (1960–), British journalist.

Quotes by John McEnroe

You can't see as well as these fucking flowers – and they're fucking plastic.

Comments made to a line judge during the US Open, 1980.

You cannot be serious!

His reaction to a referee's decision during the 1981 Wimbledon
tournament. It quickly acquired the reputation of a catchphrase,
being taken up by numerous imitators of the controversial
tennis player.

I wouldn't like to be an umpire for me, that's for sure.

Attributed.

See also APPEARANCE; FAME; SWEARING.

Manchester City

**There are three types of Oxo cubes. Light brown for chicken stock, dark
brown for beef stock, and light blue for laughing stock.**

Tommy Docherty (1928–), Scottish football manager, referring to
the light blue of Manchester City, 1988.

**I have tried to dispel the aura of invincibility at the club and I hope I have
done that by now.**

Frank Clark (1943–), English football manager. Quoted shortly
before he was sacked as manager of Manchester City in February
1998. Manchester City were relegated to the English Second
Division at the end of the 1997–98 season.

See also FOOTBALL CLUB OWNERS.

Manchester United

**In all modesty, my summing-up of 1955–56 and 1956–57 must be that no
club in the country could live with Manchester United.**

Sir Matt Busby (1909–94), Scottish football manager. *My Story* (1957).

**Peter Schmeichel says that the present Man United team would beat the
1968 European Cup winners. He's got a point, because we're over 50 now.**

Nobby Stiles (1942–), English footballer, reflecting upon a boast by
United's goalkeeper in 1997.

I get to my feet when Chelsea fans sing 'Stand up if you hate Man U'. But though I hate them, I have to admire them too.

Ken Bates (1931–), English football club owner. Speaking as chairman of Chelsea in 1997.

United will no longer be a football club but a giant Old Trafford fruit machine.

Tommy Docherty (1928–), Scottish football manager, speaking as a former Manchester United manager during Rupert Murdoch's bid to take over the club in 1998.

Manchester United Ruined my Life.

Colin Shindler (1949–), British writer and Manchester City supporter. Book title (1998).

See also Sir Matt BUSBY; David BECKHAM; George BEST; Eric CANTONA; Sir Bobby CHARLTON; Sir Alex FERGUSON; Ryan GIGGS; TRAGEDIES.

Diego MARADONA

Argentinian footballer (1960–) whose reputation as the most gifted player of his generation was marred both by the 'Hand of God' incident in the 1986 World Cup and by his involvement with drugs.

Quotes about Diego Maradona

The best one-footed player since Puskas.

Sir Stanley Matthews (1915–2000), English footballer.

If there is an effective way of killing off the threat of Diego Maradona by marking him, it probably involves putting a white cross over his heart and tethering him to a stake in front of a firing squad. Even then, there would the fear that he might suddenly drop his shoulder and cause the riflemen to start shooting one another.

Hugh McIlvanney, British sportswriter. The *Observer*, 1986.

Pelé has nearly everything. Maradona has everything. He works harder, does more and is more skilful. Trouble is that he'll be remembered for another reason. He bends the rules to suit himself.

Sir Alf Ramsey (1920–99), English football manager, 1986.

Don't cry for Maradona, Argentina.

Roddy Forsyth (1953–), British journalist. Responding to the news
that Maradona had tested positive in a drug test during the 1994
World Cup. *Sunday Telegraph*, 1994.

For me he was the perfect footballer, better than Pelé. I saw a lot of his
games when he was playing in Italy, where they'd put two men on him.
Pelé was a better team player, but I believe Maradona was better than
anyone who has played football on this planet.

Glenn Hoddle (1957–), English footballer and manager. Speaking
as England coach in 1998.

Quotes by Diego Maradona

The goal was scored a little bit by the hand of God, a little by the head of
Maradona.

Referring to the controversial goal he scored with his fist in the World
Cup finals in Mexico in 1986, as a result of which England went out of
the competition. Quoted in the *Observer*, 29 June 1986.

I was, I am and I always will be a drug addict. A person who gets involved
in drugs has to fight it every day.

Speaking after his recruitment to a government campaign against drugs in
1996. As if to underline his own words, his ongoing involvement in drugs
continued to make headlines in the press past the turn of the century.

See also The PRESS.

Marathon

It is horrible, yet fascinating, this struggle between a set purpose and an
utterly exhausted frame.

Sir Arthur Conan Doyle (1859–1930), Scottish novelist, referring to the 1908
Olympic marathon, won by the Italian Dorando Pietri who was subsequently
disqualified after he was helped across the line in an exhausted state.

If you want to run a mile, then run a mile. If you want to experience
another life, run a marathon.

Emil Zatopek (1922–), Czech middle-distance runner.

To describe the agony of a marathon to somebody who's never run it is like
trying to explain colour to a person who was born blind.

Jerome Drayton, Canadian marathon runner, 1977.

If you want to know what you'll look like in ten years, look in the mirror after you've run a marathon.

Jeff Scaff, marathon runner.

See also RUNNING; TRAINING.

Rocky MARCIANO

US heavyweight boxer (1923–1969) who was world champion 1952–56. The 'Brockton Blockbuster' was the only heavyweight champion to retire undefeated (in 49 professional fights).

Quotes about Rocky Marciano

Rocky Marciano didn't know enough boxing to know what a feint was. He never tried to out-guess you. He just kept trying to knock your brains out.

Archie Moore (1913–98), US heavyweight boxer.

Quotes by Rocky Marciano

When you become heavyweight champion, something comes between you and other people, even your family. Everybody stands back a little, not because of anything you do but because of what you are.

Reflecting upon his world title.

Marriage

A match at golf this day with Cozen Roger, and should have greatly beaten him but for what he said to me as we walked to the 15th tee, being by this time 2 upp. When he aske me: 'By the way, Sam, what is all this to go 'twixt you and your Mrs?' Which puts me in a pretty twitter as to what he has heard and what I shall best say to him, so that I did most vilely foozle my drive, and thereafter not a stroak could I strike clean.

Samuel Pepys (1633–1703), British diarist. *Diary*.

No man is fit to be called a sportsman what doesn't kick his wife out of bed on an average once in three weeks.

Robert S. Surtees (1803–64), British journalist and novelist.

A loving wife is better than making 50 at cricket, or even 99, beyond that I will not go.

J.M. Barrie (1860–1937), Scottish novelist and playwright.

My toughest fight was with my first wife, and she won every round.

Muhammad Ali (1942–), US heavyweight boxer.

If I had to make the choice between staying married and playing snooker, snooker would win.

Ray Reardon (1932–), Welsh snooker player.

It's a marriage. If I had to choose between my wife and my putter, well, I'd miss her.

Gary Player (1935–), South African golfer.

Playing with your spouse on the golf course runs almost as great a marital risk as getting caught playing with someone else's anywhere else.

Peter Andrews, sportswriter.

You can't stay married in a situation where you are afraid to go to sleep in case your wife might cut your throat.

Mike Tyson (1966–), US heavyweight boxer, after his divorce from his wife Robin Givens. Quoted in the *Daily Telegraph*, 1 February 1989.

My wife, who was in the stand, told me that at one stage the entire row in front of her stood up and gave me the V-sign. I asked her what she did and she said she didn't want them to know who she was so she stood up and joined in.

Neil Midgley (1942–), English football referee. Quoted in Derick Allsop, *The Game of Their Lives* (1995).

We interrupt this marriage to bring you the football season.

Slogan on a mug owned by Scottish football manager Kenny Dalglish (1951–) and his wife Marina.

It is more important for me to be a world-class husband than a world-class coach.

Tony DiCicco, US football coach. Quoted on resigning as coach of the US women's football team, having previously guided it to the World Cup. *The Times*, 31 December 1999.

Sir Stanley MATTHEWS

English footballer (1915–2000), nicknamed the 'Wizard of Dribble' on account of his ball skills. He is often identified as the finest footballer ever produced by England.

Quotes about Sir Stanley Matthews

Playing Stanley Matthews is like playing a ghost.

Johnny Carey (1919–), Irish-born footballer.

Last night I had the strangest dream
I've never had before
Stan Matthews on the wing for Stoke
At the age of 84.

Keele University rag record, 1964, referring to Matthews' unusually long career: he made his last appearance in first-class football at the age of 50.

The last player to score a hat-trick in a cup final was Stan Mortenson. He even had a final named after him – the Matthews final.

Lawrie McMenemy, English footballer and manager, referring to the 1953 FA Cup final, in which Mortensen played alongside Matthews for Blackpool.

They'll probably call it the Matthews funeral.

The *Guardian*, 1991, reporting on the funeral of Stan Mortensen. Another reference to the 1953 FA Cup Final, which has gone down in football history as the 'Matthews final' despite the fact that Mortensen scored three goals.

He told me that he used to play for just twenty pounds a week. Today he would be worth all the money in the Bank of England.

Gianfranco Zola (1966–), Italian footballer, recalling a conversation with Sir Stanley Matthews in the late 1990s.

Quotes by Sir Stanley Matthews

Don't ask me how I do it. It always comes out of me under pressure.

His response when asked for the secret of his skill.

I played 33 years and never got cautioned. I like that.

Television interview, 1995.

I don't know if I was all that good. I never saw myself play, so how do I know?
Said during celebrations of his 80th birthday in 1995.

Marylebone Cricket Club (MCC)

No human institution is perfect, but it would in my humble opinion be impossible to find nicer men than those who constitute the Government of Lord's.
Sir Pelham Warner (1873–1963), Trinidadian-born English cricketer.
Lord's 1787–1945 (1946).

At home and abroad, in politics and sport, Britain will do better without the Tories and their friends of the Marylebone Cricket Club. Twenty years ago Tribune first made the demand that the MCC should be nationalized. Now everyone can see the wisdom of our policy.
Michael Foot (1913–), British Labour politician. Response to the
lacklustre start to an MCC tour of Australia in 1958–59.

Popular opinion would be wrong if it ever thought that the M in MCC could stand for misogyny. Quite the reverse is the case. But it may well be that in this changing world there would be one small part of a small part of London which affords refuge for the hunted male animal.
Jack Bailey (1930–), English cricket administrator, speaking as
former Secretary (1974–87) of the MCC on the issue of allowing
women into the pavilion at Lord's in 1989.

See also LORD'S CRICKET GROUND; RELIGION AND SPORT; WOMEN IN SPORT.

Media *See* CLASSIC COMMENTARIES; COMMENTATING; COMMENTATORS;
The PRESS; RADIO; TELEVISION.

Medical treatment

I can close any cut in the world in 50 seconds, so long as it ain't a total beheading.
Adolph Ritacco, US boxing trainer, 1980.

I don't trust doctors. They are like golfers. Every one has a different answer to your problem.
Seve Ballesteros (1957–), Spanish golfer.

And he's got the icepack on his groin there, so possibly not the old shoulder injury.

Ray French (1939–), British television sports commentator. Extract
from a Sky TV rugby commentary.

Now the trainer has been called on to the pitch ... and he's having to administer artificial insemination.

Anonymous radio sports commentator. Extract of football match
commentary.

They had to take a piece of bone out of my head in order to rebuild my nose. It was kind of a pain in the ass.

Rob DiMaio (1968–), US ice hockey player, after reconstructive
surgery in 1997.

In Cameroon, healers have said they will be able to cure me in three days by burying my leg in the ground and putting fire around it. They have also recommended massage with gorilla bones while invoking the spirits of ancestors. Physiotherapy would include going on a hedgehog hunt.

Marc-Vivien Foé (1976–), Cameroonian footballer, detailing the
treatment that he was offered for the broken leg he sustained during
the 1998 World Cup finals. The *Daily Telegraph*, 'Sporting Quotes
of the Year 1998', 28 December 1998.

I've tried surgical spirit, Friar's Balsam and urine in a bucket – dip your hand in it. They are all pretty similar; they toughen the skin.

Graeme Swann (1979–), English cricketer, describing the treatments
he had tried for a bad cut on his finger, 1999.

See also INJURIES.

Mixed metaphors

I've got a gut feeling in my stomach.

Alan Sugar (1947–), British businessman and chairman of
Tottenham Hotspur.

The proof of the pudding is in the eating and Villa aren't pulling up any trees.

Tony Butler, British sports commentator. Extract from a football
match commentary.

Glenn is putting his head in the frying pan.

Ossie Ardiles (1952–), Argentinian footballer, referring to England
manager Glenn Hoddle.

The lads ran their socks into the ground.

Sir Alex Ferguson (1941–), Scottish football manager.

Wimbledon are putting balls into the blender.

Rodney Marsh (1944–), English footballer. Extract from
a football match commentary.

We didn't have any metaphors in my day. We didn't beat about the bush.

Fred Trueman (1931–), English cricketer, 1995.

If you can't stand the heat in the dressing room, get out of the kitchen.

Terry Venables (1943–), English footballer and manager.

I can see the carrot at the end of the tunnel.

Stuart Pearce (1962–), English footballer.

See also POLITICS; SPORTING SIMILES.

Money

You drive for show and putt for dough.

Anonymous.

£1 per week be ample remuneration for the best professional footballer that
ever existed.

The Field, 1886.

As I understand it, sport is hard work for which you do not get paid.

Irvin S. Cobb (1876–1944), US humorist.

It pays me better to knock teeth out than put them in.

Frank Moran (1887–1967), US boxer. Response to a question from
Theodore Roosevelt, explaining why he had given up a career in
dentistry for one in boxing.

When you're fighting, you're fighting for one thing – money.

Jack Dempsey (1895–1983), US heavyweight boxer.

Dempsey hit me hardest, 'cos Dempsey hit me two hundred eleven thousand dollars' worth, while Louis only hit me thirty-six thousand dollars' worth.

Jack Sharkey (1902–94), US heavyweight boxer, comparing his experiences in the ring against Jack Dempsey and Joe Louis.

I don't like money, actually, but it quiets my nerves.

Joe Louis (1914–81), US heavyweight boxer.

Two million dollars gate at one fight! That's some cabbage in any man's language.

Wilfrid Diamond (1931–), US sportswriter, referring to the gate money earned at the fight between Jack Dempsey and Gene Tunney on 23 September 1926. *Blood, Sweat, and Jack Dempsey* (1953).

When money enters into sport, corruption is sure to follow.

E.N. Gardiner (1864–1930), British historian, 1930.

They say money talks, but the only thing it ever says to me is good-bye.

Paul Waner (1903–), US baseball player.

I never wanted to be a millionaire, I just wanted to live like one.

Walter Hagen (1892–1969), US golfer.

Tell you what, you keep the salary and pay me the cut.

Vernon 'Lefty' Gomez (1910–), US baseball player: response when told his salary was to be cut from $20,000 to $7,500.

Johnny Haynes is a top entertainer and will be paid as one from now on. I will give him £100 a week to play for Fulham.

Tommy Trinder (1909–89), British comedian and chairman of Fulham football club, announcing his decision to award Fulham's star player a substantial pay increase in 1961 and thus breaking the existing minimum wage agreement.

An athlete cannot run with money in his pockets. He must run with hope in his heart and dreams in his head.

Emil Zatopek (1922–), Czech middle-distance runner. Quoted by Christopher Brasher in the *Observer*, 12 September 1982.

I am no longer a footballer. I am an industry.

Johann Cruyff (1947–), Dutch footballer, referring to the record
transfer fee paid to secure his move from Ajax to Barcelona in 1973.

Money is how we keep the score in motor racing nowadays.

Colin Chapman (1928–82), British motor racing team manager, 1974.

The Inland Revenue Service is the real undefeated heavyweight champion.
They show you the left. You never see the right. They'll take everything,
even your tears.

George Foreman (1948–), US heavyweight boxer, 1974.

Running for money doesn't make you run fast. It makes you run first.

Ben Jipcho (1943–), Kenyan runner, 1975.

They're selling video cassettes of the Ali–Spinks fight for $89.95. Hell, for
that money Spinks will come to your house.

Dr Ferdie Pacheco (1927–), US doctor and sports commentator.
Quoted in 'Sports Quotes of the Year', the *Guardian*, 23 December
1978.

They offered me a handshake of £10,000 to settle amicably. I told them that
they would have to be a lot more amicable than that.

Tommy Docherty (1928–), Scottish football manager, referring in
1981 to his dismissal as manager of Preston North End.

Some of our players can hardly write their own names, but you should see
them add up.

Karl-Heinz Thielen, German football manager, referring to his squad
at FC Cologne in 1982.

I came from a dirt farm, now I'm filthy rich.

Larry Holmes (1949–), US heavyweight boxer.

Real pressure in golf is playing for $10 when you've only got $5 in your
pocket.

Lee Trevino (1939–), US golfer.

The difference between an amateur and a professional athlete is the latter is
paid by cheque.

Jack Kelly Jr, US Olympics sports administrator.

I told the players we need to win so that I can have the cash to buy some new ones.

Chris Turner (1958–), English football manager, speaking as
manager of Peterborough when they played Middlesbrough in
a League Cup quarter-final in 1992.

Juninho will only need to learn three words of English: Pound, Thank You and Bye Bye.

Jan Aage Fjortoft (1967–), Norwegian footballer, responding to the
Brazilian footballer Juninho's transfer to Middlesbrough in 1995.

Not being born to parents who were accountants was probably my biggest mistake.

Chris Eubank (1966–), British middleweight boxer, 1995.

The money coming into the game is incredible. But it is just the prune-juice effect – it comes in and goes out straightaway. Agents run the game.

Alan Sugar (1947–), British businessman and chairman of
Tottenham Hotspur, 1997.

If I had known there was prize-money, I'd have won it.

Dean Macey (1977–), British decathlete. His response when,
having defied expectations by winning a silver medal at the world
championships, he learned that his medal brought with it $30,000.
The Times, 31 December 1999.

It's a simple question of supply and demand. But all of us are grossly overpaid. I think it's a ridiculous dispute.

Jim Courier (1970–), US tennis player, referring to the campaign
for equal money for men and women tennis players, 1999.

See also CORRUPTION; GAMBLING; PROFESSIONALISM; SEXISM IN SPORT.

Bobby MOORE

**English footballer (1941–93) who gained the enduring
affection and admiration of his countrymen by captaining
England to victory in the 1966 World Cup.**

Bobby Moore was great at that. Someone would come and kick a lump out of him, and he'd play as though he hadn't even noticed. But ten minutes later ... whoof! ... He had a great 'golden boy' image, Mooro. But he was hard.

Sir Geoff Hurst (1941–), English footballer. Quoted in Brian James,
Journey to Wembley (1977).

To find a way past Bobby Moore was like searching for the exit from
Hampton Court maze.

David Miller (1935–), British sportswriter, in *The Times*, 1993.

Stirling MOSS

**British racing driver (1929–) who became the most
celebrated British Formula One driver of his generation,
despite never winning the world championship.**

Quotes about Stirling Moss

If Stirling Moss had put reason before passion, he would have been World
Champion – he was more than deserving of it.

Enzo Ferrari (1898–1988), Italian motor racing constructor.

Juan Fangio was the great man of racing; whilst Stirling Moss was the
epitome of a racing driver.

Jackie Stewart (1939–), Scottish racing driver.

Quotes by Stirling Moss

It is necessary to relax your muscles when you can. Relaxing your brain
is fatal.

Detailing his driving technique in *Newsweek*, 16 May 1955.

It has taken me thirty-three years and a bang on the head to get my
values right.

Quoted in 1962, the year in which he retired from motor sport after
a bad crash at Britain's Goodwood race track.

See also Juan Manuel FANGIO; MOTOR RACING; WILLPOWER.

Motor cycling

That's all the motor cycle is, a system of concepts worked out in steel.

Robert M. Pirsig (1928–), US writer. *Zen and the Art of Motor
Cycle Maintenance* (1974).

You can always spot a motor cycle racer in a restaurant. He's the one gripping his fork with the first two fingers of his left hand.

Kenny Roberts, US motor cyclist, 1973.

It's kind of like tumbling around inside a giant clothes-drier.

Dave Aldana, US motor cyclist, describing, in 1975, the sensation of
falling off a motor cycle at speed.

I do resent giving the income tax inspector 83 per cent. I tell him he's welcome to it if he went out and got on my bike and got throwed up the road at 190 mph, be in hospital for weeks, then walk around 'alf crippled for the rest of his life ... if they did that they're welcome to my money.

Barry Sheene (1950–), British motor cyclist.

See also WEATHER.

Motor racing

RAC Rally competitors should remember not to make a noise by rushing about unnecessarily on the lower gears and generally making a nuisance.

Autocar magazine, 1931.

There's no secret. You just press the accelerator to the floor and steer left.

Bill Vukovich (1918–55), US racing driver, referring in 1954 to the
skills required to drive in the Indianapolis 500 (in which he died a
year later).

There are two things no man will admit he can't do well – drive and make love.

Stirling Moss (1929–), British racing driver.

Motor racing is dangerous; but what is danger? It is dangerous to climb a mountain. It is dangerous to cross main roads. It is dangerous to explore a jungle. One cannot frame regulations to make everything safe.

Mike Hawthorn (1929–59), British racing driver and motor cyclist.
Said in 1959, the year in which he was himself killed in a car
accident shortly after retiring from motor racing as Formula One
world champion.

Racing is 99% boredom and 1% terror.

Geoff Brabham (1952–), Australian racing driver.

Every car has a lot of speed in it. The trick is getting the speed out of it.

A.J. Foyt (1935–), US racing driver.

My first priority is to finish above rather than beneath the ground.

James Hunt (1947–93), British racing driver, 1975. He survived his
Formula One career only to die early from heart failure, hastened by
years of fast living.

You appreciate that it is very easy to die and you have to arrange your life to cope with that reality.

Niki Lauda (1949–), Austrian racing driver, reconciling the dangers
of motor sport in the *Observer*, 1982.

Some of the ravines are so deep that if you topple over, your clothes will be out of date by the time you hit the bottom.

Tony Pond, British rally driver, describing the Monte Carlo rally
course in 1986.

If you've just driven your heart out, you've got to trust that your team-mate is not then going to stick the car in a hedge.

Martin Brundle (1959–), British racing driver, discussing the
importance of team spirit in the Le Mans 24-hour race, 1997.

See also DRAG-RACING; Juan Manuel FANGIO; FORMULA ONE; Stirling MOSS;
Alain PROST; Michael SCHUMACHER; Ayrton SENNA; Murray WALKER.

·N·

Ilie NASTASE

**Flamboyant Romanian tennis player (1946–) who
attracted as much attention for his antics on court as he
did for his tennis.**

Nastase is a Hamlet who wants to play a clown, but he is no good at it; his
gags are bad, his timing is terrible and he never knows how he's going over
the top – which last drawback is the kiss of death for a comic.

Clive James (1939–), Australian writer and broadcaster. The *Observer*, 1975.

Look, Nastase, we used to have a famous cricket match in this country
called Gentlemen versus Players. The Gentlemen were put down on the
scorecard as 'Mister' because they were gentlemen. By no stretch of the
imagination can anybody call you a gentleman.

Trader Horn, British tennis umpire, explaining to Ilie Nastase at
Wimbledon why he refused to call him 'Mister'.

See also AGE; Björn BORG; SWEARING.

Martina NAVRATILOVA

**Czech-born US tennis player (1956–) who dominated the
women's game in the 1980s, winning a record nine
Wimbledon singles titles.**

Quotes about Martina Navratilova

When Martina Navratilova is tense it helps her to relax.

Dan Maskell (1908–92), British television sports commentator.

It's difficult to play against a man ... I mean against Martina. She scares you with her muscles.

Hana Mandlikova (1962–), Czech tennis player, 1984.

Quotes by Martina Navratilova

I'm not involved in tennis but committed. Do you know the difference between involvement and commitment? Think of ham and eggs. The chicken is involved. The pig is committed.

Quoted in the *International Herald Tribune*, 3 September 1982.

See also The PRESS; VICTORY; WOMEN IN SPORT.

Nerves

Every time you win, it diminishes the fear a little bit. You never really cancel the fear of losing; you keep challenging it.

Arthur Ashe (1943–93), US tennis player.

Fear was absolutely necessary. Without it, I would have been scared to death.

Floyd Patterson (1935–), US heavyweight boxer.

Fear is exciting for me.

Ayrton Senna (1960–94), Brazilian racing driver.

Nerves and butterflies are fine – they're a physical sign that you're mentally ready and eager. You have to get the butterflies to fly in formation, that's the trick.

Steve Bull, British sports psychologist. Quoted in *The Times*,
9 October 1999.

See also CONFIDENCE; COURAGE.

Netball

I didn't like netball ... I used to get wolf whistles because of my short skirts.

Princess Anne (1950–), British Princess Royal. 'Sayings of the
Week', the *Observer*, 18 September 1983.

Netball is an outlet – an escape from the humdrum. There's nothing gives me such a kick. Well, nothing except vodka.

Angela Farley, British netball player, 1989.

Newspapers *See* The PRESS.

Jack **NICKLAUS**

US golfer (1940–), nicknamed the 'Golden Bear', whose success in major tournaments made him the highest-earning golfer of his generation.

Quotes about Jack Nicklaus

Jack is playing an entirely different game, and one which I'm not even familiar with.

Bobby Jones (1902–71), US golfer, reflecting on Nicklaus's victory in the 1965 Masters.

When Nicklaus plays well he wins, when he plays badly he comes second. When he's playing terribly, he's third.

Johnny Miller (1947–), US golfer.

Quotes by Jack Nicklaus

I think I fail a bit less than everyone else.

Attributed.

See also AGE; GOLF; TECHNICAL TIPS.

Obsession

What do they know of cricket who only know of cricket?

C.L.R. James (1901–89), Trinidadian writer.

My wife had an uncle who could never walk down the nave of an abbey without wondering whether it would take spin.

Sir Alec Douglas Home (1903–95), British Conservative prime
minister. *The Twentieth Century Revisited* (1982).

As a boy I genuinely believed in the man who never ate bacon because its red and white stripes reminded him of Sheffield United – indeed in my blue and white Sheffield Wednesday heart I applauded and supported his loyalty.

Roy Hattersley (1932–), British Labour politician. *Goodbye to
Yorkshire* (1976).

I always get excited when watching football.

Marinko Janevski, retired Yugoslavian policeman: his explanation,
at his trial in 1982, for the murder of his wife after she switched
off the television set halfway through a game he was watching.
He was found guilty. Quoted in David Randall, *Great Sporting
Eccentrics* (1985).

See also FANS.

Officials

But what has come out of the chatter,
Is that the Stewards aren't really old fools.
They've run the Regatta for ages,
And are always revising the rules.

Anonymous reference to the organizers of the Henley
Regatta, 1953.

There should have been a last line of defence during the war. It would have been made up entirely of the more officious breed of cricket stewards. If Hitler had tried to invade these shores he would have been met by a short, stout man in a white coat who would have said, 'I don't care who you are, you're not coming in here unless you're a Member!'

Ray East (1947–), English cricketer. *A Funny Turn* (1983).

They bring him out of the loft, take the dust sheet off him, give him a pink gin and sit him there. He can't go out of a 30-mile radius of London because he's normally too pissed to get back. He sits there at Lord's, saying 'That Botham, look at his hair, they tell me he's had some of that cannabis stuff.'

Ian Botham (1955–), English cricketer. His view of the typical
England selector, delivered during an after-dinner speech in 1986.

At Oxford it took me weeks to convince the man on the gate that I was the manager. He always gave me the third degree before he let me in.

Jim Smith, English football manager, reflecting in 1988 on his time
as manager of Oxford United in the early 1980s.

Someone suggested that the Jockey Club Race Planning Committee consisted of a table and four chairs – and I bet they've got woodworm.

Jenny Pitman (1946–), British racehorse trainer, 1989.

If I had my way I would take him to Traitor's Gate and personally hang, draw and quarter him.

Ian Botham (1955–), English cricketer, referring to the chairman of
the England selectors Ray Illingworth in 1994.

Bloody medieval most of them.

Ian Botham (1955–), English cricketer, referring to the
administrators of English cricket in 1995.

He crossed the line between eccentricity and idiocy far too often for someone who was supposed to be running English cricket.

Ian Botham (1955–), English cricketer, criticizing English cricket administrator Ted Dexter in *Botham: My Autobiography* (1994).

See also CRICKET UMPIRES; FOOTBALL REFEREES; REFEREES AND UMPIRES.

The 'Old Firm'

Scottish football's two dominant teams – Celtic and Rangers – historically representative of, respectively, the city's Catholic and Protestant communities.

It's brilliant. Now we can beat Rangers and England at the same time.

Anonymous Celtic fan, remarking in 1987 upon the news that Rangers had signed yet another English player.

The Glaswegian definition of an atheist: a bloke who goes to a Rangers–Celtic match to watch the football.

Sandy Strang, Scottish football supporter. Quoted in Stephen Walsh, *Voices of the Old Firm* (1995).

The Old Firm match is the only one in the world where the managers have to calm the interviewers down.

Tommy Burns (1956–), Scottish football manager, speaking as manager of Celtic in 1997.

Olympic Games

Citius, altius, fortius.
Swifter, higher, stronger.

Pierre de Coubertin (1863–1937), founder of the modern Olympic Games. His choice of motto for the 1908 Olympics, held in London. Legend has it that he spotted the slogan over the doorway of a French lycée run by a friend of his, the Reverend Father Didon.

The most important thing in the Olympic Games is not to win but to take part, just as the most important thing in life is not the triumph but the struggle.

Pierre de Coubertin (1863–1937), founder of the modern Olympics. Speech at the close of the 1908 Olympic Games, held in London.

There is something in the Olympics, indefinable, springing from the soul, that must be preserved.

Chris Brasher (1928–), British middle-distance runner, 1968.

The Olympic movement is a 20th-century religion. Where there is no injustice of caste, of race, of family, of wealth.

Avery Brundage (1887–1975), US sports administrator. Quoted in
1972, while president of the International Olympics Committee.

The Montreal Olympics can no more have a deficit than a man can have a baby.

Jean Drapeau (1916–), Canadian politician. Claim made, while
mayor of Montreal, at a press conference on 29 January 1973. In
reality, the games made a substantial loss.

Go for gold!

Slogan adopted by the US Olympic team at the Winter Olympics of
1980. Several other teams, including the British squad in 1984,
subsequently adopted the slogan as part of their own campaigns.
The same slogan had, however, been used from time to time in non-
sporting contexts, the earliest instances of it including a radical
political campaign of 1832.

Murphy's Law and Parkinson's Law have both contributed to an Olympics Law which says that the bigger a thing becomes, the more problems it attracts and the sooner if hastens its own demise.

Norman Harris, British writer, in *The Sunday Times*, 12 August 1984.

A little mutant monstrosity that was born in the toxic dump of somebody's imagination.

Los Angeles Times, 1996. A reference to Whatizit, the mascot
chosen for the 1996 Atlanta Olympics.

There will never again be an official salad cream of the Olympic Games.

Michael Payne, Marketing Director of the International Olympic
Committee, quoted in the *Daily Telegraph*, 5 August 1996.

One-day cricket

For six days, thou shalt push up and down the line but on the seventh day thou shalt swipe.

Doug Padgett (1934–), English cricketer. Responding to the
introduction of limited-overs cricket on Sundays in 1969.

Throw down some sawdust, everybody put on top hats and red noses and you've got the John Player League.

Brian Close (1931–), English cricketer, 1969.

In real cricket, the player who has developed imagination and skill makes the game, but in the one-day match it is the other way round. The match dictates to the player.

Brian Close (1931–), English cricketer, 1970.

Cricket must be the only business where you can make more money in one day than you can in three.

Pat Gibson, British sportswriter, comparing the money to be made
from one-day cricket with that from three-day matches in 1975.

A Test match is like a painting. A one-day match is like a Rolf Harris painting.

Ian Chappell (1943–), Australian cricketer.

Cricketers do not expect anyone to watch three-day games.

Peter Roebuck (1956–), English cricketer, 1985.

There is a possibility that your ability as a player may well be analysed by future generations on your one-day statistics. That's the day I dread most.

Allan Border (1955–), Australian cricketer, 1985.

If there is a threat to the game of cricket, that threat lies in the first-class arena. One-day cricket, especially day–night cricket, is here to stay.

Sir Donald Bradman (1908–), Australian cricketer. Quoted in
Wisden Cricketer's Almanack (1986).

One-day cricket is like fast food. No one wants to cook.

Viv Richards (1952–), West Indian cricketer, 1988.

Sunday League cricket: multi-coloured pyjamas, two-tone umpires, and white balls with black seams. There is nothing like traditional English sport.

David Hunn, British sportswriter. Quoted in *The Sunday Times*, 1992.

One-day cricket is exhibition. Test cricket is examination.

Henry Blofeld (1939–), English cricket commentator.

Orienteering

The thought sport.

Anonymous. Quoted in Roger Smith, The *Penguin Book of Orienteering* (1982).

Cunning running.

Anonymous. Quoted in Roger Smith, *The Penguin Book of Orienteering* (1982).

Michael OWEN

Fresh-faced English footballer (1979–) who emerged as a bright new talent in the late 1990s.

Quotes about Michael Owen

Since I stopped playing, people have been comparing strikers with me. If anyone wants to say it about Michael Owen, however, they are quite welcome.

Jimmy Greaves (1940–), English footballer. Quoted in 1998.

The World Cup has at least found its juvenile lead, its Leonardo DiCaprio. And this star is leaving us after a Titanic match. Michael Owen has everything to restore England's image which was becoming that of a simple factory of tattooed hooligans and alcoholics.

Editorial, *Le Monde*, reporting on Owen's contribution to England's game against Argentina in the second round of the 1998 World Cup, in which he scored a goal of great quality.

Quotes by Michael Owen

I don't have any. I was sent to bed before the matches started.

His reply, during the 1998 World Cup campaign in which he starred, when asked for his memories of the 1990 World Cup finals.

See also YOUTH.

Jesse OWENS

US athlete (1913–80) remembered for winning four gold
medals, including one for the 100 metres, at the 1936
Olympics in Nazi Germany.

Quotes about Jesse Owens

Jesse Owens glides over the track with the grace of a streamlined express
flying over the open prairie.

Arthur Daley (1904–74), US sportswriter.

Quotes by Jesse Owens

I let my feet spend as little time on the ground as possible. From the air, fast
down, and from the ground, fast up.

Discussing his running technique.

See also RACE.

Arnold PALMER

US golfer (1929–) who established himself as one of the great post-war golfing talents with a series of major titles in the 1950s and 1960s.

Arnold Palmer is the biggest crowd-pleaser since the invention of the portable sanitary facility.

Bob Hope (1903–), US comedian.

If ever I needed an eight foot putt, and everything I owned depended on it, I would want Arnold Palmer to putt for me.

Bobby Jones (1902–71), US golfer.

Arnie would go for the flag from the middle of an alligator's back.

Lee Trevino (1939–), US golfer.

See also GOLF; LITERATURE AND SPORT; VICTORY.

Parachuting

In freefall the body can do everything an aeroplane can do except go back up!

Sally Smith, writer. *Parachuting and Skydiving* (1978).

PELÉ

Brazilian footballer (Edson Arantes do Nascimento; 1940–)
whose contribution to Brazil's World Cup victories in 1958,
1962 and 1970 earned him his reputation as the greatest
footballer of all time.

Quotes about Pelé

Di Stefano was manufactured on earth, Pele was made in Heaven.

Geoffrey Green (1911–), British sportswriter, comparing Pelé with
the great Argentinian footballer Alfredo Di Stefano (1926–).

People smoked Pelé, drank Pelé coladas, and vacationed in the Pelé islands,
but for us he never became anything more than that little guy from down
there somewhere who could bounce a ball on his head.

Dan Jenkins, US sportswriter, discussing Pelé's impact in the USA
in *Playboy*, 1985.

Quotes by Pelé

I was born for soccer, just as Beethoven was born for music.

Attributed.

People want to try to find a new Pelé. They couldn't do that. You don't find
another Beethoven, you have only one Michelangelo. In music you have
only one Frank Sinatra and in football you have only one Pelé.

'Quotes of the Year', in the *Guardian*, 24 December 1998.

See also BALLS; PENALTIES.

Penalties

It is a standing insult to sportsmen to have to play under a rule which
assumes that players intend to trip, hack and push their opponents, and to
behave like cads of the most unscrupulous kidney. The lines marking a
penalty area are a disgrace to the playing fields of a public school.

C.B. Fry (1872–1956), English cricketer, footballer and athlete,
objecting to the existence of the penalty laws in football in 1907.

A penalty is a cowardly way to score.

Pelé (Edson Arantes do Nascimento; 1940–), Brazilian footballer.

There are no opportune times for a penalty, and this is not one of those times.

Jack Youngblood, US sports commentator. From an American
football match commentary.

Penalty shoot-outs

It is loading a bullet into the chamber of a gun and asking everyone to pull
the trigger. Someone will get the bullet, you know that. And it will reduce
them to nothing. Fair? Fairness is not even an issue.

Christian Karembeu (1970–), French footballer, referring to the
penalty shoot-out.

I've only taken one penalty before, for Crystal Palace at Ipswich. It was 2–2
in the 89th minute, I hit the post and we went down that year. But I think
I'd be far more comfortable now than I was then.

Gareth Southgate (1970–), English footballer. Quoted shortly
before the doomed penalty shoot-out in a semi-final match against
Germany in the 1996 European Championship, in which Southgate's
missed shot sealed England's fate.

Pep talks

You've beaten them once. Now go out and bloody beat them again.

Sir Alf Ramsey (1922–99), English footballer and manager. His pep
talk to England players just before extra time began in the 1966
World Cup Final, with England and Germany level at 2–2 but
England having much of the best of the game. England took Ramsey
at his word and ended 4–2 victors.

Well girls, shall we go?

Dana X. Bible (1891–1980), American football coach. The full
extent of his half-time talk while coach of the Texas A&M 'Aggies'
football team.

What I said to them at half-time would be unprintable on radio.

Gerry Francis (1952–), English football manager, addressing his
Tottenham Hotspur squad in 1995.

My team talk was very simple. I said: 'Let's just have an old-fashioned match, get the right result and go out for a few drinks afterwards.' It seemed to work better than all the tactical crap.

Ron Atkinson (1939–), English football manager, speaking as
manager of Coventry City following victory against Leeds in 1996.

I told our players not to be overawed by their stars. I said: 'They're human, just like you. They pee just like you. Imagine Giggs and Cantona having a piss. They don't piss wine.'

Uri Geller (1946–), Israeli psychic. His advice to the Reading
players before an FA Cup tie with Manchester United in 1996.
Reading lost 3–0.

If Glenn Hoddle said one word to his team at half time, it was concentration and focus.

Ron Atkinson (1939–), English football manager. Commentary
during an England match under Hoddle's management.

Anyone who uses the word 'quintessentially' in a half-time talk is talking crap.

Mick McCarthy (1959–), English footballer and manager from
1996 of the Republic of Ireland football team, responding to a
comment by Niall Quinn in a half-time discussion during a Republic
of Ireland game in 1998.

Philosophy

Life is simply a cricket match, with temptation as the bowler.

Anonymous.

What is Human Life but a Game of Cricket?

Duke of Dorset (1745–99), English aristocrat. Essay title (1797).

Life was a damned muddle – a football game with everyone offside and the referee gotten rid of – everyone claiming the referee would have been on his side.

F. Scott Fitzgerald (1896–1940), US novelist.

Many continentals think life is a game; the English think cricket is a game.

George Mikes (1912–), Hungarian-born writer. *How to Be an Alien* (1946).

The understanding of being is clarified by sport.

Howard Slusher (1937–), US writer. *Man, Sport and Existence* (1967).

Great sport has intellectual beauty.

R. Carlisle. Quoted in 'Physical Education and Aesthetics' in H.T.A. Whiting and D.W. Masterson, *Readings in the Aesthetics of Sport* (1974).

Whether he is hurling a javelin, soaring off a ski-jump, performing a double back flip off a diving board, or screaming towards earth in a free fall sky dive, man is alone. He is beyond the world of public determinations; of official identities; of functions; of self-deceptions and of everydayness. And in the solitary state of oneness, man can meet himself.

William A. Harper (1944–), US sportswriter. 'Man Alone' in E.W. Gerber, *Sport and the Body: A Philosophical Symposium* (1974).

Life is an elaborate metaphor for cricket.

Marvin Cohen (1931–), British writer. 'The Time Factor' in Allen Synge, *Strangers' Gallery: Some Foreign Views of English Cricket* (1974).

Athletes have studied how to leap and how to survive the leap some of the time and return to the ground. They don't always do it well. But they are our philosophers of actual moments and the body and soul in them, and of our manoeuvres in our emergencies and longings.

Harold Brodkey (1930–96), US writer. In 'Meditations on an Athlete' (1992).

Boxing got me started on philosophy. You bash them, they bash you and you think, what's it all for?

Arthur Mullard (1910–95), British boxer and actor. Quoted in the *Independent on Sunday*, 17 December 1995.

You've got to take the rough with the smooth. It's like love and hate, war and peace, all that bollocks.

Ian Wright (1963–), English footballer, 1995.

See also Eric CANTONA.

Physique

In wrestling nimble, and in running swift;
In shooting steady, and in swimming strong;
Well made to strike, to leap, to throw, to lift,
And all sports that shepherds are among.

Edmund Spenser (1552–99), English poet.

Th' athletic fool, to whom what Heaven denied
Of soul, is well compensated in limbs.

John Armstrong (1709–79), Scottish poet and physician.
The Art of Preserving Health (1744).

His limbs were cast in manly mould,
For hardy sports or contests bold.

Sir Walter Scott (1771–1832), Scottish novelist and poet.

He was so strong that he could write his name with an eighty-four pound
weight dangling from his little finger.

Denzil Batchelor, US writer, describing the British bare-knuckle
champion John 'Gentleman' Jackson (1769–1845) in 1954.

I'm six foot eleven. My birthday covers three days.

Darryl Dawkins (1957–), US basketball player.

Quick guys get tired; big guys don't shrink.

Marv Harshman (1918–), US basketball coach, explaining his
preference for powerfully-built players over faster ones when
selecting teams.

When he sits down, his ears pop.

Don Nelson (1940–), US basketball coach, referring to the Golden
Warriors' 7ft 6in centre Shawn Bradley.

I'd like to borrow his body for just 48 hours. There are three guys I'd like to
beat up and four women I'd like to make love to.

Jim Murray, US sportswriter, referring to Muhammad Ali. Quoted in
the *Los Angeles Times*, 1964.

To be a great fast bowler, you need a big heart and a big bottom.

Fred Trueman (1931–), English cricketer.

Girls who ride horses don't necessarily have big behinds.

Ann Moore (1950–), British showjumper, 1974.

He has a neck built like a stately home staircase.

Tom Davies, British sportswriter, describing British light-heavyweight
boxer John Conteh (1951–).

Somewhere inside that flabby body was an athlete trying to get out.

Stuart Storey, British athletics commentator, referring to generously-
built British shot-putter Geoff Capes.

It is not the size of the dog in the fight that counts, but the size of the fight
in the dog.

Barry McGuigan (1961–), Irish featherweight boxer, nicknamed the
'Clones Cyclone' after his birthplace in Co. Monaghan.

We were given a choice. We can either run around the field three times or
around Tommy Lasorda once.

Steve Saxe (1960–), US baseball player, referring to the rotund Los
Angeles Dodger Tommy Lasorda.

See also APPEARANCE; BODYBUILDING.

Lester PIGGOTT

**Taciturn British jockey (1935–) who rode over
4000 winners, including 30 classics and nine Epsom
Derby wins.**

Quotes about Lester Piggott

He has a face like a well-kept grave.

Jack Leach, British jockey.

He gives the impression that if he rode facing backwards, he would still
win the races that count.

John Hislop, British sportswriter, 1980.

There should be a law against Lester Piggott.

Darrell McHargue, US jockey.

Quotes by Lester Piggott

People ask me why I ride with my bottom in the air. Well, I've got to put it somewhere.

Attributed.

See also The DERBY; FOOD; PREDICTIONS; SEXISM IN SPORT.

Playing the game

Fair play's a jewel.

Proverb.

Friendship first, competition second.

Chinese proverb.

If a man is running a race in the stadium, he ought to use every effort to win, but on no account must he cut in on a rival or push him with his hand. So too in life, it is not wrong for a man to try to satisfy his needs, but it is not right for him to take anything from another.

Cicero (106–43BC), Roman orator and statesman.

To brag a little; to show well,
To improve gently given luck.
To pay, to own up
And to shut up if beaten –
These are the virtues of the sporting man.

Walter Travis (1862–1927), Australian-born US golfer.

There's a breathless hush in the Close tonight –
Ten to make and the match to win –
A bumping pitch and a blinding light,
An hour to play and the last man in.
And it's not for the sake of a ribboned coat,
Or the selfish hope of a season's fame,
But his Captain's hand on his shoulder smote –
'Play up! play up! and play the game!'

Sir Henry Newbolt (1862–1938), British poet. 'Vitae Lampada'.

I understand that a curve ball is thrown with a deliberate attempt to deceive. Surely that is not an ability we should want to foster at Harvard?

Charles W. Eliot (1834–1926), US educator, referring, while president of Harvard University, to baseball.

It's good sportsmanship not to pick up lost balls while they are still rolling.

Mark Twain (1835–1910), US writer.

Nothing handicaps you so much in golf as honesty.

Anonymous.

Why they call a fellow that keeps losing all the time a 'Good Sport' gets me.

Charles E. Hughes (1862–1948), US politician.

If one hit the ball in an unexpected direction to the on side, intentionally or otherwise, one apologised to the bowler.

C.B. Fry (1872–1956), English cricketer, footballer and athlete, 1891.

For when the One Great Scorer comes
To write against your name
He Marks – not that you won or lost –
But how you played the game.

Grantland Rice (1880–1954), US sportswriter and poet.
'Alumnus Football', in *Only the Brave* (1941).

I wish you'd speak to Mary, Nurse,
She's really getting worse and worse.
Just now when Tommy gave her out,
She cried and then began to pout.
And then she tried to take the ball,
Although she cannot bowl at all.
And now she's standing on the pitch,
The miserable little bitch!

Hilaire Belloc (1870–1953), British poet.

Show me a good sportsman and I'll show you a player I'm looking to trade.

Leo Durocher (1906–91), US baseball manager, 1950.

Nice guys finish last.

Leo Durocher (1906–91), US baseball manager, referring to the

New York Dodgers, 6 July 1946. According to Durocher, in his book
Nice Guys Finish Last (1975), the fuller form of the quotation was
'Take a look at them. All nice guys. They'll finish last. Nice guys.
Finish last.' Also encountered as 'Nice guys don't finish first' and
'Nice guys don't play ball games.'

Last guys don't finish nice.

Stanley Keeley, US academic.

Sportsmanship, next to the Church, is the greatest teacher of morals.

Herbert Hoover (1874–1964), US Republican president. Quoted in
John Rickards Betts, *America's Sporting Heritage: 1850–1950*
(1974).

If you spend a lot of time on sportsmanship, you're going to spend a lot of time losing.

Glenn Dobbs (1920–), American football coach.

Always play a game with somebody, never against them. Always win a game, never beat an opponent.

Andrew Bailey, sportswriter. *Future Sport* (1982).

If you can't win fairly, you don't deserve to win.

Steele Bishop (1953–), Australian cyclist, 1983.

See also BALL-TAMPERING; GAMESMANSHIP.

Pole vault

Pole vaulting is a religious experience.

Dr R.V. Ganslen, US sports scientist. *Mechanics of the Pole Vault* (1973).

My first 18-foot pole vault wasn't any more of a thrill than my first clearance at 15 or 16 or 17 foot. I just had more time to enjoy it on the way down.

Roland Carter, pole vaulter, 1976.

Politics

England is unrivalled for two things – sport and politics.

Benjamin Disraeli (1804–81), British Conservative prime minister.

I would rather have won this race than be President of the United States.

Thomas Hicks (1875–), British-born US long-distance runner, on winning the Olympic marathon in 1904.

I have done nothing important or distinguished since we met except to win the handicap prize, value £4–10/– at North Berwick. This has caused more emotion and surprise in my family than did my becoming Prime Minister. Doubtless it is also more important.

Arthur Balfour (1848–1930), British Conservative prime minister, referring to his success in a recent golf club tournament in a letter to Lady Desborough early in the 20th century.

When I go to see Herr Hitler I give him the Nazi salute because that is the normal thing. It carries no hint of approval of anything he or his regime may do. And, if I do it, why should you or your team object?

Sir Neville Henderson, British ambassador to Germany, advising the England football team to greet Adolf Hitler with the Nazi salute when they played in Germany before the Second World War. The resultant photographs of the squad with raised arms caused a furore at home.

If only Hitler and Mussolini could have a good game of bowls once a week at Geneva, I feel that Europe would not be as troubled as it is.

R.G. Briscow, (1893–1957), British politician.

If the French noblesse had been capable of playing cricket with their peasants, their chateaux would never have been burnt.

George Trevelyan (1876–1962), British historian. *English Social History* (1944).

If Stalin had learned to play cricket, the world might now be a better place.

Richard Downey (1881–1953), British bishop, 1948.

Private enterprise in cricket might not be regarded as the last word, and ultimate State direction would not do it any harm.

'Manny' Shinwell (1884–1986), British Labour politician, suggesting in 1950 that English cricket would benefit from nationalization.

A pitcher who throws at a batter and deliberately tries to hit him is a Communist.

Alvin Dark (1922–), US baseball club manager, condemning violent play in baseball.

One lesson you'd better learn if you want to be in politics is that you never go out on a golf course and beat the President.

Lyndon B. Johnson (1908–73), US president.

Have you ever noticed how we only win the World Cup under a Labour government?

Harold Wilson (1916–95), British Labour prime minister, 1971, in the aftermath of England's exit from the 1970 World Cup in Mexico. England failed to make the World Cup finals in 1974, losing a key qualifying game to Poland in 1973 (under the Tory administration of Edward Heath). Labour returned to power in 1974, remaining in government until 1979, thus England's failure to make the 1978 finals cannot to be attributed to the Conservatives. 18 years of Conservative rule brought qualification for the World Cup finals in 1982, 1986 and 1990, but no trophies. Labour's belated return to power in 1997 failed to reverse the pattern, as England crashed out of the competition in the second round of the 1998 World Cup finals, losing to Argentina.

A sporting system is the by-product of society and its political system, and it is just boyhood dreaming to suppose you can ever take politics out of sport.

Peter Hain (1950–), British Labour politician. Quoted in the *Observer*, 2 May 1971.

We are very proud of him. He's our first offensive linesman to ever become President.

William Perry (1962–), American football player, referring to former American footballer and subsequent US President Gerald Ford (1913–).

The difference between golf and government is that in golf you can't improve your lie.

George Deukmajian, US Republican politician, speaking as governor of California.

Politics is like boxing – you try to knock out your opponents.

Idi Amin (1925–), Ugandan dictator and former boxer.

Sport is alienating. It will disappear in a universal communist society.

Jean-Marie Brohm (1940–), French sportswriter. *Sport – A Prison of Measured Time: Essays by Jean-Marie Brohm* (1978).

No country which has cricket as one of its national games has yet gone Communist.

Woodrow Wyatt (1918–97), British Labour politician turned right-wing journalist. Quoted in the *Sunday Mirror*, 1979.

Say that cricket has nothing to do with politics and you say that cricket has nothing to do with life.

John Arlott (1914–91), English cricket writer and commentator.

Politics governs everything we do – the games we play, the way we play them, who we play.

John Arlott (1914–91), English cricket writer and commentator, 1980.

There's a hell of a lot of politics in football. I don't think Henry Kissinger would have lasted 48 hours at Old Trafford.

Tommy Docherty (1928–), Scottish football manager, 1982.

Why runners make lousy communists. In a word, individuality. It's the one characteristic all runners, as different as they are, seem to share ... Stick with it. Push yourself. Keep running. And you'll never lose that wonderful sense of individuality you now enjoy. Right, comrade?

Advertisement for running shoes during the 1984 Los Angeles Olympics (which were boycotted by the USSR and other Eastern Bloc states). Quoted in the *Guardian*, 29 December 1984.

Cricket can be a bridge and a glue ... Cricket for peace is my mission.

Mohammed Zia ul-Haq (1924–88), Pakistani soldier and president.

Cricket shouldn't be used as a political football.

David Graveney (1953–), English cricket administrator.

The Conservatives played like English cricketers – too many rash strokes and run-outs, dropped catches and bowling anywhere but the stumps.

Norman Tebbit (1931–), British politician, speaking in the wake of disappointing Conservative results in the 1989 European elections.

In my day, governments required the occasional use of the handbag. Now it will doubtless be the cricket bat and that will be a good thing because it will doubtless be harder.

Margaret Thatcher (1925–), British Conservative prime minister.
Referring in 1991 to the love of cricket of John Major, her successor
as prime minister.

There are some remarkable parallels between basketball and politics. Michael Jordan has already mastered the skill needed for political success: how to stay aloft without visible means of support.

Margaret Thatcher (1925–), British Conservative prime minister,
referring to US basketball player Michael Jordan in 1992.

Seb Coe is a Yorkshireman. So he's a complete bastard and will do well in politics.

Daley Thompson (1958–), British decathlete, commenting upon
fellow-athlete Sebastian Coe's switch to a political career as a
Conservative in 1993.

Cricket speaks in languages far beyond that of politicians.

Nelson Mandela (1918–), South African president, greeting the
England cricket team at Soweto in 1995.

See also GOLF; MARYLEBONE CRICKET CLUB (MCC); TWICKENHAM; YORKSHIRE COUNTY CRICKET CLUB.

Polo

Let other people play at other things,
The King of Games is still the Game of Kings.

J.K. Stephen (1859–92), British journalist.

Sex – the poor man's polo.

Clifford Odets (1906–63), US playwright.

Playing polo is like trying to play golf during an earthquake.

Sylvester Stallone (1946–), US film actor, 1990.

See also WATER POLO.

Powerboat racing

There is no hope of bailing out of a speedboat racer.

Donald Campbell (1921–67), British land and water speed record-breaker. He was himself killed in his boat *Bluebird* during an attempt on the water speed record on Lake Coniston. Quoted in Douglas Young-James, *Donald Campbell: An Informal Biography* (1968).

The boats are streamlined, advertisement-spattered, potential coffins, and are controlled on a knife-edge balance of courage and sense.

Simon Barnes (1951–), British sportswriter. *The Times*, 27 August 1985.

Driving a powerboat is a bit like having one person throw a bucket of water over you while another hits you with a baseball bat.

Steve Curtis (1964–), British powerboat racer, 1989.

Predictions

Here I predict Sonny Liston's dismemberment, I'll hit him so hard, he'll forget where October–November went.

Muhammad Ali (Cassius Clay; 1942–), US heavyweight boxer. Speaking before his historic bout with Sonny Liston in 1964, in which he achieved a notable victory.

I figure I'll be champ for about ten years and then I'll let my brother take over – like the Kennedys down in Washington.

Muhammad Ali (Cassius Clay; 1942–), US heavyweight boxer, on becoming world heavyweight champion in 1964. In fact he was underestimating his own stamina: he became champion for the third and final time in 1978 and remained champion until 1980, a full 16 years later.

Listen to them moan, but those people will be going mad if we beat West Germany by a goal in the World Cup Final.

Sir Alf Ramsey (1922–99), English footballer and manager. He was referring to the sports press early in 1966, following a defeat at the hands of West Germany, a few months before his England squad successfully fulfilled his prediction. Quoted in Bryon Butler, *The Official History of the Football Association* (1986).

Unless something happens that we can't predict, I don't think a lot will happen.

Fred Trueman (1931–), English cricketer. Match commentary.

Everyone keeps asking me, 'Are you going to win?' How on earth do you know if you're going to win or not?

Lester Piggott (1935–), British jockey.

I'm not going to make a prediction – it could go either way.

Ron Atkinson (1939–), English football manager. ITV football
broadcast

Well, either side could win it, or it could be a draw.

Ron Atkinson (1939–), English football manager. Football match
commentary.

I'm not going to predict what I'm gonna do, but I'm gonna come out of there the winner.

Frank Bruno (1961–), British heavyweight boxer.

Well, I think Arsenal will either win or lose the championship this year.

Graham Taylor (1944–), English football manager.

I wouldn't be at all surprised if there's a shock result this afternoon.

John Grieg, English rugby commentator.

I never predict anything and I never will do.

Paul Gascoigne (1967–), English footballer.

People expect, because I can spin a cricket ball, I know who will win next year's AFL pennant, who'll win next year's Melbourne Cup and what the solutions to the Middle East and Indonesian crises are. I'm just a humble cricketer with no claims to omniscience or omnipotence.

Shane Warne (1969–), Australian cricketer. 'Quotes of the Year',
the *Guardian*, 24 December 1998.

See also FAMOUS LAST WORDS; HORSERACING; INCOMPETENCE.

The Press

There isn't anything on earth as depressing as an old sportswriter.

Ring Lardner (1885–1933), US humorist and writer.

I once thought of becoming a political cartoonist because they only have to come up with one idea a day. Then I thought I'd become a sportswriter instead, because they don't have to come with any.

Sam Snead (1912–), US golfer.

The popular assumption that professional boxers do not have brains comes from sportswriters, but then sportswriters' brains are themselves damaged by the obligation to be clever every day. And the quantities of booze necessary to lubricate such racing of the mental gears ends up giving sportswriters the equivalent of a good many punches to the head.

Norman Mailer (1923–), US novelist.

What's the difference between a three-week-old puppy and a sportswriter? In six weeks, the puppy stops whining.

Mike Ditka (1939–), American football coach.

I always turn to the sports section first. The sports page records people's accomplishments; the front page has nothing but man's failures.

Earl Warren (1891–1974), US chief justice. Quoted in 'Scorecard',
Sports Illustrated, 22 July 1968.

A legend in his own lunchtime.

Christopher Wordsworth (1914–), British journalist and
critic, referring to sports journalist Clifford Makins (1924–90)
in 1976, allegedly the first instance of the phrase. Also
attributed to comic writer David Climie, referring to the BBC's
Dennis Main Wilson.

The press are gin-swilling, beer-swilling slobs.

Joe Bugner (1950–), Hungarian-born heavyweight boxer.

They smile and then they stab – and they think the next time they come along for a comment you are going to forget the wounding things they write and obligingly talk to them.

Geoffrey Boycott (1940–), English cricketer. *Put to the Test* (1979).

A lot of people in football don't have much time for the press; they say they're amateurs. But I say to those people, 'Noah was an amateur, but the *Titanic* was built by professionals!'

Malcolm Allison (1927–), English football manager, 1980.

I've always said there's a place for the press but they haven't dug it yet.

Tommy Docherty (1928–), Scottish football manager, 1980.

The capacity of sporting journalists to wax lyrical in the face of the exceptional is matched only by the speed with which they run out of adjectives in doing so.

Derek Malcolm (1932–), British journalist, in the *Guardian*.

In other sports, the lateral euphemism is still in its infancy (at Wimbledon, for example, they have only just realised that 'perfectionist' can be used to represent 'extremely bad-tempered'). In soccer, the form of the encoded adjective is well developed. 'Tenacious', for example, always means 'small'.

Julian Barnes (1946–), British novelist, in the *Observer*,
4 July 1982.

Not only do they know nothing about football, but if you were to shut them up in a room by themselves, they couldn't even write a letter to mother.

Cesar Menotti (1938–), Argentinian football manager, referring to
Argentinian sports journalists. Quoted in 'Inside Track', the *Sunday
Times*, 22 August 1982.

Sure I know where the press room is – I just look for where they throw the dog meat.

Martina Navratilova (1956–), Czech-born US tennis player, 1983.

I am here to propose a toast to the sports writers. It's up to you whether you stand up or not.

Fred Trueman (1931–), English cricketer, giving a speech
at a sportswriters' dinner. Quoted in Michael Parkinson, *Sporting
Lives* (1993).

Sports-writers are probably the only individuals in our universe who actually have less constructive jobs than I do. I don't do nothing but hit people. And they don't do nothing but talk about what I do.

Randall 'Tex' Cobb (1950–), US heavyweight boxer and actor.

I would like to thank the press from the heart of my bottom.

Nick Faldo (1957–), British golfer. Said after winning the British
Open championship in 1992.

I am not talking to anyone in the British media – they are all pricks.

Allan Border (1955–), Australian cricketer, on tour in England in 1993.

He mistrusts anyone who reads past the sports pages of the tabloids.

Peter Roebuck (1956–), English cricketer, referring to the England
cricket team manager Mickey Stewart. Quoted in Ned Sherrin, *Ned
Sherrin in his Anecdotage* (1993).

I don't kick dressing-room doors, or the cat – or even journalists.

Arsène Wenger (1949–), French football manager, speaking as
manager of Arsenal in 1997.

I did it with the hand of reason.

Diego Maradona (1960–), Argentinian footballer. Quoted in
January 2000 after smashing the car window of a press
photographer's car – a reference to his famous 'hand of God'
quotation of some years before.

See also Eric CANTONA; Brian CLOUGH.

Professionalism

To think of playing cricket for hard cash! Money and gentility would ruin
any pastime under the sun.

Mary Russell Mitford (1787–1855), British novelist and playwright.
Letter to R.B. Haydon, 24 August 1823.

It is all very well to say that a man should play for the pure love of the
game. Perhaps he ought, but to the working man it is impossible.

J. J. Bentley, British football administrator.

The Nemesis of excess in athletics is professionalism, which is the death of
all true sport.

E.N. Gardiner (1864–1930), British historian, 1930.

Pray God no professional may ever captain England.

Lord Hawke (1860–1938), English cricketer. The first professional to
captain England was Sir Len Hutton, who took on the role in 1952.

Some people tell me that we professional players are soccer slaves. Well, if
this is slavery, give me a life sentence.

Sir Bobby Charlton (1937–), English footballer, 1960.

I'd kick my own brother if necessary. That's what being a professional is
all about.

Steve McMahon (1961–), English footballer, 1988.

My objective is to be the ultimate professional. Regardless of whatever
happens, the job has to be done. That's what being a professional is.

Mike Tyson (1966–), US heavyweight boxer. Quoted in the *New
York Times*, 28 June 1988.

I know we're meant to be these hard-headed, money-obsessed professionals
but we're still little boys at heart. Just ask our wives.

Rob Lee (1966–), English footballer, speaking as a midfielder with
Newcastle United and England in 1998.

See also AMATEURS; Sir Jack HOBBS; MONEY.

Alain PROST

**French racing driver (1955–) who won a record 51
Formula One victories from 199 starts, making him the
most successful driver in the history of the sport.**

I am indeed a believer, but at the start of a Grand Prix, with 156 litres of
fuel behind me, I don't entirely rely on God. I rely on Prost to negotiate the
first corner and the rest of it.

Discussing his religious beliefs.

When I drove for British teams ... they called me 'The Tadpole' because I
was too small to be a frog.

Reflecting upon his diminutive stature on being awarded an OBE by
the British government in 1994.

Race

The Americans ought to be ashamed of themselves for letting their medals be won by Negroes. I myself would never even shake hands with one of them.

Adolf Hitler (1889–1945), German dictator. Said during the 1936
Berlin Olympics. US athlete Jesse Owens, when he heard this,
responded 'I didn't come to Berlin to shake hands anyway.'

England is not ruined because sinewy brown men from a distant colony sometimes hit a ball further and oftener than our men do.

J.B. Priestley (1894–1984), British novelist and playwright, referring
to the success against England enjoyed by cricket teams from the
West Indies and elsewhere.

If I do something good then I am an American, but if I do something bad then I am a Negro!

Tommie Smith (1944–), US sprinter. Quoted in Christopher Brasher,
Mexico 1968: A Diary of the XIXth Olympiad (1968).

It's hard being black. You ever been black? I was black once – when I was poor.

Larry Holmes (1949–), US heavyweight boxer.

I strongly believe the black culture spends too much time, energy and effort raising, praising, and teasing our black children about the dubious glories of professional sports.

Arthur Ashe (1943–93), US tennis player.

Martin Luther King took us to the mountain top; I want to take us to the bank.

Don King (1932–), US boxing promoter. Referring to the black civil rights campaign led by Martin Luther King in the 1960s, specifically to a speech made by King on the day before he was assassinated in 1968, in which he spoke the words: 'I've been to the mountain top. I've looked over, and I've seen the promised land.'

An excellent player, but he does have a black side.

Gary Lineker (1960–), English fooballer and commentator, referring to Arsenal's black star Ian Wright.

Racing drivers *See* Juan Manuel FANGIO; Stirling MOSS; Alain PROST; Michael SCHUMACHER; Ayrton SENNA.

Radio

Radio football is football reduced to its lowest common denominator. Shorn of the game's aesthetic pleasures, or the comfort of a crowd that feels the same way as you, or the sense of security that you get when you see that your defenders and goalkeeper are more or less where they should be, all that is left is naked fear.

Nick Hornby (1957–), British writer and novelist. *Fever Pitch* (1992).

Did you see me on the radio?

Tony Dobbin (1976–), Irish jockey. Said in 1994, after winning a race at Cheltenham.

See also CLASSIC COMMENTARIES; COMMENTATING; COMMENTATORS.

Sir Alf RAMSEY

English footballer and football manager (1920–99) whose England squad captured the World Cup in 1966. Ramsey's achievement earned him a knighthood and the enduring gratitude of a hitherto sceptical nation.

Ramsey – tha's as much use as a chocolate teapot.

Anonymous Southampton fan, hailing Ramsey from the terraces during the latter's playing days in the 1940s.

As a manager, Alf Ramsey is like a good chicken farmer. If a hen doesn't lay, a good chicken farmer wrings its neck.

Jackie Milburn (1924–88), English footballer.

See also CLICHÉS; Diego MARADONA; PEP TALKS; PREDICTIONS.

Red Rum

**English racehorse (1965–95), winner of three Grand
Nationals.**

The greatest thing on four hooves since Pegasus.

Jean Rook (1932–91), British newspaper columnist.

Red Rum is in a stable condition.

News report of an illness suffered by Red Rum, BBC Radio 5, 1992.

Referees and umpires

When I'm right, no one remembers.
When I am wrong, no one forgets.

Larry Goetz (1900–62), US baseball umpire, 1955.

Ideally, the umpire should combine the integrity of a Supreme Court Justice, the physical agility of an acrobat, the endurance of Job and the imperturbability of Buddha.

Time magazine, referring to baseball umpires specifically.

It don't matter as long as he can count up to ten.

Sonny Liston (1932–71), US heavyweight boxer, when asked for his
views about the choice of referee for a forthcoming bout.

Trying to maintain order during a legalised gang brawl involving 80 toughs with a little whistle, a hanky and a ton of prayer.

Anonymous American football referee, defining his role.

The trouble with referees is that they just don't care which side wins.

Tom Canterbury, US basketball player. 'Sports Quotes of the Year',
the *Guardian*, 24 December 1980.

An umpire in Australia undoubtedly needs to be deaf – in both ears.

Patrick Rowley, British sportswriter, referring to hockey umpires.
World Hockey, December 1981.

I sometimes get birthday cards from fans. But it's often the same message – they hope it's my last.

Al Norman, US baseball umpire.

I can see the sun okay, and that's 93 million miles away.

Bruce Froemming (1939–), US baseball umpire. His response when
doubts were cast about his eyesight, 1987.

I wanted to have a career in sports when I was young, but I had to give it up. I'm only six feet tall, so I couldn't play basketball. I'm only 190 pounds, so I couldn't play football. And I have 20–20 vision, so I couldn't be a referee.

Jay Leno (1950–), US comedian.

See also CRICKET UMPIRES; FOOTBALL REFEREES.

Religion and Sport

Glorify God in your body.

The *Bible*, 1 Corinthians 6:20.

Sport, rightly conceived, is an occupation carried out by the whole man. It renders the body a more perfect instrument of the soul and at the same time makes the soul itself a finer instrument of the whole man in seeking for Truth and in transmitting it to others. In this way it helps a man to reach that End to which all other ends are subordinate, the service and the greater glory of His Creator.

Pope Pius XII (Eugenio Pacelli; 1876–1958), Italian-born prelate.
Speech at the Central School of Sports of the USA, 29 July 1945.

It is hard to tell where the MCC ends and the Church of England begins.

J.B. Priestley (1894–1984), British novelist and playwright. Quoted
in the *New Statesman*, 20 July 1962.

Baseball is like church. Many attend. Few understand.

Leo Durocher (1906–91), US baseball manager.

If you call on God to improve the results of a shot while it is still in motion, you are using 'an outside agency' and subject to appropriate penalties under the rules of golf.

Henry Longhurst (1909–79), British golf broadcaster and writer.

I never pray on a golf course. Actually, the Lord answers my prayers everywhere except on the course.

Billy Graham (1918–), US evangelist.

Jesus saves! But Pearson nets the rebound.

Banner waved by fans at the 1977 FA Cup Final, referring to
Manchester United star Stuart Pearson (but also applied
subsequently to many other players).

Well, that kind of puts the damper on even a Yankee win!

Phil Rizzuto (1918–), US baseball commentator. Picking up the
match commentary after breaking off to announce the death of
Pope Paul VI in 1978.

I believe in the Church of Baseball. I tried all the major religions and most of the minor ones. I've worshipped Buddha, Allah, Brahma, Vishnu, Siva, trees, mushrooms and Isadora Duncan. I know things. For instance: there are 108 beads in a Catholic rosary and there are 108 stitches in a baseball. When I learned that, I gave Jesus a chance.

Ron Shelton (1945–), US film director and scriptwriter. The opening
words of the baseball film *Bull Durham* (1988).

Prayers for Garston-based Sunday league football team urgently wanted.

Notice, *Liverpool Merseymart.*

The Saudis would struggle in Europe because of that problem with those prayers five times a day. You don't know if they're going to turn up for training. I'm being serious.

Don Howe (1935–), English football manager.

We look forward to Saturdays all week long. It's the most meaningful thing in our lives. It's a religion, really. That's how important it is to us. Saturday is our day of worship.

Anonymous Manchester United fan. Quoted in Bill Buford, *Among
the Thugs* (1991).

God created me to delight people with my goals.

Romario (1966–), Brazilian footballer, 1994.

God is a Bulgarian.

Hristo Stoichkov (1967–), Bulgarian footballer, greeting victory
against Mexico in the 1994 World Cup. When the Bulgarian side
subsequently lost against Italy, Stoichkov was moved to remark 'God
is still a Bulgarian, but the referee was French.'

I don't want players who need a shoulder to cry on.

Ray Illingworth (1932–), English cricketer and cricket administrator,
explaining in 1994 why, as chairman of the England selectors, he
had decided to dispense with the traditional team chaplain.

What's it like being in Bethlehem, the place where Christmas began?
I suppose it's like seeing Ian Wright at Arsenal ...

Simon Fanshawe, British disc jockey. Talk Radio.

It was not me making those saves, it was God.

Claudio Taffarel (1966–), Brazilian goalkeeper, referring to
sensational saves he made during his country's 1998 World Cup
campaign. 'Quotes of the Year', the *Guardian*, 24 December 1998.

See also Glenn HODDLE; Diego MARADONA; Alain PROST; SUNDAY SPORT.

Results

Win some, lose some.

Proverb.

In play there are two pleasures for your choosing;
The one is in the winning and the other the losing.

Lord Byron (1788–1824), British poet.

The game is never lost till won.

George Crabbe (1754–1832), British poet.

Every time you win, you're reborn. When you lose, you die a little.

George Allen (1922–90), American football coach.

See also DEFEAT; SCORELINES; VICTORY.

Retirement

When a jockey retires, he becomes just another little man.

Eddie Arcaro (1916–97), US jockey.

You always say, 'I'll quit when I start to slide.' Then, one morning, you wake up and you've slid.

Sugar Ray Robinson (1920–89), US welterweight and middleweight boxer.

Since I've retired, I eat less, weigh less, train less and care less.

Ray Mancini (1961–), US lightweight boxer.

You can only milk a cow so long, then you're left holding the pail.

Henry 'Hank' Aaron (1934–), US baseball player, on his retirement.

When you get to a certain age, there is no coming back. I've decided to pick my moment to quit very carefully – in about 200 years time.

Brian Clough (1935–), English football manager, 1991.

I thought I would have a quiet pint ... followed by about 17 noisy ones.

Gareth Chilcott (1956–), English rugby player, discussing the celebrations planned for his retirement from Bath RFC in 1993.

I would like to retire with my brains still intact.

Herol 'Bomber' Graham (1959–), British middleweight boxer.

I've had it. If anyone sees me near a boat they can shoot me.

Steve Redgrave (1962–), British rower. Speaking after winning a fifth Olympic gold medal at the Atlanta Olympics in 1996.

If I am fortunate enough to win next year, I will keep my mouth shut.

Steve Redgrave (1962–), British rower. Speaking in 1999 after starting training for the 2000 Olympics in Sydney. *The Times*, 31 December 1999.

I'm going to leave it to the new generation, to the crash-it-up robots that dominate the game.

David Campese (1962–), Australian rugby union player, on his retirement in 1999.

See also COMEBACKS.

Viv RICHARDS

Powerful West Indian cricketer (1952–) whose feats as a batsman included hitting over 8000 runs in Test match cricket, including the fastest-ever Test match century.

Batting for Vivian Richards is a matter of strokes, more strokes, and even more strokes.

John Arlott (1914–91), English cricket writer and commentator.
'Vivian Richards', *John Arlott's Book of Cricketers* (1979).

When you're an off-spinner there's not much point glaring at a batsman. If I glared at Vivian Richards he'd just hit me even further.

David Acfield (1947–), English cricketer and television sports commentator, 1982.

His game embraced a contempt for his fate, a foaming fury, because to him, cricket was a game of kill or be killed, a street fight in which it was left to the umpires to keep peace.

Peter Roebuck (1956–), English cricketer, 1993.

To see him take the field was to hear the beat of drums and to picture an African potentate, all chains and infernal eye, swaggering to the throne. His was a grand entrance, delayed and poised, one that said, 'See how far the little boy from a tiny island has risen, see he cannot be blown away.'

Peter Roebuck (1956–), English cricketer, 1993.

Sugar Ray ROBINSON

US welterweight and middleweight boxer (Walker Smith; 1920–89) who held world titles at both weights.

This Robinson is as sweet as sugar.

Jack Case (1918–70), US writer, referring to Sugar Ray Robinson early in his career – the origin of his nickname 'Sugar'.

I fought Sugar so many times that I'm lucky I didn't get diabetes.

Jake LaMotta (1922–), US middleweight boxer, referring to the regularity with which the two met in the ring.

See also INCOMPETENCE; RETIREMENT; VIOLENCE.

Rodeo

Rodeoing is about the only sport you can't fix. You'd have to talk to the bulls and the horses, and they wouldn't understand you.

Bill Linderman (1922–61), US rodeo champion, 1961.

Roller skating

I have recently taken up two new sports: roller skating and ankle spraining, in that order. I am getting quite good at both.

Miles Kington (1941–), British humorist. 'The Perils of Roller Skating'.

RONALDO

Brazilian footballer (1976–) who was hailed as the best player of his generation in the late 1990s.

Quotes about Ronaldo

He has the brain of a refrigerator.

Brian Moore (1932–), British football commentator, 1998.

The simplest solution is to stop the ball getting to Ronaldo in the first place. If the ball does get to him, we have to make sure he has no space to turn or knock the ball into. And if that doesn't work, we'll have to tie his shoelaces together.

John Collins (1968–), Scottish footballer, detailing Scotland's plans to contain Ronaldo before the two countries met in the 1998 World Cup tournament.

Quotes by Ronaldo

I'm not a phenomenon, just a 21-year-old footballer who still has a lot to learn.

Attempting to defuse excitable press comment about his abilities during the 1998 World Cup finals.

We lost the World Cup but I won another cup: my life.

Explaining to the press how his appearance in the 1998 World Cup final against France, which Brazil lost, had nearly been prevented by a fit he suffered just before the match. 'Quotes of the Year', the *Guardian*, 24 December 1998.

Rowing

Jolly boating weather,
And a hay harvest breeze,
Blade on the feather,
Shade off the trees.
Swing, swing together
With your body between your knees.

W.J. Cory (1823–92), British schoolmaster and poet. 'Eton Boating
Song' (1865).

All rowed fast but none so fast as stroke.

Ouida (Marie Louise de la Ramée; 1838–1908), British novelist.
Often repeated among rowers, who know full well that an oarsman
who rows at a faster rate then the rest of the crew will inevitably
cause chaos in the boat.

His blade struck the water a full second before any other: the lad had started
well. Nor did he flag as the race wore on ... as the boats began to near the
winning-post, his oar was dipping into the water *twice* as often as any other.

Captain F.T. Desmond Coke (1879–1931), British novelist. *Sandford
of Merton* (1903).

Believe me, my young friend, there is nothing – absolutely nothing – half so
much worth doing as simply messing about in boats.

Kenneth Grahame (1859–1932), Scottish writer. *The Wind in the Willows* (1908).

Eight minds with but a single thought – if that!

Sir Max Beerbohm (1872–1956), British writer, referring to a rowing eight.

See also BOAT RACE; HENLEY; RETIREMENT.

Rugby league

Rugby league is war without the frills.

Anonymous.

To play Rugby League you need three things; a good pass, a good tackle and
a good excuse.

Anonymous.

In south-west Lancashire, babes don't toddle, they side-step. Queuing women talk of 'nipping round the blindside'. Rugby league provides our cultural adrenalin. It's a physical manifestation of our rules of life, comradeship, honest endeavour, and a staunch, often ponderous allegiance to fair play.

Colin Welland (1934–), British actor and playwright, 1979.

Anyone who does not watch rugby league is not a real person. He's a cow's hoof, an ethnic or comes from Melbourne.

John Singleton, Australian businessman. *Australian* (1981).

Rugby league vs rugby union

League is much, much more physical than Union, and that's before anyone starts breaking the rules.

Adrian Hadley (1964–), Welsh rugby player with experience of both codes, 1988.

I'm 49, I've had a brain haemorrhage and a triple bypass and I could still go out and play a reasonable game of rugby union. But I wouldn't last 30 seconds in rugby league.

Graham Lowe, New Zealand rugby league coach, 1995.

Rugby union

This stone commemorates the exploit of William Webb Ellis, who, with a fine disregard for the rules of football as played in his time, first took the ball in his arms and ran with it, thus originating the distinctive feature of the Rugby game. AD 1823.

Commemorative plaque at Rugby school.

A game for ruffians enjoyed by gentlemen.

Anonymous. 19th century.

The game is so full of plot-interest and drama.

C.B. Fry (1872–1956), English cricketer, footballer and athlete.
Quoted in E.H.D. Sewell, *Rugger: The Man's Game* (1950).

Rugby football is a game I can't claim absolutely to understand in all its niceties, if you know what I mean. I can follow the broad, general principles, of course. I mean to say, I know that the main scheme is to work the ball down the field somehow and deposit it over the line at the other end and that, in order to squalch this programme, each side is allowed to put in a certain amount of assault and battery and do things to its fellow-man which, if done elsewhere, would result in fourteen days without the option, coupled with some strong remarks from the Bench.

P.G. Wodehouse (1881–1975), British comic novelist. *Very Good,*
Jeeves (1930).

The women sit, getting colder and colder, on a seat getting harder and harder, watching oafs, getting muddier and muddier.

Virginia Graham (1914–), US writer and commentator, referring to
the 'muddied oafs' image conjured up by Rudyard Kipling in his
poem 'The Islanders' (1903).

Rugby may have many problems, but the gravest is undoubtedly that of the persistence of summer.

Chris Laidlaw, New Zealand rugby player and sportswriter. *Mud in Your*
Eye: A Worm's Eye View of the Changing World of Rugby (1973).

A game played by fewer than fifteen a side, at least half of whom should be totally unfit.

Michael Green (1927–), British humorist. *The Art of Coarse Rugby* (1975).

In 1823, William Webb Ellis first picked up the ball in his arms and ran with it. And for the next 156 years forwards have been trying to work out why.

Sir Tasker Watkins (1918–), British judge, 1979.

The whole point of rugby is that it is, first and foremost, a state of mind, a spirit.

Jean-Pierre Rives (1952–), French rugby player.

A major rugby tour by the British Isles to New Zealand is a cross between a medieval crusade and a prep school outing.

John Hopkins (1945–), British sportswriter.

See also ALCOHOL; ALL-BLACKS; BITING; RULES; TACTICS; WELSH RUGBY.

Rules

The man that has no friend at court,
Must make the laws confine his sport,
But he that has, by dint of flaws,
May make his sport confine the laws.

Thomas Chatterton (1752–70), British poet.

What happens when a game of football is proposed at Christmas among a
party of your men assembled from different schools? Alas! ... The Eton man
is enamoured of his own rules, and turns up his nose at Rugby as not
sufficiently aristocratic; while the Rugbeian retorts that 'bullying' and
'sneaking' are not to his taste, and he is not afraid of his shins, or of a 'maul'
or 'scrimmage'. On hearing this the Harrovian pricks up his ears, and
though he might previously have sided with Rugby, the insinuation against
the courage of those who do not allow 'shinning' arouses his ire, and causes
him to refuse to lay with one who has offered it. Thus it is found impossible
to get up a game.

Editorial, *The Field*, 1861, reflecting the confused state of affairs that
existed in the years before rugby and football emerged as separate
disciplines.

Cricket is a game full of forlorn hopes and sudden dramatic changes of
fortune and its rules are so ill-defined that their interpretation is partly an
ethical business.

George Orwell (1903–50), British novelist. *Raffles and Miss Blandish*
(1944).

Laws may come and Laws may go, but the game goes on for ever.

Admiral Sir Percy Royds (1874–1955). *The History of the Laws of
Rugby Football* (1949).

Use every weapon within the rules and stretch the rules to breaking point,
I say.

Fred Trueman (1931–), English cricketer. *Fast Fury* (1961).

The laws of cricket tell of the English love of compromise between a
particular freedom and a general orderliness, or legality.

Sir Neville Cardus (1889–1975), British journalist and writer. Quoted
in Sir Rupert Hart-Davis, *Cardus on Cricket* (1977).

The advantage law is the best law in rugby, because it lets you ignore all the others for the good of the game.

Derek Robinson (1932–), British sportswriter, 1969.

Golf is the only game in which a precise knowledge of the rules can earn one a reputation for bad sportsmanship.

Patrick Campbell (1913–80), British writer.

To hell with the Queen of Marksbury.

Pierre Bouchard (1948–), Canadian ice-hockey player, dismissing the boxing code as stipulated by the Marquis of Queensberry, 1972.

The rules of soccer are very simple, basically it is this: if it moves, kick it. If it doesn't move, kick it until it does.

Phil Woosnam (1932–), English footballer, 1974.

There is, I believe, a time limit for playing a shot. But I think it's true to say that nobody knows what that limit is.

Ted Lowe (1920–), British television snooker commentator.
Extract of snooker commentary.

I think you enjoy the game more if you don't know the rules. Anyway you're on the same wavelength as the referees.

Jonathan Davies (1962–), Welsh rugby player, referring to rugby union referees on A Question of Sport, BBC TV, 1995.

Runners-up

No one remembers who came second.

Walter Hagen (1892–1969), US golfer.

Hell, it ain't like losing a leg!

Billy Joe Patton (1922–), US golfer, refusing to be downhearted upon narrowly losing the Masters at Augusta in 1954.

I cannot remember anyone ever asking 'Who came second?' Can you?

Ray Reardon (1932–), Welsh snooker player.

I am absolutely delighted to have come second. Who cares about winning when you can be second? I love being runner-up.

Tom Weiskopf (1942–), US golfer, 1978.

Yes, we've had bad times at Anfield; one year we came second.

Bob Paisley (1919–96), English football manager.

I feel like I want my mummy.

Bobby George (1945–), British darts player, after finishing runner-up in the World Darts Championship.

See also DEFEAT.

Running

The race is not to the swift, nor the battle to the strong.

The *Bible*, Ecclesiastes 9:11. The quotation was reworked in the late 1990s as a slogan for Nike running shoes: 'The race is not always to the swift, but to those who keep on running.'

Know ye not that they which run in a race run all, but one receiveth the prize? So run, that ye may obtain.

The *Bible*, 1 Corinthians 9:24.

Why dost thou run so many miles about?

William Shakespeare (1564–1616), English playwright and poet. *Richard III* (c.1592).

Where run'st thou so fast?

William Shakespeare (1564–1616), English playwright and poet. *The Comedy of Errors* (c.1594).

Faith, I ran when I saw others run.

William Shakespeare (1564–1616), English playwright and poet. *Henry IV Part I* (c.1596).

Now, *here*, you see, it takes all the running *you* can do, to keep in the same place. If you want to get somewhere else, you must run at least twice as fast as that.

Lewis Carroll (C.L. Dodgson; 1832–98), British writer. *Through the Looking-Glass and What Alice Found There* (1872).

One of the foulest cross-country runs that ever occurred outside Dante's *Inferno*.

P.G. Wodehouse (1881–1975), British comic novelist. *Psmith, Journalist* (1915).

Long-distance running is particularly good training in perseverance.

Mao Zedong (1893–1976), Chinese political leader and Marxist theorist, 1918.

Only think of two things – the gun and the tape. When you hear the one, just run like hell until you break the other.

Sam Mussabini (1867–1927), British athletics coach: advice to runners.

The mile has all the elements of drama.

Sir Roger Bannister (1929–), British middle-distance runner.

The Loneliness of the Long Distance Runner.

Alan Sillitoe (1928–), British novelist. Book title (1962).

Finland has produced so many brilliant distance runners because back home it costs $2.50 a gallon for gas.

Esa Tikkannen (1965–), Finnish hockey player, 1979.

Chariots of Fire.

Title of a film (1981), depicting the experiences of the British runners Harold Abrahams and Eric Liddell in the 1924 Olympics. The words came originally from William Blake's poem 'Milton', best known in the form of the hymn 'Jerusalem'. 'Chariots' is also a punning nickname of the rugby league and union wing Martin Offiah (1966–).

Running is the greatest metaphor for life, because you get out of it what you put into it.

Oprah Winfrey (1954–), US television chat show host.

If you make one mistake, it can result in a vasectomy.

Mark Rowland (1963–), British steeplechaser, on the perils of his chosen type of race.

See also AGE; Sir Roger BANNISTER; DECATHLON; DRUG-TAKING; JOGGING; Ben JOHNSON; MARATHON; MONEY; ORIENTEERING; Jesse OWENS; POLITICS.

Babe RUTH

US baseball player (George Herman Ruth; 1895–1948)
whose records included 60 home runs in a season (1927)
and a career total of 714 home runs.

Quotes about Babe Ruth

Who is this 'Babe' Ruth? And what does she do?

George Bernard Shaw (1856–1950), Irish playwright and critic.

The door opened and it was God himself who walked into the room,
straight from his glittering throne, God dressed in a camel's hair polo coat
and flat camel's hair cap. God with a flat nose and little piggy eyes, a big
grin, and fat cigar, sticking out of the side of it.

Paul Gallico (1897–1976), US journalist, novelist and short-story
writer, describing Babe Ruth.

He once asked me if Beirut was named after that famous baseball player
who hit home runs.

Brother Ray Page, US educator. Recalling Sacramento Kings star
Bobby Hurley's days at St Anthony High School, Jersey City, where
he was his teacher.

Quotes by Babe Ruth

I guess I just liked the game.

His response when asked the secret of his success.

See also TEAM SPIRIT; TECHNIQUE.

·S·

Sailing *See* YACHTING.

St Andrews

**The birthplace, in the Fife region of eastern Scotland, of
modern competitive golf.**

Until you play it, St Andrews looks like the sort of real estate you couldn't
give away.
Sam Snead (1912–), US golfer.

When it blows here, even the seagulls walk.
Nick Faldo (1957–), British golfer.

Pete SAMPRAS

**US tennis player (1971–), nicknamed 'Pistol Pete', who
dominated the men's game from the mid-1990s.**

Quotes about Pete Sampras

I think Pete Sampras has really reached his peak. About the only thing he
doesn't do is cook.
Michael Chang (1972–), US tennis player, 1994.

Quotes by Pete Sampras

I don't know how I do it, I really don't.

Quoted after a sensational performance against Andre Agassi, culminating in his sixth Wimbledon men's title. *The Times*, 31 December 1999.

School sports

I challenge all the men alive
To say they e'er were gladder,
Than boys all striving,
Who should kick most wind out of the bladder.

Charterhouse public school song, referring to football, 1794.

Follow up! Follow up! Follow up! Follow up! Follow up!
Till the field ring again and again,
With the tramp of the twenty-two men,
Follow up!

E.E. Bowen (1836–1901), British writer. 'Forty Years On', the Harrow school song.

College football is a sport that bears the same relation to education that bullfighting does to agriculture.

Elbert Hubbard (1856–1915), US writer.

The dread of beatings! Dread of being late!
And, greatest dread of all, the dread of games!

John Betjeman (1906–84), British poet. *Summoned by Bells* (1960).

Loyalty to the school to which your parents pay to send you seemed to me like feeling loyal to Selfridges: consequently I never cared in the least which team won, but only prayed for the game to be over without the ball ever coming my way.

John Mortimer (1923–), British playwright, novelist and barrister. *Clinging to the Wreckage* (1982).

All girls playing in the Wednesday hockey match will be pinned to the notice board.

Notice in a South African school.

Michael SCHUMACHER

German racing driver (1969–) who emerged as the dominant force in Formula One in the mid-1990s.

This is not a joke, nor a hoax, but confirmed information.

El Moudjahid Algerian government newspaper. Defending claims that Schumacher had been discovered to be in reality an Algerian named Farouk. 'Sports Quotes of the Year 1998', the *Daily Telegraph*, 28 December 1998.

Scorelines

We beat them five-nothing, and they were lucky to score nothing.

Anonymous.

We remember not the scores and the results in after years; it is the men who remain in our minds, in our imagination.

Sir Neville Cardus (1889–1975), British journalist and writer. *English Cricket* (1945).

There ought to be some other means of reckoning quality in this the best and loveliest of games; the scoreboard is an ass.

Sir Neville Cardus (1889–1975), British journalist and writer, referring specifically to cricket in *A Fourth Innings with Cardus* (1981).

In cricket, as in no other game, a great master may well go back to the pavilion scoreless ... In no other game does the law of averages get to work so potently, so mysteriously.

Sir Neville Cardus (1889–1975), British journalist and writer. *Cardus on the Ashes* (1989).

I never wanted to make a hundred. Who wants to make a hundred anyway? When I first went in, my immediate objective was to hit the ball to each of the four corners of the field. After that, I tried not to be repetitive.

Lord Learie Constantine (1902–71), West Indian cricketer.

For years I thought the club's name was Partick Thistle Nil.

Billy Connolly (1942–), Scottish comedian, referring to the Scottish football club Partick Thistle in 1980.

Rally points scoring is 20 for the fastest, 18 for the second fastest, right down to six points for the slowest fastest.

Murray Walker (1923–), British television motor racing commentator. BBC TV rally driving commentary, 1981.

I'm a firm believer that if you score one goal the other team have to score two to win.

Howard Wilkinson (1943–), English football manager.

Zero–zero is a big score.

Ron Atkinson (1939–), English football manager.

A triple bogey is three strokes more than par, four strokes more than par is a quadruple bogey, five more than par is a quintuple, six is a sextuple, seven is a throwuple, eight is a blowuple, and nine is a ohshutuple.

Henry Beard, US humorist. *Golfing* (1985).

See also CLASSIC COMMENTARIES; RESULTS.

Ayrton SENNA

Brazilian racing driver (1960–94) who won admiration for his great talent in Formula One, winning two world championships before his tragically early death in a crash at the 1994 San Marino Grand Prix at Imola.

Quotes about Ayrton Senna

Ayrton has this problem – he thinks that he can't kill himself.

Alain Prost (1955–), French racing driver, 1989.

Quotes by Ayrton Senna

The day it arrives, it will arrive. It could be today or 50 years later. The only sure thing is that it will arrive.

Quoted not long before his fatal crash.

It's going to be a season with lots of accidents, and I'll risk saying that we'll be lucky if something really serious doesn't happen.

Quoted at the start of his final season, 1994.

See also NERVES.

Sex

Being with a woman all night never hurt no professional baseball player. It's the staying up all night looking for one that does him in.

Charles 'Casey' Stengel (1891–1975), US baseball manager.

I got so many kisses after this goal, that they would have sufficed a modest woman for a lifetime.

Ferenc Puskas (1926–), Hungarian footballer, recalling the celebrations that followed his goal in the 1952 Olympic final.

Only the nose knows,
Where the nose goes,
When the door close.

Muhammad Ali (Cassius Clay; 1942–), US heavyweight boxer, declining to respond to press inquiries about his private life.

Of course a player can have sexual intercourse before a match and play a blinder. But if he did it for six months, he'd be a decrepit old man. It takes the strength from the body.

Bill Shankly (1919–81), Scottish football manager, 1971.

Cricket is like sex films – they relieve frustration and tension.

Linda Lovelace (1952–), US sex film actress, on a visit to Lord's in 1974.

Contrary to the old wives' tale that bloody-minded trainers put around, a little love-in before the main event can do you more good than a rub-down with *The Sporting Life*.

John Conteh (1951–), British light-heavyweight boxer.

Cornering is like bringing a woman to climax.

Jackie Stewart (1939–), Scottish racing driver.

I tend to believe that cricket is the greatest thing that God ever created on Earth ... certainly greater than sex although sex isn't too bad either. But everyone knows which comes first when it's a question of cricket or sex.

Harold Pinter (1930–), British playwright. Quoted in the *Observer*, 5 October 1980.

Women are for batsmen, beer is for bowlers. God help the all rounders!

Fred Trueman (1931–), English cricketer.

First love, second football. Maybe photo finish.

Giamperiero Masieri, Italian footballer: reponse when asked whether
sex or football was the most important thing in his life.

John Bond has blackened my name with his insinuations about the private
lives of football managers. Both my wives are upset.

Malcolm Allison (1927–), English football manager.

Don't forget, jeans are not allowed on match days or away trips. And if
you're going to get pissed or poke a girl, do it before midnight.

Mike Gatting (1957–), Middlesex and England cricketer. Part of his
team talk as Middlesex captain at the start of the 1983 cricket
season. Quoted in Simon Hughes, *A Lot of Hard Yakka* (1997).

I think it's a great idea to talk during sex, as long as it's about snooker.

Steve Davis (1957–), British snooker player, 1988.

Making love is like hitting a baseball. You just gotta relax and concentrate.

Susan Sarandon (1946–), US film actress, as the character Annie
Savoy in the baseball film *Bull Durham* (1988).

Cricket-playing nations are capable of only limited amounts of sexual
activity.

Letter published in the *Bangkok Post*, 1991.

If you want the secret of my success with women, then don't smoke, don't
take drugs and don't be too particular.

George Best (1946–), Northern Ireland footballer.

If you'd given me the choice of beating four men and smashing in a goal
from 30 yards against Liverpool or going to bed with Miss World, it would
have been a difficult choice. Luckily I had both. It's just that you do one of
those things in front of 50,000 people.

George Best (1946–), Northern Ireland footballer, 1991.

It's the boxers who attract the real women, after all, with their raw primeval
strength, beautifully toned bodies and just a touch of vulnerability.

Eamonn McCabe (1948–), British journalist. Quoted in the
Guardian/Elle Supplement, 9 January 1992.

Even though there is no question that sex is a nicer activity than watching football (no nil–nil draws, no offside trap, no cup upsets, *and* you're warm), in the normal run of things, the feelings it engenders are simply not as intense as those brought about by a one-in-a-lifetime last-minute Championship winner.

Nick Hornby (1957–), British writer and novelist. *Fever Pitch* (1992).

No sex before a race? That's a load of old cobblers. No one who knows jockeys could imagine them saying, 'Not tonight, darling, I am riding in the National tomorrow.'

Jenny Pitman (1946–), British racehorse trainer.

Football is a fertility festival. Eleven sperm trying to get into the egg. I feel sorry for the goalkeeper.

Björk (1965–), Icelandic pop singer, 1995.

After you've scored a goal it's just orgasmic ... if you asked me just after a game, I'd say it's better than sex, but if you asked me just after sex I'd say, 'forget it, mate.'

Trevor Sinclair (1973–), English footballer, 1997.

In my private life I do what I like. The night is my friend. If I don't go out, I don't score.

Romario (1966–), Brazilian footballer, responding in 1997 to attempts by the Valencia management to curb his active social life.

If it's true that men only prefer watching football to having sex because football lasts longer, then the answer lies in their own hands.

Mary Riddell, British journalist. *New Statesman*, 1997.

My soccer boots and an inflatable doll, because a month without a woman would be difficult.

Eric Deflandre (1973–), Belgian footballer, explaining what he would be taking with him to the World Cup finals in France in 1998. 'Sports Quotes of the Year 1998', the *Daily Telegraph*, 28 December 1998.

We have a game every three days. How can I be a good husband if I don't make love before each one?

Frank Leboeuf (1968–), French footballer, speaking as a Chelsea defender in *The Truth About Footballers*, ITV, 1998.

I love England, one reason being the magnificent breasts of English girls. Women are ultimately all that matters in life. Everything that we do is for them. We seek riches, power and glory all in order to make them happy.

Emmanuel Petit (1970–), French footballer. Quoted in 1998.

Football is a permanent orgasm.

Claude Le Roy (1948–), French football manager, speaking as coach of Cameroon in 1998.

I've won plenty of races after having sex.

Mario Cipollini (1967–), Italian cyclist, refuting suggestions that his eventful private life might spoil his performance in the Tour de France. *The Times*, 31 December 1999.

Football is like making love. You should not do it every night. If you make love every night you get bored. You should take your time and do it now and again, like watching football.

Gianluca Vialli (1964–), Italian footballer and football manager, 1999.

Sexism in sport

On the road to Olympia, there is a precipitous mountain with lofty cliffs; the mountain is called Typaeum. It is a law of Elis that any woman who is discovered at the Olympic Games will be pitched from this mountain.

Pausanias (2nd century AD), Greek geographer and historian. *Itinerary*.

Constitutionally and physically women are unfitted for golf. The first women's championship will be the last. They are bound to fall out and quarrel on the slightest, or no, provocation.

Horace G. Hutchinson (1859–1932), British golfer, 1893.

Let young girls ride, skate, dance and play lawn tennis and other games in moderation, but let them leave field sports and rough outdoor pastimes to those for whom they are naturally intended – men.

Badminton magazine, 1900.

Women have but one task, that of crowning the winner with garlands.

Pierre de Coubertin (1863–1937), French founder of the modern Olympic Games, 1902.

Riding as an exercise for women below forty-five years of age is to be condemned. Of the young married women who ride to hounds about sixty per cent are childless; and of the remainder few have more than one child. No girl over thirteen years of age should be allowed to ride much if at all, and then only at an amble. The reasons are obvious, but cannot be given in detail here.

James Cantlie (1851–1926), Scottish physician and writer.
Physical Efficiency (1906).

'After all, golf is only a game,' said Millicent. Women say these things without thinking. It does not mean that there is a kink in their character. They simply don't realise what they are saying.

P.G. Wodehouse (1881–1975), British comic novelist.
Order by Golf (1922).

Let us examine the proposition that women golfers are people. It requires an effort to adjust to this idea, for ever since the beheading of the first woman golfer, Mary Queen of Scots, the golf world has openly regretted that the practice didn't start a trend.

Peter Dobereiner (1925–), British sportswriter.

At Wimbledon, the ladies are simply the candles on the cake.

John Newcombe (1944–), Australian tennis player.

You should treat women the same way as any good Yorkshire batsman used to treat a cricket ball. Don't stroke 'em, don't tickle' em, just give 'em a ruddy good belt.

Fred Trueman (1931–), English cricketer.

The Ancient Greeks kept women athletes out of their games. They wouldn't even let them on the sidelines. I'm not sure but that they were right.

Avery Brundage (1887–1975), US sports administrator, 1972.

I am firmly against women riding in National Hunt races. I would deny them the equal right to cripple their limbs or disfigure their faces. Jump racing is as physically wrong for girls as boxing.

Dick Francis (1920–), British jockey and novelist, 1972.

Ladies playing cricket – absurd. Just like a man trying to knit.

Sir Len Hutton (1916–90), English cricketer.

Women should be in the kitchen, the discotheque and the boutique, but not in football.

Ron Atkinson (1939–), English football manager, 1989.

Women, by their nature, are not exceptional chess players: they are not great fighters.

Gary Kasparov (1963–), Russian chess player. Quoted in *The Times*, 9 October 1990.

Their bottoms are the wrong shape.

Lester Piggott (1935–), British jockey, dismissing the idea of women jockeys. Quoted in *The Guinness Book of Great Jockeys* (1992).

The only place for women in football is making the tea at half-time.

Rodney Marsh (1944–), English footballer, 1997.

Newcastle girls are all dogs. England is full of them.

Freddie Shepherd (1942–), English businessman and football executive, speaking as a director of Newcastle United. This unguarded comment in 1998 stirred up a storm of protest, forcing the club to apologize on behalf of Shepherd and another director, Douglas Hall. The club's new communications director tried to mend the damage, insisting 'I think North-East women are absolutely super.'

Women are a very fine species.

Colin Ingleby-McKenzie (1933–), English cricket administrator, responding, as president of the MCC, to the decision to admit women members. 'Quotes of the Year', the *Guardian*, 24 December 1998.

Even the Romans didn't put women gladiators into the Colosseum. They might have flung a few Christian women to the lions but they didn't make them fight one another.

Frank Maloney (1955–), British boxing promoter, voicing his opposition to women's boxing. 'Sporting Quotes of the Year 1998', the *Daily Telegraph*, 28 December 1998.

It's a bit greedy.

Tim Henman (1974–), British tennis player, responding to calls from women players that they should receive the same prize money as the men. 'Those Things They Said', the *Independent*, 31 December 1999.

See also Billie Jean KING; WOMEN IN SPORT.

Bill SHANKLY

Scottish footballer and manager (1919–81) renowned for his success with Liverpool, but also remembered for his oft-quoted 'Shanklyisms'.

Quotes about Bill Shankly

A man who even sees red in his dreams, and flies in imagination with the Liver bird.

Geoffrey Green (1911–), British sportswriter, alluding to Shankly's commitment to his team, red-shirted Liverpool (the Liver bird being an emblem of the city).

Bill Shankly – the man who put the 'er back into soccer.

Mike Ticher, British sportswriter. *When Saturday Comes*, 1986.

Quotes by Bill Shankly

Some people think football is a matter of life and death. I don't like that attitude. I can assure them it is much more serious than that.

'Sports Quotes of the Year', the *Guardian*, 24 December 1973.

This city has two great teams – Liverpool and Liverpool reserves.

Dismissing the claims, while Liverpool manager, of the city's other big club, Everton.

If Everton were playing down at the bottom of my garden, I'd draw the curtains.

Attributed.

When I've got nothing better to do, I look *down* the league table to see how Everton are getting along.

Attributed.

Me having no education, I had to use my brains.

Attributed.

If you're in the penalty area and aren't sure what to do with the ball, just stick it in the net, and we'll discuss your options afterwards.

Advice to his players.

Of course I didn't take my wife to see Rochdale as an anniversary present. It was her birthday. Would I have got married during the football season? And anyway it wasn't Rochdale, it was Rochdale reserves.

Attributed.

We murdered them 0–0.

Attributed.

See also Tom FINNEY; SEX; SKILL.

Alan SHEARER

English footballer (1970–) who established a reputation as the country's leading striker playing for Blackburn Rovers, Newcastle United and England during the 1990s.

A man so dull he once made the papers for having a one-in-the-bed romp.

Nick Hancock (1963–), British television presenter. From the BBC television show *They Think It's All Over*, 1997.

Alan Shearer is boring – we call him Mary Poppins.

Freddie Shepherd (1942–), English businessman and football executive. Speaking in 1998 as a director of Shearer's club Newcastle United, unaware that his words were being recorded by the *News of the World*.

See also TRANSFERS.

Bill SHOEMAKER

US jockey (1931–) whose achievements included riding a record 485 winners in a season (1953) and being the first jockey to secure 8000 victories.

Bill Shoemaker didn't ride a horse, he joined them. Most riders beat horses as if they were guards in slave-labour camps. Shoe treated them as if he were asking them to dance.

Jim Murray, US sportswriter, in the *Los Angeles Times*.

Shooting

He that's always shooting must sometimes hit.

Proverb.

See from the brake the whirring pheasant springs
And mounts exciting on triumphant wings.
Short is his joy, he feels the fiery wound,
Flutters in blood, and panting beats the ground.

Alexander Pope (1688–1744), British poet.

What he hit is history,
What he missed is mystery.

Thomas Hood (1799–1845), British poet.

A gun gives you the body, not the bird.

Henry Thoreau (1817–62), US essayist and poet.

In shooting with a young sportsman or a stranger, always allow him to precede you in getting over the fences; it may be that you save your life, or a limb, by the precaution.

Dead Shot magazine, 1861.

Deer hunting would be fine sport, if only the deer had guns.

William S. Gilbert (1836–1911), British dramatist and lyricist.

When a man wants to murder a tiger he calls it sport; when the tiger wants to murder him he calls it ferocity.

George Bernard Shaw (1856–1950), Irish playwright and critic.

I shoot the hippopotamus, with bullets made of platinum,
Because if I use leaden ones, his hide is sure to flatten 'em.

Hilaire Belloc (1870–1953), British poet.

The fascination of shooting as a sport depends almost wholly on whether you are at the right or wrong end of a gun.

P.G. Wodehouse (1881–1975), British comic novelist.

He was never, well, what I call a sportsman. For forty days he went out into the desert – and never shot anything.

Osbert Sitwell (1892–1969), British writer, assessing Jesus Christ as a sportsman in 'Old Fashioned Sportsmen' (1931).

One morning I shot an elephant in my pyjamas. How he got into my pyjamas I don't know.

Groucho Marx (Julius Henry Marx; 1895–1977), US film comedian. *Animal Crackers*, 1930 (screenplay by George Kaufman and Morrie Ryskind).

Shooting gives me a good feeling. It is faster than baseball and you are out on one strike.

Ernest Hemingway (1898–1961), US novelist.

Makes me want to yell from St Paul's steeple
The people I'd like to shoot are the shooting people.

Howard Dietz (1896–1983). 'By Myself' (1937).

The grouse are in no danger at all from people who shoot grouse.

Prince Philip, Duke of Edinburgh (1921–), Greek-born consort of Queen Elizabeth II. Quoted in *Private Eye*, 8 July 1988.

See also ANTI-BLOOD SPORTS; ARCHERY; EPITAPHS; INCOMPETENCE.

Skiing

Skiing is a battle against yourself, always to the frontiers of the impossible. But most of all, it must give you pleasure. It is not an obligation but a joy.

Jean-Claude Killy (1944–), French skier. Quoted in *Sports Illustrated*, 18 November 1968.

It is unbecoming for a cardinal to ski badly.

Pope John Paul II (Karol Wojtyla; 1920–), Polish-born pontiff, correcting a fellow-cardinal's comment that it was unbecoming for him, a cardinal, to ski.

There are really only three things to learn in skiing: how to put on your skis, how to slide downhill, and how to walk along the hospital corridor.

Lord Mancroft (1914–), British peer. *A Chinaman in the Bath* (1974).

We skiers know that falling over isn't important; it's getting up again.

Gerald Ford (1913–), US president.

There are two main forms of this sport: Alpine skiing and Nordic skiing. Alpine involves a mountain and a $5,000 to $10,000 investment, plus $300,000 for the condo in Aspen and however much you spend on drugs. It is a sport only a handful of people ever master, and those who do, do so at the expense of other skills like talking and writing their own name.

National Lampoon, 1979.

The sport of skiing consists of wearing three thousand dollars' worth of clothes and equipment and driving two hundred miles in the snow in order to stand around at a bar and get drunk.

P.J. O'Rourke (1947–), US humorist. *Modern Manners* (1984).

Ski-jumping

There are no natural jumpers, because what they do is so unnatural.

Shirley Finberg-Sullivan. Quoted by E.M. Swift in *Sports Illustrated*, 4 February 1980.

Eddie is the symbol of de Coubertin's ideal – a man whose only triumph is the struggle.

Chris Brasher (1928–), British middle-distance runner and journalist, referring to British ski-jumper Eddie 'The Eagle' Edwards' appearances in the ski jump events at the 1988 Winter Olympics, in which he predictably finished last.

Skill

I never saw Raich under pressure. He carried empty space around with him like an umbrella.

Willie Watson (1920–), English footballer and cricketer, referring to Sunderland star Horatio 'Raich' Carter (1913–94).

Lefty Grove could throw a lamb chop past a wolf.

Arthur 'Bugs' Baer (1876–1969), US sportswriter, referring to baseball pitcher Robert 'Lefty' Grove.

Dazzy Vance could throw a cream puff through a battleship.

Johnny Frederick (1902–77), US baseball player, referring to baseball
pitcher Arthur 'Dazzy' Vance.

Denis Law could dance on egg shells.

Bill Shankly (1913–81), Scottish football player and manager.

The main function of sport is that it serves as a basis for the exercise of skill,
with physical prowess.

R. Carlisle. 'Physical Education and Aesthetics' in H.T.A. Whiting and
D.W. Masterson, *Readings in the Aesthetics of Sport* (1974).

When Cookie sold you a dummy, you had to pay to get back into the ground.

Jim Baxter (1939–), Scottish footballer, referring to Chelsea's gifted
winger of the 1970s, Charlie Cook.

See also CAPTAINCY; SWIMMING; TECHNIQUE.

Smoking

You can get rid of drink, but you can never get rid of smoke.

W.G. Grace (1848–1915), English cricketer.

You can't smoke 20 a day and bowl fast.

Phil Tufnell (1966–), English cricketer, explaining, on tour with
England in 1990, why he bowled slow left-arm.

Perhaps sport should accept sponsorship from the Mafia. They kill fewer
people than smoking.

Alan Hubbard, British writer. The *Observer*, 1994.

Sam SNEAD

**US golfer (1912–) who won a record six PGA Seniors'
Championships.**

Quotes about Sam Snead

Sam Snead did to the tee-shot what Roger Bannister did to the four-minute
mile.

Byron Nelson (1912–), US golfer.

Watching Sam Snead practise hitting golf balls is like watching a fish practise swimming.
John Schlee, US golfer. *Golf Digest* (1977).

Anyone who would pass up an opportunity to see Sam Snead swing a golf club at a golf ball would pull down the shades when driving past the Taj Mahal.
Jim Murray, US sportswriter, in the *Los Angeles Times*.

Quotes by Sam Snead

The only reason I ever played golf in the first place was so I could afford to hunt and fish.
'Scorecard', *Sports Illustrated*, 22 January 1968.

See also GOLF COURSES; The PRESS; ST ANDREWS; TECHNIQUE.

Snooker

Playing snooker gives you firm hands and helps to build up character. It is the ideal recreation for dedicated nuns.
Archbishop Luigi Barbarito (1922–), papal emissary. Said while
watching a snooker tournament at Tyburn convent. Quoted in the
Daily Telegraph, 15 November 1989.

If snooker hadn't existed, TV would surely have had to invent it.
Geoffrey Nicholson (1929–), British sportswriter.

Whoever called snooker 'chess with balls' was rude, but right.
Clive James (1939–), Australian writer and broadcaster.

See also BILLIARDS; CLASSIC COMMENTARIES; Steve DAVIS; MARRIAGE; RULES; SEX; TELEVISION.

Sir Gary SOBERS

West Indian cricketer (Garfield St Aubrun Sobers; 1936–),
generally considered to be the greatest all-rounder in
cricket history. His feats as a batsman included the then
world record individual score of 365 not out against
Pakistan in 1958, and a maximum 36 runs off a single over
off the hapless Glamorgan bowler Malcolm Nash at
Swansea in 1968.

His immense power is lightened by a rhythm which has in it as little
obvious propulsion as a movement of music by Mozart.

Sir Neville Cardus (1889–1975), British journalist and writer.

Gary Sobers was unsurpassed as an all-rounder, he always played cricket
the way the Gods intended – absolutely straight, absolutely hard, but
never with malice.

Trevor Bailey (1923–), English cricketer and journalist.

When he walked out to bat, six feet tall, lithe but with adequately
wide shoulders, he moved with long strides which, even when he was
hurrying, had an air of laziness, the hip joints rippling like those of a
great cat.

John Arlott (1914–91), English cricket writer and commentator.
'Sir Garfield Sobers', *John Arlott's Book of Cricketers* (1979).

See also COUNTY CRICKET.

Soccer *See* FOOTBALL (ASSOCIATION).

Songs

Kick-off, throw it in, have a little scrimmage,
Keep it low, a splendid rush, bravo, win or die,
On the ball, City, never mind the danger,
Steady on, now's your chance,
Hurrah! We've scored a goal.

Albert T. Smith, British songwriter. Music hall song that was
subsequently adopted by fans of Norwich City. Written around
1890, it is sometimes identified as the oldest football anthem still in
use today.

Why does everybody stand up and sing 'Take Me Out to the Ballgame' when they're already there?

Larry Andersen (1953–), US baseball player, referring to baseball's most famous anthem, written by Jack Norworth and Harry Von Tilzer in 1908.

Nice one, Cyril!

Football song associated with fans of Tottenham Hotspur from 1973, referring to the team's left-back Cyril Knowles (1944–91). It was inspired by a television advertisement for Wonderloaf, first screened in 1972, in which a baker named Cyril was thus praised for his wonderful bread. Tottenham Hotspur fans picked the phrase up with enthusiasm and in 1973 the Cockerel Chorus released a single with the refrain 'Nice one, Cyril, nice one, son; nice one, Cyril, let's have another one!'

In your Liverpool slums, in your Liverpool slums
You look in the dustbin for something to eat,
You find a dead rat and you think it's a treat,
In your Liverpool slums.

English football song, directed against Liverpool. Sung to the tune 'My Liverpool Home', 1980.

And so this is Burnley, and what have we done,
We've lost here already, would you like a cream bun?

English football song, adopted by Burnley fans in the 1980s and sung to the tune of John Lennon's 'Happy Xmas (War is Over)'.

Me brother's in borstal,
Me sister's got pox,
Me mother's a whore down Hartlepool docks,
Me uncle's a pervert
Me aunty's gone mad
And Jack the Ripper's me dad,
La, la, la ...

English football song, adopted by Hartlepool fans in the 1980s.

We're all mad, we're insane,
We eat Mars bars on the train.

English football supporters' song associated with fans of Leyton Orient.

It's a weird thing, 'You Never Walk Alone' being a big football fans' anthem, because it comes from an old musical. I'd like to go down to Millwall and hear them singing 'How Do You Solve a Problem Like Maria?'

Jo Brand (1958–), British comedienne, 1996.

Speed records

The world land speed record requires the minimum of skill, and the maximum of courage.

Tommy Wisdom (1907–72), British racing driver and motoring journalist. Quoted in Phil Drackett, *The Story of Malcolm and Donald Campbell* (1969).

We did it for Britain and for the hell of it.

Richard Noble (1946–), British land speed record holder. Said in 1983 after establishing a new land speed record in *Thrust 2*. Quoted in 'The Week in Words', the *Sunday Times*, 9 October 1983.

Spitting

He dribbles a lot and the opposition don't like it: you can see it all over their faces.

Ron Atkinson (1939–), English football manager. Atkinson was, of course, referring to the player's ball skills.

If somebody in the crowd spits at you, you've just got to swallow it.

Gary Lineker (1960–), English footballer and commentator, 1995. Although now associated with Lineker, the original source was apparently Lineker's former manager at Leicester City, Gordon Milne.

You have to consider the socio-cultural value of spitting, the depth of insult that it conveys. It's a non-manly thing to do. It's the sort of thing a woman might do. Most of the insults in football are to do with de-masculinising – you call them a poof. Spitting is a non-masculine thing. And we all know that most foreign footballers are homosexuals anyway!

Peter Marsh, British academic and football club director. Reflecting upon a controversial incident in which Frenchman Patrick Viera spat in the face of West Ham defender Neil 'Razor' Ruddock. Quoted in the *Sunday Times*, 10 October 1999.

Sport

In sports and journeys, men are known.

Proverb.

He will never be dull to strangers who joins in sport with his own family.

Plautus (254–184 BC), Roman playwright.

A summer's day will seem an hour but short
Being wasted in such time-beguiling sport.

William Shakespeare (1564–1616), English playwright and poet.
Venus and Adonis (1593).

There's no such sport as sport by sport o'erthrown.

William Shakespeare (1564–1616), English playwright and poet.
Love's Labours Lost (c.1594).

If all the year were playing holidays,
To sport would be as tedious as to work.

William Shakespeare (1564–1616), English playwright and poet.
Henry IV, Part I (c.1596).

It is a poor sport that is not worth a candle.

George Herbert (1593–1633), English poet.

Games lubricate the body and mind.

Benjamin Franklin (1706–90), US statesman and philosopher.

He learned the arts of riding, fencing, gunnery,
And how to scale a fortress – or a nunnery.

Lord Byron (1788–1824), British poet.

Sport went hand in hand with science.

Alfred Lord Tennyson (1809–92), British poet.

Man is a sporting as well as a praying animal.

Oliver Wendell Holmes (1809–94), US jurist.

If it were not for the running-ground at Eton, the towing-path at Oxford,
the Thames swimming baths, and the yearly circuses, humanity would

forget the plastic perfection of its own form, and degenerate into a race of short-sighted professors, and spectacled *précieuses*!

Oscar Wilde (1854–1900), Irish writer and wit. *London Models.*

The sports of the people afford an index to the character of the nation.

Frederick W. Hackwood, British sportswriter, 1907.

Were cricket and football abolished, it would bring upon the masses nothing but misery, depression, sloth, indiscipline and disorder.

Lord Birkenhead (1872–1930), British lawyer and politician, 1911.

It may be that all games are silly. But then, so are humans.

Robert Lynd (1879–1949), Anglo-Irish essayist and critic.

Almost any game with any ball is a good game.

Robert Lynd (1879–1949), Anglo-Irish essayist and critic.

Sports do not build character. They reveal it.

Heywood Broun (1888–1939), US humorist.

There is a vast difference between games and play. Play is played for fun, but games are deadly serious and you do not play them to enjoy yourself.

Maurice Baring (1874–1945), British journalist, 1922.

In sport, in courage, and in the sight of Heaven, all men meet on equal terms.

Winston Churchill (1874–1965), British Conservative prime minister.

I remain of the opinion that there is no game from bridge to cricket that is not improved by a little light conversation; a view which ... is shared only by a small and unjustly despised minority.

Osbert Lancaster (1908–80), British cartoonist. *All Done From Memory* (1953).

No human being is innocent, but there is a class of innocent human actions called Games.

W.H. Auden (1907–73), Anglo-American poet. 'Dingly Dell and The Fleet', *The Dyer's Hand* (1962).

There is only one emotion that I know of which has absolutely no place in spectator sport and death to it – laughter.

René Maheu, Director-General of the United Nations.
'Cultural Anthropology' in E. Jokl and E. Simon, *International Research in Sport and Physical Education* (1964).

People understand contests. You take a bunch of kids throwing rocks at random and people look askance, but if you go and hold a rock-throwing contest – people understand that.

Don Murray. Quoted by Gilbert Rogin in *Sports Illustrated*,
18 October 1965.

I love sport because I love life, and sport is one of the basic joys of life.

Yevgeny Yevtushenko (1933–), Russian poet. Quoted in *Sports Illustrated*, 19 December 1966.

Athletes hang loose, but tough. They relax and let sport turn them on.

Howard Slusher (1937–), US writer. *Man, Sport and Existence* (1967).

There is something for everyone in sports.

Arnold Beisser (1925–85), US psychologist, 'Modern Man and Sports' in George H. Sage, *Sport and American Society: Selected Readings* (1970).

When you play a sport, you have two things in mind. One is to get into the Hall of Fame and the other is to go to heaven when you die.

Lee Trevino (1939–), US golfer.

All sports are games of inches.

Dick Ritger (1938–), US bowler, in the *New York Times*, 17 April 1977.

I am in favour of soccer passion as I am in favour of drag racing, of competition between motorcycles on the edge of a cliff, and of wild parachute jumping, mystical mountain climbing, crossing oceans in rubber dinghies, Russian roulette, and the use of narcotics. Races improve the race, and all these games lead fortunately to the death of the best, allowing mankind to continue its existence serenely with normal protagonists, of average achievement.

Umberto Eco (1932–), Italian semiologist and novelist. 'The World Cup and its Pomps' (1978).

What is sport? I suppose it's anything they can make competitive or entertaining enough to be good television.

The *Observer*, 22 August 1982.

Sport is life to the nth degree.

Neil Offen, US writer. Quoted by Richard Lipsky in
National Forum, Winter 1982.

Unlike any other business in the United States, sports must preserve an
illusion of perfect innocence. The mounting of this illusion defines the
purpose and accounts for the immense wealth of American sports. It is the
ceremony of innocence that the fans pay to see – not the game or the match
or the bout, but the ritual portrayal of a world in which time stops and all
hope remains plausible, in which everybody present can recover the
blameless expectations of a child, where the forces of light always triumph
over the powers of darkness.

Lewis H. Lapham (1935–), US essayist. *Money and Class in America* (1988).

I've been around a lot of heavy, degenerate gamblers, so I can see what it
does to people. It's a lifestyle. People killing each other over games. There's
more passion at a Wembley soccer match than in St Patrick's Cathedral.

Abel Ferrara (1952–), US film-maker. Interview, *Sight and Sound*, February 1993.

I'm fanatical about sport: there seems to me something almost religious
about the fact that human beings can organise play, the spirit of play.

Simon Gray (1936–), British playwright. Interview, *Independent on
Sunday*, 19 February 1995.

Sport is the only entertainment where, no matter how many times you go
back, you never know the ending.

Neil Simon (1927–), US playwright.

See also AMATEURS; ANTI-SPORTS; BUSINESS AND SPORT; PLAYING THE GAME;
RELIGION AND SPORT; SKILL.

Sporting royals

I will that every man be entitled to his hunting in wood and in field of his
possession, and let everyone forego my hunting.

Canute (994–1035), king of England, Denmark and Norway.

They say Princes learn no art truly, but the art of horsemanship. The reason
is the brave beast is no flatterer. He will throw a Prince as soon as his groom.

Ben Jonson (1573–1637), English playwright and poet.

To the Tennis Court, and there saw the King play at tennis and others; but to see how the King's play was extolled, without any cause at all, was a loathsome sight.

Samuel Pepys (1633–1703), British diarist, recording his experience
of watching Charles II at real tennis. *Diary*, 4 January 1664.

Cricket is not illegal, for it is a manly game.

Queen Anne (1665–1714), queen of England, 1710.

King Charles I is said to have been fond of the exercise of the golf. While he was engaged in a party of golf on the Links of Leith, a letter was delivered into his hands, which gave him the first account of the rebellion in Ireland.

William Tytler (1711–92), Scottish historian, 1792.

Mary Queen of Scots appears to have practised this game, for it was made a charge against her by her enemies, as an instance of her indifference to Darnley's fate, that she was seen playing at golf and pall-mall in the fields beside Seton a few days after his death.

Inventories of Mary Queen of Scots (1863).

If you can't ride, I'm afraid people will call you a duffer.

George V (1865–1936), king of England, addressing his son, the
future Edward VIII.

When I'm approaching a water jump, with dozens of photographers waiting for me to fall in, and hundreds of spectators wondering what's going to happen next, the horse is just about the only one who doesn't know I am a Royal!

Princess Anne (1950–), British Princess Royal.

There is a commotion in the stands. I think it has something to do with a fat lady ... I've just been informed that the fat lady is the Queen of Holland.

Jay 'Dizzy' Dean (1911–74), US baseball player and commentator.
Baseball commentary.

I never heard a minute's silence like that.

Glenn Hoddle (1957–), English footballer and manager,
commenting upon the minute's silence observed by a Wembley
crowd in tribute to the late Princess Diana in 1997.

One is not amused at that.

Elizabeth II (1926–), queen of Great Britain and Northern Ireland.
Her alleged response when a disallowed goal by Sol Campbell
against Argentina spelt England's exit from the 1998 World Cup.
According to the Lord Provost of Edinburgh, Eric Milligan, who was
also present in the royal box, the Queen 'was very excited at the
quality of England's performance' and was deliberately sending
herself up when she mimicked Queen Victoria's celebrated 'We are
not amused'. 'Sporting Quotes of the Year', the *Daily Telegraph*, 28
December 1998.

See also ANTI-SPORTS; EPITAPHS; JOCKEYS AND RIDERS; SUNDAY SPORT.

Sporting similes

A bad football team is like an old bra – no cups and little support.

Anonymous.

He loved to walk sideways towards them, like a grimly playful crab.

R.C. Robertson-Glasgow (1901–65), English cricket writer,
describing the batting technique of George Gunn when faced
with fast bowlers. *Cricket Prints* (1943).

Hoffman knocked off triples with the awesome precision of a fighter pilot swatting flies. He made the same artistic impresssion as a fringe theatre company producing a minor play by Brecht in the back room of a pub.

Clive James (1939–), Australian broadcaster and writer, referring to
ice skater Jan Hoffman during the 1980 Winter Olympics.

He has a swing like an octopus falling out of a tree.

Anonymous golf commentator.

That Randall! He bats like an octopus with piles.

Unidentified Australian cricket fan to journalist Matthew Engel, referring to
the England cricketer Derek Randall during the 1982–83 England tour of
Australia. Quoted in *Wisden Cricketers' Almanack* (1994).

See also CLASSIC COMMENTARIES; MIXED METAPHORS.

Sportsmanship *See* PLAYING THE GAME.

Sportswriting *See* The PRESS.

Squash

Squash is boxing with racquets.

Jonah Barrington (1941–), British squash player.

Before I arrived, no one trained specifically for squash; it was just a means of keeping fit for other sports such as rugby and football.

Jonah Barrington (1941–), British squash player.

Squash – that's not exercise, it's flagellation.

Noël Coward (1899–1973), British playwright, composer and actor.

Crystallizing my feelings about the game, I find that squash is less frustrating than golf, less fickle than tennis. It is easier than badminton, cheaper than polo. It is better exercise than bowls, quicker than cricket, less boring than jogging, drier than swimming, safer than hang gliding.

John Hopkins (1945–), British sportswriter. *Squash: A Joyful Game* (1980).

If you think squash is a competitive activity, try flower arranging.

Alan Bennett (1934–), British playwright. *Talking Heads* (1988).

Statistics

Baseball is an island of activity amidst a sea of statistics.

Anonymous.

Say you were standing with one foot in the oven and one foot in an ice bucket. According to the percentage people, you should be perfectly comfortable.

Bobby Bragan (1917–), US baseball player and sportswriter, discussing baseball statisticians, 1963.

Statistics are used like a drunk uses a lamp post – for support, not illumination.

Vince Scully (1927–), US sports commentator. 'Coaches' Corner', *Scholastic Coach*, January 1983.

So that's 57 runs needed by Hampshire in 11 overs and it doesn't need a calculator to tell us that the run rate required is 5.1818 recurring.

Norman de Mesquita, English cricket commentator.

The only things that really keep me going are statistics.

Sir Richard Hadlee (1951–), New Zealand cricketer. His own
statistical feats included a world record of 431 Test wickets, achieved
in 1990. *At the Double* (1985).

See also Sir Donald BRADMAN.

Streakers

Well, the streakers are at it again. This time at a local football game just
outside of Boston. I can't figure out this type of behaviour – I guess it's their
way of showing they're nuts.

Laddy Glick, US radio sports commentator.

Don't know. They were wearing a bag over their head.

Lawrence 'Yogi' Berra (1925–), US baseball player. His response
when asked if some streakers had been male or female.

Bill, there's a guy just run on the park with your backside on his chest.

Steve Smith (1951–), English rugby player. Speaking to England's
Bill Beaumont in 1982 on the appearance of a naked Erica Roe
during a match at Twickenham, suggesting a resemblance between
his rear end and her ample bosom.

There was a slight interruption there for athletics.

Richie Benaud (1930–), Australian cricketer and commentator,
responding to the appearance of a streaker at Lord's.

It is a sign of decreasing self-esteem and increasing moral turpitude.

Wes Hall (1937–), West Indian cricketer, responding to an
outbreak of streaking while on tour in England in 1995.

I've never got to the bottom of streaking.

Jonathan Agnew (1960–), English cricket commentator. *Test Match
Special* commentary. 'Quotes of the Year', the *Guardian*, 24
December 1998.

Our brief was to let the ladies run around as long as they liked, otherwise
we might have antagonized the crowd. But we were told to get the guys to
ground as quickly as possible.

Mark Pink, English rugby official. Quoted as coach of the Brunel
University 'anti-streaking squad' employed at Twickenham during the
1999 Rugby World Cup. *The Sunday Times*, 10 October 1999.

Success *See* VICTORY.

Sunday sport

Lord, remove these exercises from the Sabaoth. Any exercise which
withdraweth from godliness either upon the Sabaoth or on any other day, is
wicked and to be forbidden.

Philip Stubbes (*fl*.1583–91), English Puritan pamphleteer.
Anatomie of Abuses in the Realme of England (1583).

Na inhabitants, be thameselffis, thair chiildren, servands, or fameleis, be
sene at ony pastymes or gammis within or without the toun upoun the
Sabbath day, sic as golf, aircheies, rowbowliss, penny stayne, katch pullis,
or sic other pastymes.

Order of Edinburgh Council, 1592.

Walter Hay, goldsmith, accusit for playing at the boulis and golff upoun
Sondaye in the tyme of the sermon.

Elgin court record, 1596.

John Gardiner, James Bowman, Laurence Chalmers, and Laurence Cuthbert
confess that they were playing at the golf on the North Inch in time of
preaching after noon on the Sabbath. The Sesion rebuked them, and
admonished them to resort to the hearing of the Word diligently on the
Sabbath in time coming, which they promised to do.

Records of the Perth Kirk Sessions, 1599.

Any golfer can be devout on a rainy Sunday.

Anonymous.

A decision of the courts decided that the game of golf may be played on a
Sunday, not being a game within the view of the law, but being a form of
moral effort.

Stephen Leacock (1869–1944), Canadian humorist. 'Why I Refuse to
Play Golf', *Over the Footlights* (1923).

If it were not for my Archbishop of Canterbury I should be off in my plane to Longchamp every Sunday.

Elizabeth II (1926–), queen of Great Britain and Northern Ireland.

See also GOLF; ONE-DAY CRICKET.

Super Bowl

The climactic game in the annual American football calendar.

Do you know what happens after you lose a Super Bowl? The world ends. It just stops.

Joe Kapp (1938–), American football player and coach, describing the sensation of losing the Super Bowl, 1970.

If the Super Bowl is the 'Ultimate Game', why are they playing it again next year?

Duane Thomas (1947–), American football player, speaking as one of the Dallas Cowboys squad in the 1970s.

Superstition

My only feeling about superstition is that it's unlucky to be behind at the end of the game.

Duffy Daugherty (1915–87), American football player.

Maybe he thinks the gypsies have put a curse on me – he's very superstitious you know.

Stan Bowles (1948–), English footballer, speculating on the reasons why he was not included in an England team selected by Don Revie in 1976.

I'm not superstitious or anything like that, but I'll just hope we'll play our best and put it in the lap of the Gods.

Terry Neill (1942–), English football manager, speaking as manager of Tottenham Hotspur in the mid-1970s.

I always used to put my right boot on first, and then obviously my right sock.

Barry Venison (1964–), English footballer and sports commentator.
ITV television commentary.

The whole of our national sport is not doing very well. We may be in the wrong sign or something. Venus may be in the wrong juxtaposition to somewhere else.

Ted Dexter (1935–), English cricketer and cricket administrator,
reflecting upon the latest in a run of England defeats in 1993.

When I made my debut for Besiktas they even sacrificed a lamb, which is a sacred animal, on the pitch. Its blood was then daubed on my forehead and boots to bring me good luck. They never did that at QPR.

Les Ferdinand (1966–), English footballer, referring to his
experience of football in Turkey, 1995.

See also LUCK.

Surfing

A surfer is an American lemming.

Jacob Bronowski (1902–74), Polish-born scientist.

The surfer projects himself upon the wave as the matador before the bull ...

W. Cleary. Quoted by Roselyn E. Stone in 'Perceptual Studies:
Sources and Kinds of Meaning in the Acts of Surfing and Skiing' in
H.T.A. Whiting, *Readings in Sports Psychology* (1972).

Swearing

If I lose at play, I blaspheme; if my fellow loses, he blasphemes. So, God is always the loser.

John Donne (1571–1631), English poet, 1623.

Good shot, bad luck and hell are the five basic words to be used in a game of tennis, though these, of course, can be slightly amplified.

Virginia Graham (1914–), US writer and commentator. *Say Please*
(1949).

American professional athletes are bilingual; they speak English and profanity.

Gordie Howe (1926–), Canadian ice hockey player, 1975.

When Ilie Nastase plays John McEnroe, it's the only time the crowd call for silence.

Jerry Girard, 1979.

You don't go to an X-rated movie if you don't want to watch it.

Ilie Nastase (1946–), Romanian tennis player, rejecting the
controversy aroused by his use of bad language on court, 1981.

Swearing at the polo club? It's a load of bollocks!

Major Ronald Ferguson, father of the Duchess of York, 1987.

The thing about sport, any sport, is that swearing is very much part of it.

Jimmy Greaves (1940–), English footballer and commentator.
'Sayings of the Year', the *Observer*, 1 January 1989.

Famous midsouth resorts include Pinehurst and Southern Pines, where it is said there are more golf curses per square mile than anywhere else in the world.

North Carolina tourist brochure.

I do swear a lot, but the advantage is that having played abroad, I can choose a different language from the referee's.

Jürgen Klinsmann (1964–), German footballer, 1995.

Well to be honest, the fackin' facker's fackin' facked.

John Emburey (1952–), Middlesex and England cricketer. His
reported response to a journalist's enquiry after the state of his
injured back. Quoted in Simon Hughes, *A Lot of Hard Yakka* (1997).

Swimming

Good swimmers are oftenest drowned.

English proverb.

Like an unpractis'd swimmer plunging still,
With too much labour drowns for want of skill ...

William Shakespeare (1564–1616), English playwright and poet.
The Rape of Lucrece (1594).

If he fall in, good night, or sink or swim!

William Shakespeare (1564–1616), English playwight and poet.
Henry IV, Part I (c.1596).

Who foremost now delight to cleave
With pliant arm thy glassy wave?

Thomas Gray (1716–71), English poet. 'Ode on a Distant Prospect
of Eton College' (1747).

And I have loved thee, Ocean! and my joy
Of youthful sports was on thy breast to be
Borne, like the bubbles, onward: from a boy
I wantoned with thy breakers.

Lord Byron (1788–1824), British poet. *Childe Harold's
Pilgrimage* (1812).

Wet, she was a star – dry she ain't.

Joe Pasternak (1901–91), Hungarian-born film producer, referring to
US swimmer Esther Williams and her relatively unremarkable career
as a film actress. Quoted in Leslie Halliwell, *The Filmgoer's Book of
Quotes* (1973).

Do men who have got all their marbles go swimming in lakes with their
clothes on?

P.G. Wodehouse (1861–1975), British comic novelist. *Cocktail
Time* (1958).

When Captain Webb the Dawley man,
Captain Webb from Dawley,
Came swimming along the old canal
That carried the bricks to Lawley
We saw the ghost of Captain Webb,
Webb in a water sheeting,
Come dripping along in bathing dress
To the Saturday evening meeting.

John Betjeman (1906–84), British poet. 'A Shropshire Lad' (1960).

There is a world of difference between what the diver thinks he is doing
and what he is in fact doing.

Wally Orner. 'Diving' in *The Official Coaching Book of the E.S.S.A.,
Swimming and Diving* (1972).

A person drowns if he allows the water to win.

Michael Bettsworth (1943–), writer. *A Technique for Water
Survival: Drownproofing* (1976).

It was the fastest-ever swim over that distance on American soil.

Greg Phillips in the *Portsmouth News*.

What on earth has this synchronised swimming got to do with anything, let
alone sport?

Frank Keating (1937–), British sportswriter, in the *Guardian*,
8 August 1984.

The swimmers are swimming out of their socks.

Sharron Davies (1962–), British swimmer. BBC TV commentary.

See also EXERCISE; FAMOUS LAST WORDS.

Synchronised swimming *See* SWIMMING.

·T·U·

Tackles

It isn't necessary to see a good tackle. You can hear it.

Knute Rockne (1888–1931), American football player.

I give 'em the hip, then I take it away.

Jim Thorpe (1886–1953), American football player, explaining how
he managed to dodge tackles so effectively.

I love tackling, love it. It's better than sex.

Paul Ince (1967–), English footballer, 1997.

Every time I went to tackle him, Horrocks went one way, Taylor went the
other, and all I got was the bloody hyphen.

Mick English, Irish rugby union player. Describing his attempts to
tackle Phil Horrocks-Taylor, British rugby player, in a Five Nations
match in the late 1950s.

Tactics

Slow but sure wins the race.

Proverb.

Let's be getting at them before they get at us.

W.G. Grace (1848–1915), English cricketer, explaining why he
always chose to bat first.

When you win the toss – bat.
If you are in doubt, think about it – then bat.
If you have very big doubts, consult a colleague – then bat.

W.G. Grace (1848–1915), English cricketer.

We'll get 'em in singles.

George Hirst (1871–1954), English cricketer. Speaking to his partner
Wilfred Rhodes when the pair were faced with making a last-wicket
stand of 15 runs in order to beat Australia in 1902. Hirst denied ever
saying such a thing.

Find out where the ball is, get there; hit it.

Prince Ranjitsinhji (1872–1933), Indian cricketer.

The tactical difference between Association Football and Rugby with its
varieties seems to be that in the former the ball is the missile, in the latter
men are the missiles.

Alfred E. Crawley (1869–1924), British social anthropologist. *The
Book of the Ball* (1913).

Never change a winning game: always change a losing one.

Bill Tilden (1893–1953), US tennis player.

Attack is only one half of the art of boxing.

Georges Carpentier (1894–1975), French light-heavyweight boxer,
nicknamed 'The Orchid Man'.

I once saw a bowler in Australia thunder to the wicket and bowl a flat-out
underarm to the batsman. No warning given. Quite right, too. In my
profession you have to mystify the enemy.

Bernard Montgomery, 1st Viscount Montgomery of Alamein
(1887–1976), British soldier.

We try to equalize before the others have scored.

Danny Blanchflower (1926–93), Northern Ireland footballer. Said in
1958 while captain of Northern Ireland.

Football tactics are rapidly becoming as complicated as the chemical formula
for splitting the atom.

Jimmy Greaves (1940–), English footballer, 1963.

It was a very simple team talk. All I used to say was: 'Whenever possible, give the ball to George.'

Sir Matt Busby (1909–94), Scottish football manager, recalling the team talks he gave at Manchester United when his star players included George Best. Quoted in Michael Parkinson, *Sporting Lives* (1993).

Championships are won on defence.

Vince Lombardi (1913–70), American football coach. Quoted by Tex Maule in *Sports Illustrated*, 1967.

Get your retaliation in first.

Carwyn James (1929–83), Welsh rugby coach, addressing the British Lions team in 1971. Quoted in the *Guardian*, 7 November 1989.

When you've got your man down, rub him out.

Rod Laver (1938–), Australian tennis player.

I think Ally MacLeod believes that tactics are a new kind of peppermint.

Anonymous reference to Scottish manager Ally MacLeod, 1978.

Football wasn't meant to be run by linesmen and air traffic control.

Tommy Docherty (1928–), Scottish football manager, protesting against the current popularity of the 'long ball' game, 1988.

We're totally committed to defence. I'm not sure our defence is committed to defence, but the rest of our team is.

Lou Holtz (1937–), American football coach, speaking as coach of Notre Dame.

If all else fails, you could wait for the first corner and tie his dreadlocks to the goalpost.

Vinny Jones (1965–), Welsh footballer, discussing the best way to restrain the dreadlocked Dutch player Ruud Gullit.

Hump it, bump it, whack it! It might be a recipe for a good sex life, but it won't win the World Cup.

Ken Bates (1931–), English football club owner, referring to the tactics favoured by England manager Graham Taylor in 1993.

We need to forget about all these tactics and just play football.

Hristo Stoichkov (1967–), Bulgarian footballer, commenting on life with Barcelona under Louis van Gaal, 1997.

See also COACHING; BODYLINE; FAST BOWLING; GAMESMANSHIP; Sir Richard HADLEE; LEG SPIN BOWLING; TECHNIQUE.

Tantrums *See* Jimmy CONNORS; John McENROE; Ilie NASTASE.

Graham TAYLOR

**English football manager (1944–) whose successful career
as a manager of domestic clubs ran into trouble when he
was appointed England coach (1990–93).**

Quotes about Graham Taylor

As well as being England's first managerial turnip, Graham Taylor has prime ministerial qualities, combining the personality of John Major with the gift of prophecy of Neville Chamberlain.

Steve Grant, British writer. *Time Out*, 1994.

Quotes by Graham Taylor

Being an ex-England manager, one that failed to qualify for the World Cup, is like being a dead politician.

Reflecting upon his failure to secure England a place in the 1994
World Cup Finals, a disappointment that resulted in his own
resignation from the post of England manager in 1993.

See also AGENTS; LUCK; PREDICTIONS.

Team selection

Of all the talking points which make international sport fascinating, selecting a team to represent the country surely takes pride of place.

E.W. Swanton (1907–2000), British sportswriter.

Terry has a choice of Gascoigne, Beardsley and Ince. Any of those would be in the Swiss side. I've got to pick between Sforza, Sforza and Sforza. I usually pick Sforza.

Roy Hodgson (1947–), English football manager. As manager of
the Swiss national side, comparing the talent at his disposal with
that available to England's Terry Venables, 1995.

Team spirit

The way a team plays as a whole determines its success. You may have the greatest bunch of individual stars in the world, but if they don't play together, the club won't be worth a dime.

Babe Ruth (1895–1948), US baseball player.

Individual commitment to a group effort, that is what makes a team work, a company work, a society work, a civilization work.

Vince Lombardi (1913–70), American football coach.

Every batsman must realize that his duty is first, last, and all the time to his side and not to himself.

MCC Cricket Coaching Book (1976).

Football isn't necessarily won by the best players. It's won by the team with the best attitude.

George Allen (1922–90), American football coach.

I would have thought that the knowledge that you are going to be leapt upon by half-a-dozen congratulatory, but sweaty team-mates would be inducement not to score a goal.

Arthur Marshall (1910–89), British journalist and writer.

If I'd wanted to be an individual, I'd have taken up tennis.

Ruud Gullit (1962–), Dutch footballer and manager.

Ask not what your teammates can do for you. Ask what you can do for your teammates.

Earvin 'Magic' Johnson (1959–), US basketball player, parodying the famous quotation by US President John F. Kennedy.

A player who conjugates a verb in the first person singular cannot be part of the squad, he has to conjugate the verb in the first person plural. We. We want to conquer. We are going to conquer. Using the word 'I' when you're in a group makes things complicated.

Wanderley Luxemburgo (1952–), Brazilian football manager. His justification for leaving Edmundo and Romario out of the Brazilian national side, 1999.

Technical tips

Bowling

1. Should you desire to bowl leg-breaks, close the right eye.

2. Off-breaks are obtained by closing the left eye.

3. To bowl straight, close both.

Jos A. Knowlson. 'The Lady Cricketer's Guide', *Punch*, 29 August 1906.

Tee the ball high. Because years of experience have shown me that air offers less resistance to dirt.

Jack Nicklaus (1940–), US golfer, 1977.

Never go for a 50/50 ball unless you are 80/20 sure.

Ian Darke, British television sports commentator. Football commentary, Sky Sports TV.

See also ADVICE.

Technique

'Babe' Ruth and Old Jack Dempsey,
Both Sultans of Swat,
One hits where the other people are,
The other where they're not.

Ring Lardner (1885–1933), US humorist and writer.

The greens are so fast I have to hold my putter over the ball and hit it with the shadow.

Sam Snead (1912–), US golfer.

The poetic temperament is the worst for golf. It dreams of brilliant drives, iron shots laid dead, and long putts holed, while in real golf success waits for him who takes care of the foozles and leaves the fine shots to take care of themselves.

Sir Walter Simpson (1843–1898), British writer. *The Art of Golf*.

I never had technique.

Al Oerter (1936–), US discus thrower and winner of four Olympic gold medals. Quoted in the *New York Times*, 16 May 1978.

Technique is the servant of tactics.

Jack Barnaby (1909–), US squash and tennis player and
coach. *Winning Squash Racquets* (1979).

The really great batsmen fall into two categories. One comes to the wicket
saying to the bowlers 'I am going to slaughter you'. The other comes to the
wicket saying 'You can't get me out'.

Ben Travers (1886–1980), British playwright. *94 Declared Cricket
Reminiscences* (1981).

My golf swing is like ironing a shirt. You get one side smoothed out, turn it
over and there is a big wrinkle on the other side. You iron that side, turn it
over and there's another wrinkle.

Tom Watson (1949–), US golfer, 1987.

See also SKILL; TACTICS; TECHNICAL TIPS.

Television

And when you rub the ball on rump or belly,
Remember what it looks like on the telly.

A.P. Herbert (1890–1971), British humorist.

A rabid sports fan is one that boos a TV set.

Jimmy Cannon (1910–73), US sportswriter.

It was when old ladies who had been coming into my shop for years started
talking about sweepers and creating space that I really understood the
influence of TV.

Jack Taylor (1932–), English football referee, 1974.

There is a tendency with television for people to just sit there with feet up,
eating pizza and drinking beer and that is their participation in sports. I
don't think that is bad.

Richard Nixon (1913–94), US president.

Griffiths is snookered on the brown, which, for those of you watching in
black and white, is the ball directly behind the pink.

Ted Lowe (1920–), British television snooker commentator.

When television first focused a Cyclopean eye on American professional golf the matchplay form of the game was turned to stone.

Peter Dobereiner (1925–), British sportswriter, the *Observer*, 15 January 1984.

Television turns players into people and uniform numbers into personalities.

Steve Miller, US sportswriter. 'Television and Sports: The Ties that Bind', *USA Today*, November 1984.

I'd have looked even faster in colour.

Fred Trueman (1931–), English cricketer, speaking on BBC Radio in the 1990s.

I would rather play Hamlet with no rehearsal than TV golf.

Jack Lemmon (1925–), US film actor.

See also ACTION REPLAYS; CLASSIC COMMENTARIES; COUCH POTATOES.

Tennis

When we have match'd out rackets to these balls,
We will, in France, by God's grace play a set.

William Shakespeare (1564–1616), English playwight and poet. *Henry V* (1599). The form of tennis alluded to here would have been 'real tennis' and not lawn tennis, the latter not being invented until the 19th century.

A vain, idle and sinful game at which there was much of the language of the accursed going on.

James Hogg (1770–1839), Scottish poet.

Anybody on for a game of tennis?

George Bernard Shaw (1856–1950), Irish playwright and critic. Possibly the original source of the oft-repeated 'Anyone for tennis?' tag. *Misalliance* (1910).

What a polite game tennis is. The chief word in it seems to be 'sorry' and admiration of each other's play crosses the net as frequently as the ball.

J.M. Barrie (1860–1937), Scottish novelist and playwright.

In a sport where 'love' means nothing, it's not surprising that etiquette means everything.

Molly Tyson, US writer. Quoted in the *New York Times*, 15 May 1978.

The only possible regret I have is the feeling that I will die without having played enough tennis.

Jean Borotra (1898–1994), French tennis player, nicknamed the 'Bounding Basque'

An otherwise happily married couple may turn a mixed doubles game into a scene from *Who's Afraid of Virginia Woolf.*

Rod Laver (1938–), Australian tennis player.

The serve was invented so that the net could play.

Bill Cosby (1937–), US comedian.

Tennis doesn't encourage any kind of intellectual development. The dumber you are on court, the better you're going to play.

Jim Courier (1970–), US tennis player, 1999.

See also WIMBLEDON.

Tennis players *See* Björn BORG; Jimmy CONNORS; Billie Jean KING; John McENROE; Ilie NASTASE; Martina NAVRATILOVA; Pete SAMPRAS.

Tenpin bowling

The pins become an object of frustration, not just to be knocked down, but to be conquered.

Don Russell, US bowling coach and writer. *Bowling Now* (1980).

Daley THOMPSON

British decathlete (1958–) who won Olympic gold medals in 1980 and 1984.

Quotes about Daley Thompson

As a runner he is excellent, as a jumper he is excellent, and as a thrower he is an excellent runner and jumper.

Cliff Temple, British sportswriter, referring to Daley Thompson in 1978.

Quotes by Daley Thompson

Being a decathlete is like having ten girlfriends. You have to love them all, and you can't afford losing one.

Attributed

When I lost my decathlon world record I took it like a man. I only cried for ten hours.

Quoted in 1980.

Jeff THOMSON

Australian cricketer (1950–). 'Thommo' established a fearsome reputation as one of the fastest bowlers ever to play Test cricket.

Quotes about Jeff Thomson

Broken marriages, conflicts of loyalty, the problems of everyday life fall away as one faces up to Thomson.

Mike Brearley (1942–), English cricketer, describing what it was like to face Thomson's bowling. Quoted in Ned Sherrin, *Cutting Edge* (1984).

Quotes by Jeff Thomson

I was once timed at 99.97 mph, but that's rubbish, I was miles faster than that.

Attributed.

He'll cop it too.

Thomson's prediction of the fate awaiting the veteran England batsman Colin Cowdrey when he belatedly joined the England side in Australia, 1974–75. Quoted in David Frith, *The Fast Men* (1975).

I couldn't wait to have a crack at 'em [England]. I thought: 'Stuff that stiff upper lip crap. Let's see how stiff it is when it's split.'

Thommo Declares (1986).

See also Ian BOTHAM; FAST BOWLING; HARD MEN; WEATHER.

Tragedies

At six o'clock, out of pure curiosity, I turned on my television set. As the news came on, the screen seemed go black. I sat listening with a frozen brain to that cruel and shocking list of casualties that was now to give the word Munich an even sadder meaning than it had acquired on a day before the war, after a British Prime Minister had come home to London waving a pitiful piece of paper and most of us knew that new calamities of war were inevitable.

H.E. Bates (1905–74), British novelist, referring to the Munich air
crash of 1958, in which eight members of the Manchester United
squad were among the 23 dead. *FA Yearbook 1958–59*.

Maybe we weren't the greatest team in the world. We may never have
become the greatest. But we were certainly the most loved. The team had
youth, glamour and, above all, modesty ... The magic of United could have
died at Munich, but the emotions that team aroused still draw in the crowds
20 years after the last championship.

Harry Gregg (1932–), Irish footballer, recalling in 1988 his
memories of the Manchester United team involved in the 1958
Munich air crash.

Maybe it was a goal. Anyone can make a mistake.

Eduardo Angel Pazos, Uruguayan football referee. Remark
made after his refusal to allow a goal in the closing minutes of a
match between Argentina and Peru in 1964 which provoked riots
and the deaths of 301 people. David Randall, *Great Sporting
Eccentrics* (1985).

If this is what soccer is to become, let it die.

Editorial, *L'Equipe*. Reporting the 1985 Heysel Stadium disaster, in
which 39 football fans died as the result of panic following clashes
between Juventus and Liverpool supporters.

The saddest and most beautiful sight I have ever seen.

Kenny Dalglish (1951–), Scottish footballer and manager, referring to
the tributes of wreaths and scarfs that covered much of the pitch at
Anfield following the Hillsborough football disaster in 1989.

It's all changed now, which is why it mattered to those young men from
Liverpool that they should be there to support their team. What other group
is going to troop their colours for them, present them with scarves and
emblems? To what other section of society should they owe allegiance? Not
to country; we're going into Europe. Not to community; we're all isolated,
shut in little boxes, high-rise or low, watching another box. Not to God;
science has got rid of him. Not to guilt; Freud shoved that out of the
window.

Beryl Bainbridge (1934–), British novelist, writing in the wake of
the Hillsborough football disaster of 1989.

See also DEATH.

Training

The man who wishes to achieve the longed-for victory in a race must as a boy have trained long and hard, have sweated and groaned, and abstained from wine and women.

Horace (65–8BC), Roman poet and satirist.

For every pass I caught in a game, I caught a thousand passes in practice.

Don Hutson (1913–), American football player.

Train little, train hard, train often.

Jim Peters (1919–99), British runner, 1955.

If you are playing a match for an hour and a half on Saturday, you shouldn't spend two hours a day training. You don't want to leave all your vitality on the training track.

Danny Blanchflower (1926–93), Northern Ireland footballer, 1960.

One day of practice is like one day of clean living. It doesn't do you any good.

Abe Lemmons, US basketball coach, 'Coaches' Corner', *Scholastic Coach*, April 1979.

You don't run 26 miles at five minutes a mile on good looks and a secret recipe.

Frank Shorter (1947–), US marathon runner.

In the USA, unlike China and Russia, you cannot tell an athlete he has to go to the gym.

Francis Allen, US gymnastics coach.

If you train hard, you'll not only be hard, you'll be hard to beat.

Herschel Walker (1962–), American footballer.

It's not necessarily the amount of time you spend at practice that counts; it's what you put into the practice.

Eric Lindros (1973–), Canadian ice hockey player.

If you don't practice you don't deserve to dream.

André Agassi (1970–), US tennis player.

I read Billy Schwer had this tennis ball tied to his head and was punching it. It made me think of James Green's trainer in the eighties. He used to blow bubbles and make the fighter punch them.

Miguel Diaz, Argentinian-born boxing trainer, in *The Times*, 31
December 1999.

To be No. 1, you must train like you are No.2.

Maurice Greene (1974–), US sprinter. Speaking as 100 metres
world champion and record-holder. *The Times*, 31 December 1999.

Transfers

It took me five years to learn to spell Chattanooga – and then we moved to Albuquerque.

Joe Morrison (1937–), American football coach.

I had mixed feelings – like watching your mother-in-law drive over a cliff in your car.

Terry Venables (1943–), English footballer and manager,
referring to Paul Gascoigne's transfer from Tottenham Hotspur
to Lazio in 1992.

The most important thing is to get Rangers into the Premiership.

Paul Gascoigne (1967–), English footballer. Quoted in 1998, apparently
forgetting he had just been transferred from Rangers to Middlesbrough.
'Quotes of the Year', the *Guardian*, 24 December 1998.

I've never wanted to leave. I'm here for the rest of my life, and hopefully after that as well.

Alan Shearer (1970–), English footballer, referring to Newcastle
United after his transfer from Blackburn Rovers in 1996.

See also FOREIGN SIGNINGS.

Lee TREVINO

**US golfer (1939–) who won the British and US Open
championships in the same year (1971).**

Golf isn't just my business, it's my hobby.

Attributed.

I plan to win so much money this year, my caddie's gonna finish in the Top 20 money winners.
Attributed.

They say I'm famous for my delicate chip shots. Sure, when I hit 'em right, they land, just so, like a butterfly with sore feet.
Attributed.

They say, 'Trevino is wondering whether to play a five- or six-iron to the green', when all the time I'm gazing at some broad in the third row of the gallery, wondering where my wife is.
Attributed.

I adore the game of golf. I won't ever retire. I'll play until I die. Then I want them to roll me into a bunker, cover me with sand and make sure nobody's ball lands in there for a while.
Quoted in 1985.

See also AGE; FORM; INCOMPETENCE; INTELLIGENCE; JOGGING; MONEY; Arnold PALMER; SPORT; WEATHER.

Triple jump

It's only jumping into a sandpit.
Jonathan Edwards (1966–), British triple jumper, on breaking the triple jump world record in 1995.

Fred TRUEMAN
English cricketer (1931–). 'Fiery Fred' was greatly respected as a fast bowler, taking 307 Test wickets, and has become notorious for his outspoken views on the game.

Quotes about Fred Trueman
Fast bowlers are a breed apart, and Fred Trueman was apart from the breed.
Denis Compton (1918–97), English cricketer.

Fred Trueman the mature fast bowler was a sharply pointed and astutely directed weapon; Fred Trueman the man has often been tactless, haphazard, crude, a creature of impulse.
John Arlott (1914–91), English cricket writer and commentator. *Fred* (1971).

… once, when Sam Pothecary was standing at Taunton, Trueman felled him, as he passed, with a blow of his steel right toe-cap on the ankle so savage as to leave that mildest of umpires limping for a fortnight.

John Arlott (1914–91), English cricket writer and broadcaster, describes the aggressive run-up of the England fast bowler and its effects on a hapless umpire. 'Fred Trueman', *John Arlott's Book of Cricketers* (1979).

It's a different game now but people won't accept it … Trueman would still be a good bowler but he wouldn't be called Fiery Fred.

Ian Botham (1955–), English cricketer. Ian Botham and Peter Roebuck, *It Sort of Clicks* (1986).

Quotes by Fred Trueman

I need nine wickets from this match, and you buggers had better start drawing straws to see who I don't get.

Remark made to an opposing team as they prepared to bat. Quoted in Ned Sherrin, *Ned Sherrin in his Anecdotage* (1993).

The definitive volume on the finest bloody fast bowler that ever drew breath.

Suggesting a title for his autobiography, 1971.

See also ADVICE; BASEBALL; BASEBALL-BASHERS; Ian BOTHAM; Geoffrey BOYCOTT; FAST BOWLING; MIXED METAPHORS; PHYSIQUE; PREDICTIONS; The PRESS; RULES; SEX; SEXISM IN SPORT; TELEVISION; VANITY.

Twickenham

The headquarters, in west London, of the Rugby Football Union, and the home base of the England rugby union team.

An international at Twickenham is more than mere spectacle. It is the gathering of the clan.

John Morgan (1892–1947), Welsh rugby player.

A bomb under the West car park at Twickenham on an international day would end fascism in England for a generation.

Philip Toynbee (1916–81), British writer.

Mike TYSON

US heavyweight boxer (1966–), a brutally powerful puncher and the youngest-ever world heavyweight champion, notorious as much for his activities outside the boxing ring – including a prison term for rape – as for his boxing prowess.

Quotes about Mike Tyson

When Mike Tyson gets mad, you don't need a referee, you need a priest.

Jim Murray, US sportswriter, in the *Los Angeles Times*, 1986.

Nothing is going to stop Mike Tyson that doesn't have a motor attached.

David Brenner, US comedian and writer, in the *New York Times*, 1988.

Mike fights like you stole something from him or said something nasty about his family.

Mike Acri, US boxing promoter.

Mike Tyson's not all that bad. If you dig deep ... dig real deep, dig, dig, dig, dig, dig, deep, deep, go all the way to China ... I'm sure, you'll find there's a nice guy in there.

George Foreman (1948–), US heavyweight boxer.

Mike's like a Gershwin or Beethoven. You go for the quality of the performance, not the longevity of it.

Don King (1932–), US boxing promoter, remarking upon the speed with which Tyson usually disposed of his rivals in the ring. 1989.

Mike Tyson dropped me and when I looked up, the count was on five. I said to myself, 'Damn, whatever happened to one to four.'

Buster Mathis Jr (1970–), US boxer, 1995.

Everything Tyson's got has 'goodnight' written on it.

Mills Lane (1940–), US boxing referee. He was referee for the notorious 1998 bout between Tyson and Evander Holyfield, in which Tyson bit off part of Holyfield's ear.

I'm not sure we need him in the state of Nevada any longer.

Lorenzo Fertitta, US boxing administrator, following an official

investigation into allegations that Tyson threw a late punch at the
close of a bout in Nevada in 1999. Quoted in *The Times*, 30
October 1999.

Quotes by Mike Tyson

Hydrogen bombs! I threw hydrogen bombs out there! Every punch with
murderous intent.

Quoted in 1986.

See also BOXING; MARRIAGE; PROFESSIONALISM.

Umpires *See* CRICKET UMPIRES; REFEREES AND UMPIRES.

Vanity

I'm not God – but I am something similar.

Roberto Duran (1951–), Panamanian middleweight boxer.

Hector Camacho's great dream is to someday die in his own arms.

Irving Rudd, US boxing publicist, referring to Puerto Rican super-
featherweight boxer Hector 'Macho' Camacho.

There's only one head bigger than Tony Grieg's and that's Birkenhead.

Fred Trueman (1931–), English cricketer, referring to the South
African-born cricketer and England captain Tony Grieg (1946–).

If Graeme Souness was a chocolate drop, he'd eat himself.

Archie Gemmill (1947–), Scottish footballer, referring to the
Scottish footballer and football manager Graeme Souness (1953–).

If only I had a little more humility, I would be perfect.

Ted Turner (1941–), US media tycoon and owner of the Atlanta
Braves baseball club.

The British press hate a winner who's British. They don't like any British
man to have balls as big as a cow's like I have.

Nigel Benn (1964–), British middleweight boxer.

You have to try to reply to criticism with your intellect, not your ego.

Mike Brearley (1942–), English cricketer, 1995.

Nelson Mandela was as disappointed as I was.

Ruud Gullit (1962–), Dutch footballer and manager, commenting
on the cancellation of a planned meeting with South African
president Nelson Mandela. 'Quotes of the Year', the *Guardian*,
24 December 1998.

People will say this is not before time. Who am I to argue?

Brian Clough (1935–), English football manager. His response on
learning that a stand at Nottingham Forest's ground was to be
named after him, 1999.

See also Muhammad ALI.

Victory

It is a silly game where nobody wins.

English proverb.

Hey, Ma, your bad boy did good!

Rocky Graziano (1922–90), US middleweight and welterweight
boxer, on winning the world middleweight championship in 1947.

Winning is not the most important thing; it's the only thing.

Vince Lombardi (1913–70), American football coach.

Winning isn't everything, but making the effort is.

Vince Lombardi (1913–70), American football coach.

Winning isn't everything, but wanting to is.

Arnold Palmer (1929–), US golfer.

When you win you eat better, sleep better and your beer tastes better. And your wife looks like Gina Lollobrigida.

Johnny Pesky (1919–), US baseball manager. 'Scorecard', *Sports
Illustrated*, 20 May 1963.

The goddess of sport is not Beauty but Victory, a jealous goddess who demands an absolute homage.

R.K. Elliott. Quoted in 'Aesthetics in Sport' in H.T.A. Whiting and
D.W. Masterson, *Readings in the Aesthetics of Sport* (1974).

When you win, nothing hurts.

Joe Namath (1943–), American football player.

Americans are experts at winning, but still amateurs at losing.

Edward R. Walsh, US writer, *New York Times*, 20 March 1977.

Australia's national sport – winning.

John A. Daley. Title of an article in William Johnson, *Sport and Physical Education* (1980).

In real life, of course, it is the hare who wins. Every time. Look around you. And in any case it is my contention that Aesop was writing for the tortoise market ... Hares have no time to read. They are too busy winning the game.

Anita Brookner (1926–), British novelist, referring to Aesop's fable about the tortoise and the hare. *Hotel du Lac* (1984).

The moment of victory is much too short to live for that and nothing else.

Martina Navratilova (1956–), Czech-born US tennis player. Quoted in the *Guardian*, 21 June 1989.

Winning is everything. The only ones who remember you when you come second are your wife and your dog.

Damon Hill (1960–), British racing driver. *The Sunday Times*, 18 December 1994.

The world looks a totally different place after two wins. I can even enjoy watching *Blind Date* or laugh at *Noel's House Party*.

Gordon Strachan (1957–), Scottish football manager, speaking as manager of Coventry City in 1996.

Winning doesn't really matter as long as you win.

Vinny Jones (1965–), Welsh footballer.

I don't know what to do with myself. I'm normally in the dressing room feeling sorry for myself at this stage, but I can't get the smile off my face.

Angus Fraser (1965–), English cricketer. Quoted in 1998 when, after a long series of international defeats, England finally won a Test match (against South Africa). 'Sports Quotes of the Year 1998', the *Daily Telegraph*, 28 December 1998.

See also DEFEAT; RUNNERS-UP; WINNING STREAKS.

Village sports

It becomes our painful duty to record the death of the Right Honourable
Game Football, which melancholy event took place in the Court of Queen's
Bench on Wednesday, No. 14th, 1860. The deceased Gentleman was, we
are informed, a native of Ashbourn, Derbyshire, at which place he was
born in the Year of Grace, 217, and was consequently in the 1643rd year of
his age. For some months the patriotic Old Man had been suffering from
injuries sustained in his native town, so far back as Shrovetide in last year;
he was at once removed (by appeal) to London, where he lingered in
suspense till the law of death put its icy hand upon him, and claimed as
another trophy to magisterial interference one who had long lived in the
hearts of the people. His untimely end has cast a gloom oer the place,
where the amusement he afforded the inhabitants will not soon be
forgotten.

Anonymous handbill published in protest against attempts made in
the courts to prohibit the often riotous playing of Shrovetide football
in Ashbourne, Derbyshire, and elsewhere. 'Death of the Right
Honourable Game Football', 1860.

Village cricket spread fast through the land. In those days, before it became
scientific, cricket was the best game in the world to watch – each ball a
potential crisis.

George Trevelyan (1876–1962), British historian.

Few things are more deeply rooted in the collective imagination of the
English than the village cricket match. It stirs a romantic illusion about the
rustic way of life, it suggests a tranquil and unchanging order in an age of
bewildering flux.

Geoffrey Moorhouse (1931–), British writer. *The Best Loved Game* (1979).

Villagers do not think village cricket is funny.

John Arlott (1914–91), English cricket writer and commentator.
Foreword to Gerald Howat, *Village Cricket* (1981).

The rolling pin throwing contest was won by Mrs Upsall ... Mr Upsall won
the 100 yards dash.

Kingston Star.

See also CRICKET.

Violence

Sports begets tumultuous strife and wrath, and wrath begets fierce quarrels.

Horace (65–8BC), Roman poet and satirist.

Football, wherein is nothing but beastly fury and extreme violence, whereof proceedeth hurt, and consequently rancour and malice do remain with them that be wounded.

Thomas Elyot (1499–1546) British politician and writer. *Book Named the Governor* (1531).

For as concerning football playing, I protest unto you it may be rather called a friendly kind of fight than a play or recreation, a bloody or murmuring practice than a fellowly sport or pastime.

Philip Stubbes (*fl.*1583–91), English Puritan pamphleteer. *Anatomie of Abuses in the Realme of England* (1583).

Football causeth fighting, brawling, contention, quarrel-picking, murder, homicide, and a great effusion of blood, as daily experience teaches.

Philip Stubbes (1543–93), English Puritan pamphleteer. *Anatomie of Abuses in the Realme of England* (1583).

Rules of Football: No. 3 – Kicks must be aimed only at the ball.

J.C. Thring. *The Simplest Game* (1862).

I don't believe in stopping fights. Even if a guy is getting too much of a beating. If he's done, let him be done ... it's just like a mercy killing.

Jake LaMotta (1922–), US middleweight boxer.

Why should I? When somebody insulted Caruso, did he sing an aria for him?

Joe Louis (1914–81), US heavyweight boxer, explaining why he did not hit a motorist after the latter abused him following an accident.

I ain't never liked violence.

Sugar Ray Robinson (1920–89), US welterweight and middleweight boxer.

The more violent the body contact of the sports you watch, the lower the class.

Paul Fussell (1924–), US historian and writer.

Soccer is a man's game; not an outing for mamby-pambies.

Jack Charlton (1935–), English footballer and manager, justifying
violent play in professional football in *For Leeds and England* (1967).

Pro football is like nuclear warfare; there are no winners, only survivors.

Frank Gifford (1930–), US television sports commentator.

My idea of a good hit is when the victim wakes up on the sidelines with
train whistles blowing in his head. I like to believe that my best hits border
on felonious assault.

Jack Tatum (1948–), American football player.

You can run on a football field but you can't hide out there. Sooner or later
you are going to get hit.

Sam Huff (1934–), American football player, reworking the 'he can
run but he can't hide' line of boxer Joe Louis.

If me and King Kong went into an alley, only one of us would come out.
And it wouldn't be the monkey.

Lyle Alzado (1949–92), American football player.

There's more violence in one football game than there is in an entire hockey
season, and nobody ever talks about that.

Keith Allen (1923–), US hockey official, comparing violence in
professional hockey with that in American football.

If a fast bowler is allowed to strike a batsman on the head with the ball,
why shouldn't the batsman be allowed to retaliate by giving the bowler a
crack on the head with his bat?

Lambert Jeffries, British writer.

It's the first time, after a match, that we've had to replace divots in the players.

Ron Atkinson (1939–), English football manager. Quoted as
manager of Manchester United after a particularly fierce encounter
with the Spanish club side Valencia in 1982.

If you can't take a punch, you should play table tennis.

Pierre Berbizier (1958–), French rugby union player. 1995.

See also BITING; BOXING; HARD MEN; INJURIES; TACKLES; Mike TYSON.

Volleyball

Volleyball is a dandy game and more besides.

Peter Wardale. *Volleyball: Skill and Tactics* (1964).

Volleyball is a Jewish sport. It's fun, and nobody can get hurt.

Gail Parent (1941–), US writer. *Sheila Levine is Dead and Living in New York* (1972).

·W·

Murray WALKER

British television motor racing commentator
(1923–) famed for his enthusiastic style of commentary
and numerous gaffes.

Quotes about Murray Walker

Murray sounds like a blindfolded man riding a unicycle on the rim of the pit of doom.

Clive James (1939–), Australian broadcaster and writer, in the
Observer.

Even in moments of tranquillity, Murray Walker sounds like a man whose trousers are on fire.

Clive James (1939–), Australian broadcaster and writer. *Glued to
the Box* (1984).

Quotes by Murray Walker

Unless I'm very much mistaken ... I *am* very much mistaken.

Television commentary.

Anything happens in Grand Prix racing and it usually does.

Television commentary.

The lead car is absolutely unique, except for the one behind it, which is identical.

Television commentary.

Patrick Tambay's hopes, which were nil before, are absolutely zero now.

Television commentary.

And Nakano tries to avoid being passed by his team-mate Trulli, which should in fact be quite easy, because Trulli is going more slowly than his team-mate Nakano.

Television commentary.

Mansell is slowing it down, taking it easy. Oh no he isn't! It's a lap record.

Television commentary.

Do my eyes deceive me, or is Senna's car sounding a bit rough?

Television commentary.

You can cut the tension with a cricket stump.

Television commentary.

The battle is well and truly on if it wasn't on before, and it certainly was.

Television commentary.

I imagine that the conditions in those cars today are totally unimaginable.

Television commentary.

He is shedding buckets of adrenalin in that car.

Television commentary.

There is Michael Schumacher. He's actually in a very good position. He's in last place.

Television commentary. Quoted in 'Those Things They Said', the *Independent*, 31 December 1999.

I don't make mistakes. I make prophecies which are immediately proved wrong.

Attributed.

See also SCORELINES.

Walking

After dinner rest a while,
After supper walk a mile.

Proverb.

It is a fact that not once in all my life have I gone out for a walk. I have
been taken out for walks; but that is another matter.

Sir Max Beerbohm (1872–1956), British writer. 'Going Out
for a Walk'.

I like long walks, especially when they are taken by people who annoy me!

Fred Allen (1894–1956), US comedian.

The 880-yard heel and toe walk is the closest a man can come to
experiencing the pangs of childbirth.

Avery Brundage (1887–1975), US sports administrator, 1956.

There are times when you feel you simply can't go on. The last five miles
of every stage are awful. Terrible. That is the point where you are like a
human cabbage: you can see the destination but it just won't come any
closer. It is then that I pinch myself and remind myself just what I am
doing, why I am on this road.

Ian Botham (1955–), English cricketer, referring to his experience of
long-distance sponsored walks in aid of charity in *Botham: My
Autobiography* (1994).

War

My successes in the Army are owing in a great measure to the manly sports
of Great Britain, and one sport above all – cricket.

Arthur Wellesley, 1st Duke of Wellington (1769–1852), British
soldier and Tory prime minister.

The battle of Waterloo was won on the playing fields of Eton.

Arthur Wellesley, 1st Duke of Wellington (1769–1852), British soldier
and Tory prime minister. Attributed in Count Charles de Montalembert,
De l'Avenir politique de l'Angleterre (1856). According to US baseball
legend Babe Ruth, however, 'Duke Ellington said the battle of Waterloo
was won on the playing fields of Elkton.'

You have played with one another and against one another for the Cup. It is now the duty of everyone to join with each other and play a sterner game for England.

Lord Derby (1865–1948), British Conservative politician. Addressing Sheffield United and Chelsea players as he presented the FA Cup in 1915. The match, which was the last for four years because of World War I, was dubbed the 'Khaki Cup Final' because of the large number of uniformed men in the crowd.

No Lord's this year: no silken lawn on which
A dignified and dainty throng meanders.
The schools take guard upon a fiercer pitch
Somewhere in Flanders.

Bigger the cricket here: yet some who tried
In vain to earn a colour while at Eton
Have found a place upon an England side
Which can't be beaten.

E.W. Hornung (1866–1921), British novelist. Referring to the absence of many cricketers from the country's pitches during World War I. 'Lord's Leave: 1915'.

On through the hail of slaughter,
Where gallant comrades fall,
Where blood is poured like water,
They drive the trickling ball.
The fear of death before them
Is but an empty name
True to the land that bore them
The Surreys play the game.

'Touchstone', referring to reports that the 8th Battalion of the East Surrey Regiment dribbled four footballs through no man's land as they attacked German positions on the Somme on 1 July 1916, suffering heavy losses. *Daily Mail*, 1916

1. Players are asked to collect bomb and shrapnel splinters to save these causing damage to the mowing machines.

2. In competitions, during gunfire or while bombs are falling, players may take cover without penalty for ceasing play.

3. The position of known delayed-action bombs are marked by red flags at a reasonably, but not guaranteed, safe distance therefrom.

4. Shrapnel and/or bomb splinters on the fairways, or in bunkers within a

club's length of a ball, may be moved without penalty and no penalty shall be incurred if a ball is thereby caused to move accidentally.

5. A ball moved by enemy action may be replaced, or if lost or destroyed, the ball may be dropped not nearer the hole without penalty.

6. A ball lying in a crater may be lifted and dropped not nearer the hole, preserving the line to the hole, without penalty.

7. A player whose stroke is affected by the simultaneous explosion of a bomb may play another ball from the same place. Penalty one stroke.

Richmond (Surrey) Golf Club rulebook. Special rules introduced in 1940, during the Battle of Britain. When reports of the club's actions reached Josef Goebbels in Berlin he expressed his outrage in a radio broadcast to the nation, roundly condemning the measures as 'ridiculous reforms' and the golfers themselves as 'English snobs'. In David Randall, *Great Sporting Eccentrics* (1985).

I was playing golf the other day
That the Germans landed;
All our troops had run away,
All our ships were stranded;
And the thought of England's shame
Altogether spoilt my game.

Anonymous ditty of World War II vintage.

They bombed my granny's chippie, left it completely flat. I'll have her for that.

Jane Couch (1970–), British boxer. Quoted as the first women to receive a professional boxing licence in the UK shortly before her fight against German boxer Simona Lukic: Lukic lasted four minutes. 'Sporting Quotes of the Year 1998', the *Daily Telegraph*, 28 December 1998.

Shane WARNE *See* LEG SPIN BOWLING; PREDICTIONS.

Water polo

Marilyn Monroe: Water polo? Isn't that terribly dangerous?
Tony Curtis: I'll say! I had two ponies drown under me.

Billy Wilder (1906–), US film-maker. *Some Like It Hot* (1959), screenplay (written in collaboration with I.A.L. Diamond).

Weather

I shall stay no longer than to wish him a rainy day to read this ... discourse; and that if he be an honest angler, the east wind may never blow when he goes a-fishing.

Izaak Walton (1593–1683), English writer. 'Epistle to the Reader',
The Compleat Angler (1653).

The weather for catching fish is that weather, and no other, in which fish are caught.

William Blake (1757–1827), British poet.

It was an ideal day for football – too cold for the spectators and too cold for the players.

Red Smith (1905–82), US sportswriter. Match report, 1963.

The elements are cricket's presiding geniuses.

Sir Neville Cardus (1889–1975), British journalist and writer.
A Fourth Innings with Cardus (1981).

If I'm on the course and lightning starts, I get inside fast. If God wants to play through, let him.

Bob Hope (1903–), US comedian.

Hold up a one-iron and walk. Even God can't hit a one-iron.

Lee Trevino (1939–), US golfer. His advice to fellow-golfers on how
to avoid being struck by lightning while on the golf course. He was
struck by lightning himself in 1975.

The advantage of the rain is, that if you have a quick bike, there's no advantage.

Barry Sheene (1950–), British motor cyclist.

Folks, this is perfect weather for today's game. Not a breath of air.

Curt Gowdy (1919–), US television sports commentator. TV
baseball commentary.

I'm glad to say that this is the first Saturday in four weeks that sport will be weather-free.

David Coleman (1926–), British television sports commentator. *Grandstand*, BBC TV.

It's a perfect day here in Australia, glorious blue sunshine.

Christopher Martin-Jenkins (1945–), British radio sports
commentator. BBC radio commentary, 1979.

It is extremely cold here. The England fielders are keeping their hands in
pockets between balls.

Christopher Martin-Jenkins (1945–), British radio sports
commentator. BBC radio commentary.

We're not used to weather in June in this country.

Jimmy Hill (1928–), English football manager and commentator.

You know it's summertime at Candlestick when the fog rolls in, the wind
kicks up, and you see the centre fielder slicing open a caribou to survive the
ninth inning.

Bob Sarlette, US comedian.

I can't see, unless the weather changes, the conditions changing
dramatically.

Peter Alliss (1931–), British television sports commentator. BBC TV
golf commentary, 1995.

Jeez, it's not even as cold as this in my fridge back in Brisbane.

Jeff Thomson (1950–), Australian cricketer, commenting on the
temperature early in the English cricket season. Quoted in Simon
Hughes, *A Lot of Hard Yakka* (1997).

Weightlifting

The guy with the biggest butt lifts the biggest weights.

Paul Anderson (1932–), US Olympic champion weightlifter.

Welsh rugby

I wanted a play that would paint the full face of sensuality, rebellion and
revivalism. In South Wales these three phenomena have played second
fiddle only to the Rugby Union which is a distillation of all three.

Gwyn Thomas (1913–81), British writer. 'Jackie the Jumper', *Plays
and Players*, 19 January 1963.

When it comes to the one great scorer,
To mark against your name,
He'll not ask how you played the game,
But ... whether you beat England.

Max Boyce (1945–), Welsh entertainer.

Wembley

Football stadium in London, chosen in 1997 as England's new National Sports Stadium. It was closed for long-overdue rebuilding in 2000.

A vast white elephant, a rotting sepulchre of hopes and the grave of fortunes.

Anonymous sportswriter's view of Wembley at the end of the British Empire Exhibition in 1925. Quoted by British sportswriter David Lacey in the *Guardian*, 1989.

You could hardly be worse off sitting on your food and eating your seat. The nutritional value could not be any lower, nor the view any worse.

Colman's Food Guide, referring to Wembley Stadium in 1997.

Willpower

Winners never quit and quitters never win.

Anonymous.

Do not let what you cannot do interfere with what you can do.

John Wooden (1910–), US basketball coach.

I believe that if a man wanted to walk on water, and was prepared to give up everything in life, he could do it.

Stirling Moss (1929–), British racing driver.

Mind is everything. Muscle – pieces of rubber. All that I am, I am because of my mind.

Paavo Nurmi (1897–1973), Finnish runner, nicknamed 'The Flying Finn'.

You have to expect things of yourself before you can do them.

Michael Jordan (1963–), US basketball player.

Wimbledon

The home of lawn tennis in England, in London's southwestern suburbs.

A traditional fixture at Wimbledon is the way the BBC TV commentary box fills up with British players eliminated in the early rounds.

Clive James (1939–), Australian broadcaster and journalist.

New Yorkers love it when you spill your guts out there. Spill your guts at Wimbledon and they make you stop and clean it up.

Jimmy Connors (1952–), US tennis player. Quoted in the *Guardian*, 24 December 1984.

Winning streaks

Winning is a habit.

Leo Durocher (1906–91), US baseball manager.

When players are used to winning, they put out a little more.

Red Auerbach (1917–), US basketball coach.

Winning all the time is not necessarily good for the team.

John Toshack (1950–), Welsh footballer.

See also FORM; LOSING STREAKS; VICTORY.

Women in sport

A tyme there is for all,
My mother often sayes,
When she, with skirt tuck't very high,
With girls at football playes.

Sir Philip Sidney (1554–86), English poet and soldier.

Women never look so well as when one comes in wet and dirty from hunting.

Robert S. Surtees (1803–64), British novelist and journalist. *Mr Sponge's Sporting Tour* (1853).

Pam, I adore you, Pam, you great big mountainous sports girl
Whizzing them over the net, full of the strength of five:
That old Malvernian brother, you zephyr and khaki shorts girl,
Although he's playing for Woking,
Can't stand up to your wonderful backhand drive.

John Betjeman (1906–84), British poet. 'Pot Pourri from a Surrey
Garden', in *Old Lights for New Chancels* (1940).

Miss J. Hunter Dunn, Miss J. Hunter Dunn,
Furnish'd and burnish'd by Aldershot sun,
What strenuous singles we played after tea,
We in the tournament – you against me.

Love-thirty, love-forty, oh! weakness of joy,
The speed of a swallow, the grace of a boy,
With carefullest carelessness, gaily you won,
I am weak from your loveliness, Joan Hunter Dunn.

John Betjeman (1906–84), British poet. 'A Subaltern's Love-Song', in
New Bats in Old Belfries (1945).

The game of cricket is no joke
To us who neither drink or smoke
Games are won and runs are made
By girls who stick to lemonade.

Nat Gubbins, poet, 1951.

If a woman can walk, she can play golf.

Louise Suggs (1923–), US golfer.

We have nothing against man cricketers. Some of them are quite nice
people, even though they don't win as often as we do.

Rachael Heyhoe-Flint (1939–), English cricketer, 1975.

Women will not be talking about football unless one of them is in love with
a football player, and then suddenly you discover that they know
everything that is to be known about it.

Jeanne Moreau (1929–), French actress, 1976.

The reason women don't play football is because 11 of them would never
wear the same outfit in public.

Phyllis Diller (1917–), US comedienne.

It's rumoured that a well-known New England newspaper is to sponsor a topless female basketball team – to be called the Boston Globes.

Playboy magazine, 1981.

People in the States used to think that if girls were good at sports their sexuality would be affected. Being feminine meant being a cheerleader, not being an athlete. The image of women is changing now. You don't have to be pretty for people to come and see you play. At the same time, if you're a good athlete, it doesn't mean you're not a woman.

Martina Navratilova (1956–), Czech-born US tennis player.
Martina Navratilova – Being Myself (1985).

The stereotype footballer – big and butch – is a thing of the past. Players look more feminine today. We've got one blonde player who won't even train without checking her hair is OK.

Sheila Edmonds (1916–), British physician, speaking as physiotherapist for the Doncaster Belles women's football team, 1997.

Men always want to talk about the standard of women's football, which isn't and couldn't be as high as the men's game. But they've had 100 years' more practice.

Maureen McGonigle, Scottish Women's FA administrator, 1997.

See also SEXISM IN SPORT.

Tiger WOODS

US golfer (1975–) whose precocious talent prompted comparisons with the great Bobby Jones.

I don't know. I've never played there.

Sandy Lyle (1958–), Scottish golfer. His response, in 1992, when asked his opinion of Tiger Woods.

When Tiger was six months old, he would sit in our garage, watching me hit balls into a net. He had been assimilating his golf swing. When he got out of the high chair, he had a golf swing.

Earl Woods (1932–), father of Tiger Woods.

World Cup

The World Cup – truly an international event.

John Motson (1945–), British television sports commentator. BBC television commentary.

The World Cup is every four years so it's going to be a perennial problem.

Gary Lineker (1960–), English footballer. BBC Radio Four, 1998.

The World Cup, believe it or not, was brought to my house and I held it in my hands and closed my eyes, and I energized it for England. To be very honest with you, I even managed to bend it ever so slightly.

Uri Geller (1946–), Israeli psychic, recalling how he held football's
World Cup before the 1998 tournament. His efforts unfortunately
failed to have much of a positive effect upon England's performance
in the competition, the team going out before the final stages.

Winning the World Cup is the most beautiful thing to have happened to France since the Revolution.

Emmanuel Petit (1970–), French footballer. 'Quotes of the Year', the *Guardian*, 24 December 1998.

Wrestling

If it's all-in, why do they wrestle?

Mae West (1893–1980), US film actress.

Professional wrestling's most mysterious hold is on its audience.

Luke Neely, British writer, 1953.

There are people who think that wrestling is an ignoble sport. Wrestling is not sport, it is a spectacle, and it is no more ignoble to attend a wrestled performance of suffering than a performance of the sorrows of Arnolphe or Andromaque.

Roland Barthes (1915–80), French semiologist, *Mythologies* (1957).

It's excitement, it's show business, it's chic.

Andy Warhol (1927–88), US artist and film director.

I don't know what it is, but I can't look at Hulk Hogan and believe that he's the end result of millions and millions of years of evolution.

Jim Murray, US sportswriter.

·X·Y·Z·

Yachting

There is one good rule in helmsmanship – let the boat do the sailing.

Peter Heaton (1919–), British writer. *Sailing* (1949).

Good seamanship is eight parts common sense.

Jack Knights, yachtsman and writer, *Sailing: Step by Step* (1961).

Coarse sailing is not mucking around in boats, but boating around in muck.

Michael Green (1927–), British humorist. *The Art of Coarse Sailing* (1962).

One who in a crisis forgets nautical language and shouts, 'For God's sake turn left!'

Michael Green (1927–), British humorist, defining the 'Coarse
Sailor' in *The Art of Coarse Sailing* (1962).

There is never a 'right' time to sail across the Atlantic alone. There is only 'now' or 'never'.

David Blagden, British yachtsman and writer. *Very Willing Griffin* (1973).

I have no interest in sailing round the world. Not that there is any lack of requests for me to do so.

Edward Heath (1916–), British Conservative prime minister and
yachtsman. Quoted in the *Observer*, 19 June 1977.

Ocean racing is like standing under a cold shower tearing up £5 notes.

Edward Heath (1916–), British Conservative prime minister and
yachtsman.

Yorkshire County Cricket Club

Don't tell me his average or his top score at Trent Bridge. How many runs,
how many wickets, did he get against Yorkshire?

Douglas Jardine (1900–58), English cricketer. His test in selecting
players for England in the 1930s.

In an England cricket eleven, the flesh may be of the South, but the bone
is of the North, and the backbone is Yorkshire.

Sir Len Hutton (1916–90), English cricketer.

I don't know of any other club in history which finished bottom of the
league, sacked its star player and left the manager in the job.

Brian Clough (1935–), English football manager, reacting in 1983
to the news that Yorkshire, then managed by Ray Illingworth, had
responded to a prolonged loss of form by dismissing star batsman
Geoffrey Boycott.

The Yorkshire County Cricket Club has behaved like the Labour Party in
its worst periods. Every time there's a little dispute, everybody attacks
each other in public.

Roy Hattersley (1932–), British Labour politician. Speaking as a
supporter of Yorkshire in 1983, responding to the furore surrounding
the sacking of Geoffrey Boycott.

I would have died for Yorkshire. I suppose once or twice I nearly did.

Brian Close (1931–), English cricketer.

It can be absurd, cantankerous, self-destructive and pompous, but it is
never crass.

Peter Roebuck (1956–), English cricketer, referring to Yorkshire
cricket in 1995.

See also Geoffrey BOYCOTT.

Youth

Years lost in early life are irrecoverable, particularly where cricket is
concerned.

Les Ames (1905–90), English cricketer.

He's a great kid and shows lots of ability.

Michael Owen (1979–), English footballer, commenting, at the
advanced age of 19, upon Aston Villa's 17-year-old star Gareth
Barry. 'Sporting Quotes of the Year 1998', the *Daily Telegraph*, 28
December 1998.

Gianfranco ZOLA

Italian footballer (1966–) who established a reputation as
one of the best players of his generation, joining England's
Chelsea in the late 1990s.

Quotes about Gianfranco Zola

Like so many of the current Chelsea team, Zola is unique.

Barry Venison (1964–), English footballer and sports commentator.
ITV commentary, 1998.

Quotes by Gianfranco Zola

It's best that I hide my real personality. I cannot tell you what it is because
I don't want to go to prison.

1997.

See also ITALIAN FOOTBALL.

Index

Roman numerals indicate that the person, team or club listed is the *source of the quotation*.

Bold numerals indicate that the person, etc. is the *subject of the quotation*.